CURRICULUM, SYLLABUS DESIGN AND EQUITY

Curriculum scholars and teachers working for social justice and equity have been caught up in acrimonious and polarizing political debates over content, ideology and disciplinary knowledge. At the forefront in cutting through these debates and addressing the practical questions involved, this book is distinctive in looking to the technical form of the curriculum rather than its content for solutions. The editors and contributors, all leading international scholars, advance a unified, principled approach to the design of syllabus documents that aims for high quality/high equity educational outcomes and enhances teacher professionalism.

Stressing local curriculum development capacity and professional responses of teachers to specific community and student contexts, this useful, practical primer introduces and unpacks definitions of curriculum, syllabus, the school subject and informed professionalism; presents key principles of design; discusses a range of approaches and offers clear, realistic guidelines for the tasks of writing curriculum documents and designing official syllabi and professional development programs at system and school levels. Providing a foundational structure for syllabus design work, *Curriculum, Syllabus Design and Equity* is relevant for teachers, teacher educators and curriculum policy workers everywhere who are engaged in the real work of curriculum writing and implementation.

Allan Luke is Research Professor in the Faculty of Education at the Queensland University of Technology, Brisbane, Australia.

Annette Woods is Senior Lecturer in the Faculty of Education at Queensland University of Technology in Brisbane, Australia.

Katie Weir is Senior Lecturer at Griffith University's Gold Coast campus in Queensland, Australia.

CURRICULUM, SYLLABUS DESIGN AND EQUITY

A Primer and Model

Edited by
Allan Luke, Annette Woods
and Katie Weir

Routledge
Taylor & Francis Group

NEW YORK AND LONDON

First published 2013
by Routledge
711 Third Avenue, New York, NY 10017

Simultaneously published in the UK
by Routledge
2 Park Square, Milton Park, Abingdon, Oxon OX14 4RN

Routledge is an imprint of the Taylor & Francis Group, an informa business

Library of Congress Cataloging in Publication Data
Curriculum, syllabus design, and equity : a primer and model / edited by Allan Luke, Annette Woods, Katie Weir.
p. cm.
Includes bibliographical references and index.
1. Curriculum Planning- -methodology. 2. Educational equalization.
3. Social justice- -Study and teaching. I. Luke, Allan. II. Woods, Annette.
III. Weir, Katie.
LB2806.15.C886 2012
375'.001- -dc23
2012006745

ISBN: 978-0-415-80319-9 (hbk)
ISBN: 978-0-415-80320-5 (pbk)
ISBN: 978-0-203-83345-2 (ebk)

Typeset in Bembo
by Taylor & Francis Books

SUSTAINABLE FORESTRY INITIATIVE

Certified Sourcing
www.sfiprogram.org
SFI-01234

Printed and bound in the United States of America on sustainably sourced paper by IBT Global

CONTENTS

PREFACE

Three decades ago, Michael Apple (1978) made the case that the over-specification of curriculum through directive syllabi, packaged materials and instructional scripts has the potential to deskill teachers, deterring their professionalism and inhibiting the quality and equity of instruction. One of the paradoxes of our current educational context is that three decades later curriculum policy continues to ignore this case as our systems push toward increased accountability of teacher and student work in ways that deprofessionalize and limit what is possible in classrooms, and prescriptive curriculum that aim to produce consistency of practice rather than of expectations and access. And all this in the name of social justice, equity and quality.

This book was written and assembled in the context of a national curriculum debate in Australia. We (see Luke, Weir & Woods, 2008) were asked to develop a defensible position on how our particular education jurisdiction, the state of Queensland, should respond to the issues around the form and contents of a national curriculum. The national debate in Australia – like those elsewhere – is explicitly politicized. In our context it has entailed successive federal and state governments planting clear ideological flags in the ground over issues such as phonics and "the basics", Shakespeare and the literary canon, revisionist versus traditional approaches to the history of the nation and its peoples, the rightful place of indigenous knowledge and cultures, vocational education and pathways to work in a crisis-ridden globalized economy and, of course, the inclusion of digital and technological capacities for what was termed, before the global financial crisis, "the knowledge economy". The terms of the debate would be familiar to readers who work in varied contexts, from Europe to Asia, from large emergent systems of the Americas and Africa, to the current policy contexts of the US and UK.

The chapters in this book are brought together to make the case that some forms of curriculum policy and syllabus or curriculum guideline design and prescription deter the achievement of high quality and high equity systems, and that others enhance teacher professionalism and, accordingly, improve the prospects of quality and equity of outcomes. We argue that the technical form of syllabi or other official curriculum documents matters. The arguments made are relevant for teachers, teacher educators and curriculum policy workers – those that are engaged in the dirty work of curriculum writing and implementation.

The technical form of the curriculum sets the "locus of curriculum authority". This locus can rest by degrees with the mandated curriculum commodity package, with the mandated approach, with the "test" in test-driven systems, or it can, optimally, rest with informed professionals interpreting informed central prescription. This book is different from others in that it looks to the technical form of the curriculum rather than the content of the curriculum for solutions to our need as educators to produce equitable education systems.

As such, the chapters in this book do not either prescribe or describe content. While the authors recognise the importance of cultural, intellectual, cognitive, social and economic questions about which school subjects, knowledges, skills, competences and capabilities should be included in the curriculum, they are not addressed here. In Chapter 1 Luke presents an introduction to curriculum policy work as experienced by the editors and their colleagues over many years. In Chapter 2, Luke, Woods and Weir build on this introduction as they lay out their argument for low-definition syllabi documents with clear, accessible and balanced prescription that enables teacher and system professionalism. This chapter sets the foundation for the next four chapters by Deng, Connelly and Connelly, Shannon and Klenowski, all of whom deal with different aspects of curriculum making and policy. In Chapter 7 through 9, Grieshaber deals with the particulars of curriculum documents for early childhood settings, Alverman and Marshall with the middle years of schooling, and finally Levin with the particularities of reform for secondary schools. The volume is brought to an end by Luke, who discusses issues related to the current push for transnational curriculum standards.

The strength of the volume is that while each chapter proposes very different approaches, they all have one thing in common; they all support the educational goal of achieving a high quality and high equity system, and clearly propose ways to ensure this achievement through the balance of informed prescription and informed professionalism (Schleicher, 2008).

References

Apple, M. (1978). Curricular form and the logic of technical control. In M. Apple (Ed.) *Cultural and economic reproduction in education* (pp. 247–74). London: Routledge & Kegan Paul.

Schleicher, A. (2008). Seeing school systems through the prism of PISA. In A. Luke, K. Weir and A. Woods (Eds) *Development of a set of principles to guide a P-12 syllabus framework*. Brisbane, Queensland: Queensland Studies Authority.

Luke, A., Weir, K. and Woods, A. (2008) *Development of a set of principles to guide a P-12 syllabus framework*. Brisbane, Queensland: Queensland Studies Authority.

ACKNOWLEDGMENTS

This book has taken time and we appreciate the patience of all involved. What is interesting is that even though some time has passed since the report that served as the original impetus for producing this collection was delivered, the issues raised in the volume are as important and relevant to current education as they have ever been. Curriculum matters in the push for equitable education outcomes for all children.

We thank the authors of the chapters in this volume for their insights and willingness to participate, and also Nerida Spina and Di Weiss for their expert editing and formatting. We thank our partners at the Queensland Studies Authority – especially Paul Herschel, Janice Chee and Kim Bannicoff – for their insight as policy workers to request and engage with research about their day-to-day work. We also owe our thanks to the many teachers, administrators, children and community members who continue to work with us in the quest to improve schooling for all students, but especially those for whom access to equitable schooling is often denied.

The support of the Australian Research Council is also acknowledged, as are the insights of our Linkage Grant team Lesley McFarland, John McCollow, Paul Herschel and Janice Chee, and our partners on the "What teachers do with the official curriculum" grant – the Queensland Teachers' Union and the Queensland Studies Authority.

To all at Routledge who have been involved in the production of this book we thank you for your work and patience. Special thanks must go to Naomi Silverman for her professionalism and never ending patience and belief that we would deliver. Thank you Naomi.

Finally to our families and to the many colleagues who have contributed to our knowledge and thinking about curriculum, we thank you for much of what appears in this work.

1

INTRODUCTION

The Practical Problem of Curriculum Making

Allan Luke

Debates over curriculum have durable histories and tend to work in binary arguments that caricature and distort complex educational positions and curriculum strategies: the basics versus the postmodern, traditional versus politically correct literature, rote knowledge versus constructivism and so forth. There is often little sense of the conceptual ironies, practical contradictions and empirical anomalies that the resultant settlements may generate. In current debates, these tend to be welded together into a dual set of claims: that the resultant teaching and learning, knowledge and power relations will contribute to (1) the growth and global competitiveness of domestic human capital and economy; and, since 9/11 and the global financial crisis, (2) national and regional social cohesion, affiliation and security. In the context of many OECD countries such as Australia, Canada, New Zealand and Nordic and European states, we would add to this the national concern that the curriculum settlement will contribute to, rather than deter, an equitable and "fair" transmission and distribution of knowledge, skill and capacity to students, regardless of their ethnic, linguistic and social class background or location.

It would be convenient to dismiss such debates as a recurrent set of pendulum swings. This is the approach of the media, and often involves a harking back to mythological periods where the basics were taught, the intergenerational transmission of dominant cultural traditions ensued and meritocratic value was properly recognized. The industrial curriculum settlement of the last century was forged on two grounds. First, on the existence of a corpus of universal "skills" and "knowledges" that could be psychologically defined, transmitted through schooling and assessed through standardized instruments. Second, that these skills and knowledges were considered to be universally transferable and of exchange value in the social fields of work, civic life and community. Access to and use of these universal skills was not seen to depend on variable student background, insofar as the early

20th-century curriculum settlement was premised upon a consensually-derived, common monoculture: that the "dominant culture" valued the aforementioned universal skills, and that cultural, linguistic, social class characteristics of students and cohorts would not influence the desirability or accessibility of these skills. Hence, the late 20th-century curriculum settlement was predicated on stable and expanding industrial and service workforces, fair and non-discriminatory workplaces and civic spaces, culturally homogeneous populations and focused on the redesign of schooling to optimally ensure the acquisition of this corpus of universal skills.

This model has proven to be remarkably durable to critique – despite the social facts of population change and the emergence of technologically driven economic globalization. The results are ubiquitious multiculturalism and multilingualism in North America and Europe spurred by decolonization, large scale immigration and economic globalization. The historical lineage and persistence of the postwar industrial model of schooling is discussed by Patrick Shannon later in this volume and is well documented in curriculum history. Yet such historical moments blend and hybridize residual with emergent cultural traditions. They are not pendulum swings, but dialectically constitute new historical settlements, new social and cultural formations of knowledge and power – always partial and contested and, in effect, making and remaking what counts as knowledge, skill and competence, human cognition and sociocultural action.

So, however extreme and polemical such curriculum debates may be, they come to ground in a documentary and textual settlement that has an empirical con-sequence in the shaping of what teachers and students do in schools and classrooms, a process that occurs anew each and every day. While the actual official curriculum – the syllabus or curriculum guideline – cannot determine the curriculum in any direct and unmediated way, it nonetheless provides grounds for constraint, delimitation and prescription and, in our current accountability-focused contexts, enforcement, sur-veillance and monitoring of what occurs in classrooms and, indeed, in student learning, knowledge and consciousness. The normative goals and material outcomes of an equitable education remain matters for rigorous and multidisciplinary empirical scrutiny and principled theoretical and political debate (Luke, Green & Kelly, 2010).

As you read this book, in some national or state or regional educational system, teachers, consultants, union representatives, teacher educators, systems bureaucrats, along with discipline and subject-area experts are undertaking the practical task of making an official curriculum. We have participated in such gatherings in hotel conference rooms and corporate board rooms, in staffrooms and classrooms in Australia, North America and Asia and in villages and community halls in the South Pacific.

These meetings aim for professional exchange, consultation and consensus upon contents, standards, goals and objectives for teaching and learning in schools. At the onset of such meetings, marching orders are laid out: the technical parameters for the lists of skills and contents, standards and outcomes to be compiled are displayed on powerpoint slideshows or large sheets of butchers' paper. But there are other, not so subtle messages also being passed around these rooms. To those who might want to debate larger issues of philosophy and ideology – the implicit message is something like "leave your curriculum theory at the door" and get on with the practical task of specifying what should be taught to whom and when; inevitably arguments arise – between advocates of this curriculum content and that; between those who want basic skills and those who want more space for problem solving or hands on activities; between those who see their task as representing those "excluded" by the curriculum and those who take up the voice of the supposedly oft forgotten "majority." But in terms of the technical vocabulary, taxonomies and categories to be used, these gatherings are more often than not *fait acompli*. Key decisions about curriculum philosophy and paradigm have already been made prior to these meetings beginning. Typically, the boxes to be filled in have been determined. An overall grid or map of the curriculum has already been set well before people sit down to debate. And it is in this grid that the political, cultural and ideological parameters of the curriculum are set.

These are moments in the formation of "official knowledge" (Apple, 1990). They are the actual sites where the textual work of constructing and construing regional, state and national curriculum settlements is done. Where tensions arise, they are over curriculum content: over the "selective traditions" (Apple, 1978) of human knowledge and wisdom to be taught. Historically, curriculum content has been and remains the focal point of public, political and media debate. In part this is because questions over which versions of historical events, of politics, of religion, of science and, indeed, of the state, are readily accessible to public scrutiny and media debate. It is also because matters of the representation of the "facts" of history, society and cultures, science and religion, the representation of national formation and human virtue, models of "quality" thought, writing and belief are necessarily contentious in secular, democratic societies. This is especially the case in media saturated societies, where versions of scientific and moral truth – of evolution, climate change, ecology, economics, war and peace, race relations, friend and foe, core cultural values – are under continual public scrutiny.

Consider, for example: the century-long US debate over evolution and creationism in the school curriculum, foregrounded again in the *Louisiana Science Education Acts* of 2008; the postwar argument in Japan over the representation of World War II (Nozaki & Inokuchi, 2000); the recent Texas discussons of the portrayal of cultural minorities, immigration and multiculturalism; the Australian disputes over the first contact of Aboriginal peoples and British colonizers in 1788 as settlement or invasion; or the ongoing debate over the uses and abuses of *Huckleberry Finn* as an historical, literary representation of slavery. Which texts and discourses and which versions of history and science will be represented in the official curriculum, and whose lingua franca will be the medium of instruction are important, core ideological and sociocultural decisions by education systems and by societies. These often generate full-blown paradigm wars – where competing visions of a particular curriculum field, and indeed particular normative versions of what will count as being literate, or as "play," as "early childhood," as "middle years," or, for that matter, "learning" and "teaching" generate tension. Open contestation over the selective curricular traditions of schooling is, by definition, a central element of what democratic schooling should be about – of the robust and, more often than not, divisive search for common and uncommon cultural touchstones, values and beliefs in culturally, linguistically and historically heterogeneous and heteroglossic societies. This contrasts sharply with autocratic societies where the decisions about what will count as knowledge are made in closed, inaccessible and incontestable contexts by elite interests.

These curriculum conversations, then, are crucial. But in the midst of such debates we hear little about the technical form of the curriculum. To return to the actual site of curriculum making – typically, the basic definitions and taxonomic categories of the curriculum are determined well before the curriculum writing process begins. The categories for curriculum developers, writers and consultants charged with developing state and system syllabus documents are more often than not "given," fixed a priori in both philosophic and political senses and presented as beyond criticism. This means that the "naming of the parts" of the curriculum is never problematized: those of us engaged in this curriculum work are asked to identify and "fill in" state-ments of "outcomes," "content," or "skills." Over the past two decades, depending on jurisdiction, this nomenclature has varied: with the emergence of categories such as "skills," "behaviours," "knowledge," "competencies," "capacities" and more recently general capabilities or cross curricular dimensions or priorities, and other attempts to name what should be taught, how and in what sequence. These are the core categories and levels of specification used by state systems.

Consider this example: In one such meeting around the development of an Australian state government's syllabus, the task at hand was to develop "outcome statements" for infancy to Year 3. The task, we and other curriculum consultants were told, was to name "behaviourally observable" and "measurable" outcomes. The result included items such as "can hold head upright without assistance." There is a great deal that can be said about the breaking down and parcelling of human development and cultural practice into discrete behaviours, much less about their ultimate measurability. Suffice to say, the description of the phenomena of infancy and early childhood into "outcomes" qua "observable behaviours" reflected core behaviourist assumptions. There is substantive sociological debate to be had about the extension of official knowledge into what were previously domains of family and community – the extension of official knowledge to preschool settings (Fuller, 2007). This further raises important issues about the extent to which such standards and approaches may or may not intrude upon, for example, the ways of childrearing and childhood of indigenous communities (Romero-Little, 2006). Finally, the "periodicization" or segmentation of "childhood" (cf. Grieshaber, this volume on "early childhood" and Alvermann and Marshall, this volume, on "adolescence") was presented as a naturalized, commonsense unit or segment of curriculum. Yet these "larger" issues were quickly swept to the side by the curriculum bureaucrats chairing these meetings as impediments to the technical task at hand; the filling in the developmental continuums of children's growth and maturation. This event, as with so many similar events, was a "consultative" process.

This volume is addressed to all those who work in scenes like this, making curriculum documents, resource materials, guidelines and policies and official syllabi. Our principal argument here, supported by our many colleagues across these chapters, is that the technical form of the curriculum matters. Critical curriculum studies has focused largely on normative theoretical assumptions curriculum and overt ideological content as the objects of critique and reconstruction. The prevailing assumption has been that issues of equity and social justice are focal matters of curriculum content – of the actual skills, ideas, facts, beliefs, histories and cultural scripts that are represented and sanctioned in the written, spoken and visual texts of schooling. Yet this has led to a neglect of the educational effects of the technical form of the curriculum, and left curriculum developers, consultants and experts – practical curriculum workers – without clear grounds to analyze the effects of the different taxonomic categories, grids and technical specifications of the curriculum. In what follows we and our colleagues begin to unpack possible parameters for an official curriculum that aims for high quality *and* high equity education.

References

Apple, M. (1978). *Ideology and curriculum*. New York: Routledge.

Apple. M. (1990). Is there a curriculum voice to reclaim? *Phi Delta Kappan, 71*(7), 526–30.

Fuller, B. (2007). *Standardized childhood*. Stanford, CA: Stanford University Press.

Luke, A., Green, J. and Kelly, G.J. (2010). What counts as evidence and equity? *Review of Research in Education, 34*(1), vii–xvi.

Nozaki, Y. and Inokuchi, H. (2000). Japanese education, nationalism and Lenaga Saburo's textbook lawsuits. In L. Hein and M. Selden (Eds) *Censoring history: Citizenship and memory in Japan, Germany and the United States*. (pp. 96–126). Armonk, New York: M.E. Sharpe Inc.

Romero-Little, M. E. (2006). Honoring our own: Rethinking indigenous languages and literacy. *Anthropology & Education Quarterly, 37*(4), 399–402.

2

CURRICULUM DESIGN, EQUITY AND THE TECHNICAL FORM OF THE CURRICULUM

Allan Luke, Annette Woods and Katie Weir

Introduction

This is a volatile period for curriculum settlements in many nations, states and regions. System curriculum documents – usually in the form of a formal syllabus, curriculum guideline[1] or course of study – are often the first port of call for media and political analysts and critics in intellectual paradigm wars over content. This is because the documents exist as a publically accessible texts. Unlike the "enacted curriculum" that occurs every day in student/teacher discourse, interaction and relationships, the official curriculum contains normative statements about what should be learned, and these are recoverable and available for ideological and cultural scrutiny. Hence, in periods of economic and social uncertainty and upheaval, in periods of cultural conflict and transformation, curriculum documents are often held accountable for the academic and social outcomes of schooling.

While public firestorms over education may begin with claims about falling levels of basic skills, declines in graduate outcomes and employer and media complaints about the general quality of graduates, the trail generally leads to two sources of the ostensible problem: the curriculum and teachers. That is, public attention turns to what is being taught – and who is doing the teaching. Bureaucratic incoherence or lack of political vision and will are rarely mentioned or critiqued in these public outcries.

The official curriculum and the official presentation of this curriculum in syllabus documents, what Michel Foucault (1972) referred to as "grids of specification", that is an institutional structure for mapping human knowledge and human subjects; the divisions and categories used to specify what the curriculum will be at this time and in this context. These grids are taxonomic and categorical systems used for describing a potentially unlimited universe of human knowledge and practice. The

systems divide, contrast, regroup and derive what
valued school knowledge, now, from the unlimite
chapter, we refer to this taxonomy as the *technical*
argument here is that the technical form of the curri:
of enabling and disenabling particular kinds of teac
and face-to-face-interaction in schools and classrooms.
(Luke, 1988), it encourages and discourages teacher an
critical analyses of local contexts, teachers' bending :
respond to particular students' needs and to particular school and community con-
tingencies. We will argue and attempt to demonstrate that *high definition*, or extremely elaborated, detailed and enforced technical specifications and *low definition*,
that is, less elaborated, detailed and constrained curriculum act as degrees of central
prescription. We suggest that these levels of prescription – from high through to
low – in turn set the conditions for local teacher professionalism or workforce
deprofessionalization. The case we make is that over-prescription in the technical
form of the curriculum has the effect of constraining teacher professionalism and
eventually deskilling teachers, and that as a consequence less equitable educational
outcomes ensue.

Curriculum theory and research provide ample theoretical tools for debating and
contesting "whose knowledge should count": whose versions of human wisdom
and knowledge should and can be made to count in teaching and learning. These
range from the foundational questions raised by the "new sociology of education"
(Young, 1971), through "critical multiculturalist" work of the 1990s (e.g., Nieto,
1999), to the ongoing reconceptualist work of feminists, poststructuralist and queer
theorists (e.g., Pinar, 2001). These are matters of the tension between educational
hegemony and recognitive justice (Fraser, 1997): that is, between the representation
of "dominant" views of culture, ideology and science; and of bids for the recognition
and representation of "other", minority views of the world, of cultural and linguistic
practice, of everyday forms of life, human existence and experience. Such tensions
play out regularly during curriculum reform processes and are evident in current
curriculum debates in the US and Australia, particularly as that nation moves toward
implementing its first national curriculum. Debates over "black arm band" history
versus a more sanitized, less culpable version, of whether to cut content according to temporal categories or themes in history, and a revisiting of the grammar
debates between traditional and functional versions continue in consultation meetings, organized to provide a wider group of interests a voice in the ultimate selections made.

At this historical moment, curriculum content is an issue of contestation and
debate. There is a call for the representation of the lives and discourses of minority
communities as part of a broader, half-century push for an approach that highlights
both redistributive and recognitive social justice in schools (e.g., Connelly with
He & Phillion, 2008). These attempts are counterposed against a new educational
"fundamentalism" (Luke, 2006) that argues for a supposed self-evident corpus of the

persistent call for a return to canonical classical knowledges, and the call
w disciplinarity that focuses on explicit access to the specialized techniques,
istic forms and cognitive strategies of scientific disciplinary knowledge (e.g.,
reebody, Martin & Maton, 2008).

Taken together, these are robust and culturally-warranted debates over curriculum
content. However at the same time, contemporary curriculum theory provides
little theoretical or practical advice on the technical form of the curriculum, for the
definition and specification of hierarchical and taxonomic categories or descriptive
categories. As illustrated in a series of recent handbooks and encyclopaedias of
curriculum, there is a broad critique of Neo-Tylerian assumptions and limitations,
persistent debates over the political and social contexts of curriculum – but little
substantive engagement with the institutional processes of curriculum making
(see, for example, essays in Connelly with He and Phillion, 2008).

This marking out of the categories, imposing the grids used to divide and contrast
the content is the core, unglamorous "dirty work" of curriculum reform. It is the textual
organization and work of making official syllabus documents. The default mode is
that official documents will proceed with anywhere from six to eight core curriculum areas (e.g., school subjects, disciplinary fields or key learning areas), and that
these will be "filled in" with essential skills, processes and contents that correspond
to specific age/grade/developmental stage (Deng & Luke, 2008). To accommodate those
general competences or skills that are seen to traverse the curriculum areas and,
most recently, what are referred to as "21st century" skills and competences, additional grids are added, generally for coverage in a range of grades and
subjects (Reid, 2005). These range, depending on the national and regional context,
from capacities with new information technology or textual modes, to overarching
cognitive and textual strategies (e.g., critical thinking, higher order problem solving),
to more specific cultural and linguistic capacities often, but not always, linked to
achievement across core school subjects and increasingly linked to citizenship of
some order (e.g., civics and ethical behaviors).

Curriculum theory enables principled arguments for curriculum content. Yet while
we could identify and critique the root assumptions of particular approaches to
technical form (e.g., behaviorist skills versus traditional knowledge content statements),
we have little programmatic theory or empirical evidence on the efficacy of one
programmatic approach to another. Simply, there is little in the curriculum studies
literature and research that actually makes the case for any particular technical form
of curriculum. There has been little interest in or problematizing of the shape,
format and form of the curriculum – beyond teachers' practical notions of use and
ease of working with this frame or that.

If we follow Dewey's (1915) analogy about the curriculum as a journey or a
map – those of us actually involved in making the curriculum in official syllabus
documents too often proceed without map or compass. We may have varying
views about the nature of the terrain, and, indeed, the eventual destination and
be willing to argue for these views and beliefs. But we have tended to have a

limited technical sense of the effects of different approaches to the cartography – of the implications of variable options in nomenclature, conventions for describing the terrain or the journeys eventually traversed. We have often found in our travels, that these categories were tabled by Departments and Ministries of Education on the basis of precedent, previous syllabi or those of other jurisdictions, and in some contexts on the very real necessities of printing and page counts for systems relying on external support. In many instances these decisions are made on the latest received wisdom about what kinds of formats teachers found useful and that they would comply with and work within, or which formats would enable accountability requirements to be met. Across all the contexts where curriculum work remains a key feature of education systems there continues to be little principled or robust debate on how to actually structure and write a curriculum document.

The history of curriculum is written as a debate over content. Whether we construe that content in terms of dominant ideologies, available discourses, disciplinary and knowledge paradigms or cultural narratives and values – at any historical moment, the process of reaching a curriculum settlement in democratic educational systems is subject to academic, public, media and political contestation. The ongoing debates in Japan over the textbook representation of WWII, the recent revisionist approach to the representation of Stalinism in Russian history texts and the ongoing debates in the US over the representation of immigration and migrant cultures are cases in point. Since the civil rights and feminist movements in the US, and more recently in relation to the land and knowledge claims of indigenous peoples, much of the controversy over curriculum has centered on the inclusion of revisionist histories, and the voices and experiences of cultural and linguistic minority groups, women and others who have historically been marginalized in official knowledge. Additionally, and of immediate relevance to our task here, the hundred-year debate in the US over the optimal way to teach reading (Chall, 1967) – phonics versus word recognition, whole language versus direct instruction and so forth – has been a focus of "back to the basics" movements in the US, Canada, Australia, New Zealand and the UK. Curriculum settlements are by definition unstable, contingent and volatile.

These are the debates of this chapter. We frame an approach to curriculum writing that foregrounds the technical form of the curriculum. While we do not diminish the importance of content in curriculum theory, we do claim that the identified gap in research that has investigated the very material effects of the technical form of the curriculum has left curriculum writers, policy makers, teachers and educators with little to call on as they make decisions about the shape and structure of curriculum documents and syllabi. We also make the claim that technical form matters for equity and for the quality of a system, even though it has been ignored within the curriculum field more generally. Before moving to these arguments however we take the time to define curriculum, syllabus and school subject as key terms for the chapter and for this volume.

Curriculum and Syllabus: Curriculum and Selective Tradition in Documents

We define the official curriculum document, a syllabus, as a map and a descriptive overview of the curriculum. It stands as a structured summary or outline of what should be taught and learned across the schooling years. The syllabus is *not* the curriculum per se.

Instead we define *curriculum* as the sum total of resources – intellectual and scientific, cognitive and linguistic, textbook and adjunct resources and materials, official and unofficial – that are brought together for teaching and learning by teachers, students and in the best case community, in classrooms and other learning environments. Curriculum is simply what is taught and learned in schools (Kelly, 2004). It is the very constitutive cultural and scientific "stuff" of education that is "transmitted" by the message systems of instruction and assessment (Bernstein, 1990). The syllabus, or official curriculum documentation, is a bid to shape and set the parameters of the curriculum, in a particular place and time.

As a decade of research on the enacted curriculum tells us, the official curriculum document cannot, by its very definition, contain and express, control and micro-manage what goes on in the classroom. It might constrain and enable certain practices and processes and not others – but the written document is never the same as the lived experience of the curriculum constructed and enacted by teachers and students in classrooms.

Westbury (2008) defines the syllabus as a "guide" to the curriculum while Schwartz (2006) describes the syllabus as a "written curriculum" that acts as an action-oriented "guide" or "tool" for teachers. The *Oxford English Dictionary* tells us that the term "syllabus" has evolved to refer to a "summary" of what is to be taught and learned. The syllabus has been used in fields such as literature and law to refer to an outline of curriculum. In all of these definitions there is some sense of the syllabus as an authoritative outline, schema or structure for courses of study. We have found it useful to define the syllabus as an official map of a school subject (Woods, Luke & Weir, 2010). That is, it is a document that provides teachers with a rationale and outline of the school subject in question, an overview and specification of preferred expected content to be taught and learned and a description of operational ways of appraising standards for gauging student performance. The expected learning(s) can and are stated in various forms such as key knowledge and understandings, skills, competences, processes and experiences.

So by drawing on Dewey's (1902) seminal definitions, we argue that the syllabus constitutes a map of the terrain to be covered over course or schooling phase. Accordingly the syllabus is not an exhaustive view of the territory, but it sets the grounds for teachers' and students' actual educational journey through the terrain. Teachers' professional judgement necessarily is called into play in the shaping of curriculum work programs, pedagogical approaches and classroom assessment as this will allow and enable individuals and cohorts to take different routes through the terrain. By this account the official curriculum document or syllabus is not and cannot be comprehensive or exhaustive, and it cannot and should not prescribe and dictate pedagogic method, approach, style and instructional interaction. This is optimally the domain of school and teacher professional judgement (Newmann & Associates, 1996; Fullan, 2008). So as Connelly and Connelly (in this volume) insist, the function of a quality syllabus should be to enhance teacher professionalism, and not as is the case with overly authoritative and prescriptive curriculum documents and adjunct policies, to constrain, regulate and deprofessionalize teaching.

Our case here then is that the syllabus is an outline of preferred expected knowledges, skills, performances and competences, with affiliated specification of expected standards. It should act as a guide and detail what is valued in a system's context. Such a document is optimally supported by diverse, well-developed professional training and development resources and targeted professional development and support (for reviews, see Feinman-Nemser, 2001; Timperley, Wilson, Barrar & Fung, 2007). These resources can then be assembled, developed and applied by teachers in local curriculum planning and designing processes. Such curriculum work by teachers and local authorities is a key element of successful systems in Finland and Ontario. Yet there is evidence that other systems are ignoring this evidence, shifting instead to overly prescriptive, narrowly defined notions of curriculum support.

What occurs in teaching and learning is shaped by a range of factors. The official curriculum documents are only one of these factors, although they remain key. Other factors include the background knowledge, cognitive and cultural resources that students bring to classrooms; teacher expertise gained through pre and in-service teacher education and practical experience; textbook selection and content; availability of further training and professional resources; school leadership; system governance and accountability structures; high stakes testing and examination; classroom assessment; available financial resources; the physical site of the classroom and so forth (see articles in Pinar, 2005; Connelly, He & Phillion, 2008). Even if educational science can identify "effective" and "appropriate" curricular programs and teaching methods, real change in pedagogy, and therefore change in student outcome patterns, is dependent upon how these come together in the social ecology of schools and classrooms (Raudenbush, 2005).

The confusion of the "curriculum" and the syllabus is part of the continued trend toward control and regulation of teachers and teachers' work. A document that attempts to *be* the curriculum in its entirety leads to a situation where the document itself and its implementation become difficult and overly complex, where teachers' professionalism and the local configurations of school and community relations and values are ignored. Instead, we argue that the official curriculum document or the syllabus should be seen as a defensible map of core skills, knowledges, competences and capacities to be covered, with affiliated statements of standards. These, in turn, need to be visibly aligned with systemic, school and classroom-level assessment practices.

School Subjects and their Discipline Heritage

Each syllabus or official curriculum document then is the map of a school subject. We define a school subject as an institutionally defined field of knowledge and practice for teaching and learning (Stengel, 1997; Deng, 2007; see also Deng in this volume). Unlike disciplines, school subjects are "uniquely purpose-built educational enterprises, designed with and through educational imagination towards educative ends" (Deng & Luke, 2008, p. 83).

The current and recurring debates over curriculum content have polarized opinion between disciplinary experts (e.g., scientists, literary theorists, historians, geographers, mathematicians) and educational experts (e.g., teacher educators and curriculum developers). These debates have confused "school subjects" – key learning areas in specific fields – with "disciplines", and so taking the time to clarify these terms is necessary here.

School subjects are different from but related to disciplines and practical applied fields of knowledge (see Deng, this volume). For school syllabi, the traditional, operational and practical unit of study is the school subject – not the "discipline" or "field" of knowledge per se. School subjects have different connections to disciplines and disciplinary knowledge (Shulman, 1986), to culturally or scientifically important tools, artefacts and texts (Cole, 1996) and to particular cultures and cultural knowledges (Ladson-Billings & Brown, 2008).

School subjects also reflect particular "versions" of related disciplines and applied fields. The syllabus, therefore, involves a motivated selection from identifiable intellectual, scientific and aesthetic paradigms within a traditional or emergent field or discipline and also from particular approaches to an applied domain of practice (e.g., workplace or professional competence). The contents of a syllabus are a "selective tradition" (Apple, 1978), with conscious and deliberate inclusions and exclusions from a vast range of possible disciplinary contents available. As Deng argues in this volume, school subjects are distinctive and purpose-built for particular contexts, times and spaces. School subjects are related to, but not the same as, disciplines and practical fields.

Disciplines are ways of thinking about, construing and describing the world (Cole, 1996; Freebody, 2006). As defined by Aristotle, disciplines are built to address scientific and cultural problems, to describe and explain a particular domain or field in the world. They entail specific epistemological stances on the world, commensurate first principles, relevant procedures and methods and distinctive goals and aims (McKeon, Owen & McKeon, 2001). They are also constructed and structured through purpose-built discourses, technical vocabulary, spoken and written genres and ways of representing the world (Lemke, 1990). By definition and necessity, disciplines evolve and change in response to new theories, new problems and changes in the phenomena they attempt to describe. This applies to both scientific fields (Kuhn, 1962) and to cultural and aesthetic fields (Dewey, 1938). At any given time, there is both consensus and dissensus — shared and contested claims among the practitioners of any field or discipline.

Unlike disciplines, school subjects occur in a distinctive institutional context (schools and classrooms), and they mark out a particular set of social and cultural educative goals (a social logic) for distinctive groups of people (a psychologic) (Dewey, 1902). They will likely draw upon the stances, principles, procedures, goals and aims of particular disciplines (Tyler, 1949). Therefore, as purpose-built and targeted units of study for schools, their technical form and contents must address specific institutional imperatives and contexts. They set the grounds and directions for the social interaction and knowledge-making that occurs in teacher/student classroom interaction.

The school subject has a variable relationship to disciplinary knowledges or to applied fields of knowledge, and this depends in part at least on the subject and school phase that they are a part of. In a key work, Stengel (1997) argues that school syllabi and curriculum can take different stances in relation to their foundational disciplinary fields. Curriculum can be based on the assumptions that:

(1)   academic disciplines precede school subjects
(2)   school subjects precede academic disciplines
(3)   the relation between the two is dialectic (Stengel, 1997).

In all cases it is important to consider the implications of these assumptions on the resultant curriculum work than to categorize the relationships according to such a framework.

The New Curriculum Settlement and Equitable Schooling

Having set the definitions of syllabus, curriculum and school subject we turn to larger questions. For the past five decades, western democratic education systems have attempted to strike a balance between the goals of economic development and competitiveness, on the one hand, and social and cultural development and cohesion on the other. What does it mean to argue for a syllabus design, a curriculum system, that achieves equity? We share with the other authors of this volume a broad commitment to social justice in education. Definitions and dialogue around educational equity have been the object of both complex social theory and everyday practice for the past four decades. By equity, we refer to what was broadly termed "equality of educational opportunity" in the post-1968 reframing of education as part of the civil rights movement, feminism, and, later, broadly liberationist debates around emergent and postcolonial education. Following Bowles and Gintis (1976) we suggest that education systems should be held to their meritocratic ideals: that students should have the opportunity to achieve to their optimal abilities regardless of their specific community background or dispositional characteristics. We take a strong stance that the contract between a school system and its students and their families and communities should be based on the democratic right to achieve at least at a threshold level of knowledge, skills and dispositions that will enable effective and useful citizenship.

To translate this for large educational systems requires a framework for understanding justice as it pertains to rights and responsibilities. The work of philosopher Nancy Fraser (1997) is regularly called upon by us and other educational researchers as a way to talk about such issues. She distinguishes between "recognitive" justice and "redistributive" justice, and more recently "representational" justice (Fraser, 2003). In curriculum terms, we can index the former concept to notions of "recognition" and the general move towards including, and thereby recognizing, those cultures and histories, knowledges and skills that have previously been marginalized in mainstream curriculum (Gale & Densmore, 2000). This is a matter of recognizing the different cultural backgrounds, linguistic competences, histories and approaches to learning of women, indigenous peoples, immigrants and those sub-communities of learners with special needs and interests. To date, issues of recognitive justice arise in cultural debates over curriculum content, but have rarely been dealt with in ways that alter mainstream curriculum in ways that are more than token.

On the other hand, redistributive justice, following Fraser, entails the equitable and fair distribution of material wealth, access to services, opportunities to participate in civic and economic life and so forth (Gale & Densmore, 2000). Education stands as a democratic entitlement. In educational terms, the OECD's concern with "high equity" systems aligns with redistributive justice: the more equitable achievement of conventionally-defined achievement outcomes, retention and participation rates and credentialing.

The OECD approach has been to argue for a new version of the human capital model, that stresses both relevant skills for the new economies and the development of social and cultural capital (McGaw, 2006). In the technical analysis of PISA data, the OECD has developed a terminology to describe the relative efficacy of systems. The tables of comparative national performance in literacy, maths and science provide evidence of relative "quality" of systems at producing conventionally-measured test achievement. The OECD (2005) describes equity both in terms of the spread of achievement across a population (e.g., through standard deviations), but also the relative performance of identifiable equity groups (e.g., migrants/second language learners) and the relative impact of socio-economic background on test performance (through regression analysis). While many systems achieve high average means in performance, they also have steep equity slopes, indicating that socio-economic background remains a strong predictor of performance (e.g., most developing countries, but notably, the US, UK and Germany). Other systems generate both high average means in performance but also flatter equity slopes, indicating that within those systems background has less of an impact on determining performance (e.g., Finland, Sweden, Canada, Ireland, Korea). These analyses demonstrate that quality and equity do not have to be traded off against each other. This is what Fraser (2003) refers to as a two dimensional model of justice – one that achieves both redistributive and recognitive justice and thus results in high quality and high equity outcomes within a system.

The pursuit of redistributive justice entails a fairer, more equitable distribution of conventional educational goods. However, as we have detailed, recognitive social justice also matters. Debates over the actual substantive intellectual, cultural and ideological contents of curriculum remain crucial. The focus of a good deal of curriculum research in the past twenty-five years has been on recognition – that is the representation of "other" knowledge, skills and capacities in the curriculum. There has been a determined effort by critical curriculum scholars to document the exclusion, marginalization, literary and historical misrepresentation of women and girls, cultural and ethnic minorities and indigenous peoples. Each curriculum settlement by definition is selective (Apple, 1990), a purposive set of inclusions and exclusions from a vast and potentially unlimited archive of human knowledge and thought, skill and capacity, history and technology. These selections, Apple's groundbreaking work goes on to suggest, are not arbitrary but have historically tended to mirror the interests of particular ruling cultures and class. In this regard, Apple's framing of the critical sociology of the curriculum in the early 1980s begins from Marx's prototypical political economy of knowledge: that the dominant ideas of an age, or in this case, of a curriculum settlement, reflect the interests of the ruling class. To take the argument a step further, school knowledge as ruling class "ideology" tends to be a systematic distortion, a misrepresentation in the interests of that class. This is most obviously the case in the representation of indigenous peoples in colonial and post-colonial contexts, and women in literature (see for example Ashcroft, Griffiths & Tiffin, 1989; Nieto, 2010). In a recent statement of this position, Nieto and colleagues argue for a stronger inclusion of minority "voice" in the curriculum – taken up by systems in attempts to embed indigenous knowledges and languages into the curriculum. Taken together, such critiques constitute the grounds for a social reconstruction of curriculum: for a reconstruction of textual contents, representations and discourses that better and more accurately express the aspirations, histories and values of hitherto marginalized social and cultural groups. The point of Apple's work relevant to us here, however, is that there will always be a selective tradition in action. If this is the case, then by definition there will always be contestation over the exclusions and inclusions, representations and revisioning of content. As curriculum theorists we have ample evidence and writing in our field to support these claims. First, as Michael Young (2008) has argued, not all knowledge selection is arbitrary, but may also include and entail representation of scientifically and aesthetically valuable information. Of course, we can turn such arguments into questions of "who decides" which knowledge is of developmental, scientific and aesthetic value. Young's current position does not solve this practical dilemma – but nor does the necessarily socially situated and politicized process of curriculum selection necessarily preclude Young's claim. Just because all content selection by definition must be done from a class invested position and standpoint, and therefore all curriculum is "socially constructed", this does not preclude the fact that that there may be dominant cultural knowledges, technologies and sciences that are potentially of educational value and power for everybody.

But there are two other critical caveats that are more central to our current task. First, while it undoubtedly addresses issues of "recognitive justice", there is the question about whether reconstruction of the ideological and cultural content of the curriculum will necessarily lead to "redistributive justice". That is, even where we modify the content of curriculum to better represent the histories and futures of marginalized communities and students – will this necessarily contribute to stronger and fairer patterns of the distribution of conventional achievement to these same groups? Many critical educators have provided qualitative case evidence that changing the content of curriculum will increase motivation, relevance, engagement and participation of marginalized students. Yet others have argued, following Gramsci, that empowerment consists of direct and transparent access not to minority, diasporic and marginalized knowledge, but to mainstream codes and canon, the "secret English" and disciplinary knowledge of dominant societies. This view is contra feminist views about calling on the "master's tools" for social transformation. While we would agree that it is difficult to critique discourse from within, we also know that the drive for equity and access cannot focus exclusively on revisionist curriculum content, as there remains a need to focus on ensuring greater access to conventional, canonical disciplinary and field knowledge – regardless of its historical origins and uses. The hazard is to ensure that providing access to the dominant curriculum does not lead to the revisionist curriculum being dealt with in token ways – both dimensions should be key elements of mainstream curriculum.

Despite the fact that these curriculum content arguments continue, what is rarely argued and remains unclear is the effect of the technical form of the curriculum and the determinate effects of this on the patterns of acquisition – and eventually transmission – of educationally acquired skills and knowledge, conventionally defined. In dealing with this educational problem the concepts of prescription and professionalism as they relate to curriculum policy and syllabus design are pertinent here.

Standarization of Education and Informed Prescription and Informed Professionalism

Modern science is predicated upon the establishment of uniform systems of measurement, common technical nomenclature and replicable procedures. Western science and governance alike work through the construction of grids of specification for the mapping of human subjects (Foucault, 1972). This push to standardization is central to the logics of education systems also. Over the past two to three decades the culture of accountability has redefined performance, outcomes and values of education.

What cannot be counted seems to no longer count. The general trend is toward increased authority and control by those agencies with the power to set standards for all manner of performance and capacity indicators, the establishment of competitive markets for educational knowledge products and ensuing extension of the reach and power of publishing institutions through billion dollar textbook markets, the deprofessionalization of the teaching workforce and a narrowing of the curriculum (see for example Spring, 2004; Nichols & Berliner, 2007).

In such a context the aim of education systems should be for a balance of informed prescription and informed professionalism. It is in this way that high quality and high equity educational outcomes may be achieved (Schleicher, 2008). Schleicher (2008) describes the conditions that characterize high quality, high equity systems as requiring a balance of accountability and professionalism. Specifically, he describes accountability as having central curriculum and evaluation systems that enable the steering of teachers' and schools' work toward particular educational outcomes. He calls this informed prescription. In terms of professionalism, he refers to schools' and teachers' relative degrees of autonomy in using professional judgement to shape and modify curriculum and pedagogy. This he calls informed professionalism.

An over-emphasis on high stakes accountability without a comparable investment in school autonomy and teacher professional capacity may lead to a form of prescription that generates uninformed professionalism. According to an increasing number of small and large-scale research projects, this has been the result of the US No Child Left Behind reforms (see Luke & Woods, 2009 for a much larger review of the research in this field). These reforms and those under the auspices of more recent initiatives such as *Race to the Top*, have generally taken the form of more explicitly scripted and directive pedagogy. In effect there is a bid in the United States to norm and standardize classroom pedagogy and the enacted curriculum in primary schools (Abedi, 2002). This is despite the fact that there are extensive studies that demonstrate that the effects of such approaches are mixed at best, leading variously to test score plateau effects, teacher deskilling and uneven outcomes patterns. In a major study of National Assessment of Educational Progress (NAEP) longitudinal test results, Nichols, Glass and Berliner (2005) claim that increased accountability through testing and prescriptive curricula has in fact deterred closing the "equity gap" in the US. The Harvard Civil Rights Project undertook a similar study, reanalysing state test score reports in relation to NAEP data. In that study, Lee (2006) reported that there had been no consistent or sustainable closure in the equity gap which, in some cases, had widened and notably, in the states with the longest-running high-stakes testing and accountability system, had had little sustained effects in terms of test score gains or improved achievement of students of minority groups. In a reanalysis of NAEP data, former US Assistant Secretary of Education Mike Smith (2007) reached similar findings. Recent reporting of evaluations of the NCLB initiatives present a similar picture with little or no evidence that the equity gap has been narrowed and continuing evidence that there has been collateral damage as a result of the policy. In Australia, early signs from similar policy trends suggest narrowing of curriculum and scarce improvements in the equity of the system. As restrictions tighten in 2012 with the implementation of the new Australian curriculum, new research is required to monitor the impacts of these moves in our system.

Our position is that the technical form of the official curriculum document in any system is at least as important as the curriculum content, and that when properly supported, it is possible that the technical form of the curriculum can set the school and classroom conditions for improving outcomes and results for all students. Uniform or excessively "hard" prescription as the basis for curriculum documents can decrease the level of, and possibility for, professionalism, and as a consequence deter both quality and equity.

School efficacy and systems results entail complex alignments of not just the variable factors studied in PISA, but also of historical, cultural and social trends, patterns and forces. Hence, direct comparison or adaptation of one national approach to another are never easy. Because of the complexity of policy and curriculum, each comparative case needs to be considered in terms of its overall systems policies and cultural and historical context (Alexander, 2001) (Luke considers these points more fully in the final chapter of this volume).

In Finland and Ontario, systems that are currently judged across a variety of measures as having highly successful schooling systems, the content statements included in official curriculum documents or syllabi blend and mix descriptions of traditional knowledge contents, behaviours and skills, global competences and more general capabilities, essential educational experiences and processes. While they provide general statements of the philosophy of the school subject and learning phase, these systems do not restrict themselves to strict statements of behavioural objectives or disciplinary/field contents and their syllabi do not describe or prescribe pedagogical approach in any detail. In both systems, the local adaptation of curriculum pace, unit planning and actual classroom pedagogical choices and instructional methods are left to teachers' professionalism, with adjunct resource materials available from various authorized sources.

Using these recognized quality systems as examples it is possible to make some claims about high quality and high equity systems and their general characteristics. To begin with, the technical form of the curriculum document or syllabus is relatively low definition in both cases. That is, it outlines expected coverage and standards without attempting to script or control pedagogy. So there is an expectation that teachers will exercise informed and autonomous professionalism – but there is also space provided for this. Teacher professionalism is supported at multiple levels through aligned preservice training, professional resources, inservice training and annual local system of school curriculum planning. The prescription of the system is enforced not through high stakes testing, but rather through parsimonious testing and assessment that enables schools to diagnostically assess their performance relative to comparable schools, through strong system's messages about standards and equity and through the official provision of a range of professional development resources from various sources and at multiple levels of the system.

An axiom of curriculum studies is that the *curriculum-in-use* generates efficacy and outcomes. The syllabus or other official curriculum documents may enable and constrain, but do not necessarily reflect or index what is taught and learned in classrooms. The principal way that national debates have dealt with this is to debate the political, cultural and scientific values and truth claims of different stances on content – and to augment this with criticism of teacher workforce capability and professionalism. This approach usually leads to a dual policy approach: fix and mandate new (or old) content (change the prescription); enforce this through increased accountability pressure, incentives and disincentives for teachers (change the professionalism). Schleicher (2008) refers to responses of this sort as uninformed prescription that is linked to uninformed professionalism. Uninformed prescription, he argues, may entail strong centralized accountability without the resources or the opportunities for building strong knowledge-based and evidence-based teacher professionalism. He stresses the need for an approach to curriculum that lays out informed prescription centrally (through the syllabus setting core learnings and specification of standards) but that also sets the conditions for local teacher professionalism, school and classroom-based developmental diagnostic use of evidence (see Klenowski in this volume for a more detailed discussion) and the exercise of local curriculum interpretation and translation, development and implementation. This is part of a process of upping the bar for all students to achieve and raising expectations for learners while encouraging a range of relevant pedagogical approaches. Schleicher refers to this as informed prescription.

Schleicher's (2008) proposed solution model favours the production of adaptive professionalism over reproductive professionalism (Darling-Hammond & Bransford, 2005). He claims that in high quality, high equity systems, teachers use professional knowledge and evidence to make informed and relevant decisions about teaching and learning. In other words, informed prescription depends upon teachers' professional capacity to locally interpret, adapt and adjust curriculum content, pacing, presentation, interaction and structure to particular institutional, community settings and student cohort characteristics (e.g., Cochran-Smith, 1999). It includes a capacity to use evidence on student background, prior achievement, developmental and diagnostic progress, school and classroom-based assessment to make curricular and instructional decisions.

With strong, targeted professional development and powerful system-based messages about equity, a specific focus on instructional adaptation of the curriculum for those students traditionally least well served by schooling makes a difference (OECD, 2005; Schleicher, 2008). The literature on effective curriculum for students of cultural and linguistic minority backgrounds, indigenous students and students from low SES backgrounds offers a clear lesson, that being, that teacher quality and professionalism at the school and classroom level makes the most substantive difference to student achievement (Newmann & Associates, 1996; Ladson-Billings, 1997;

Cochran-Smith, 2001; Gore, Williams & Ladwig, 2006; Ladwig, 2010). It also suggests that a clear system-wide focus on equity can work, when enacted through school-based curriculum and pedagogical foci.

According to Darling-Hammond and Bransford (2005) (and also Levin in this volume), adaptive professionalism entails the capacity to modify curriculum and generate new curriculum in relation to student cohort variables, and changing contexts and demands of knowledge fields. The uninformed prescription model, reinforced by testing for purposes of surveillance and quality control, mandates that teachers reproduce existing, mandated programs and approaches. Its most extreme form is in commodified curriculum packages, teacher-proof or scripted instruction, where the system attempts to micromanage teacher to student interaction in the interests of quality assurance and accountability through curriculum prescription (see Shannon in this volume). In the US context this has led to, at best, mixed effects on National Assessment of Educational Progress testing performance (Lee, 2006; Smith, 2007), and at worst a host of collateral effects that include narrowing of the curriculum, teaching to the test, teacher deskilling and attrition, documented test score fraud and manipulation at the state and school level – with no visible sustainable effects at improving equity outcomes (Nichols & Berliner, 2007).

Schleicher (2008) argues that an emphasis on centralized standards and curriculum mandates must be balanced against high levels of workforce curriculum professional decision-making. Informed prescription requires well-resourced teacher professional capacity. His argument is that the high quality and high equity systems tend to strike a balance on the informed axis (e.g., Finland, Canada, Sweden). Using PISA data, it is possible to claim that highly marketized systems with strong accountability, testing and compliance foci can lead to uninformed prescription and uninformed professionalism. The approach of high quality and high equity systems then, entails a balance of systemic standard setting and accountability with well-resourced, local school leadership, with a strong focus on building teacher capacity at curriculum, pedagogy and assessment.

These are crucial caveats on syllabus design. Syllabi in and of themselves never have direct, hypodermic and unmediated effects on classroom instruction and assessment. But they are part of the complex message systems of education (Bernstein, 1990), of curriculum, instruction and assessment. These in turn can be differentially aligned, enabled and disenabled by other elements of educational structure and practice, ranging from teacher capacity and knowledge, professional support structures and school administration structures to system governance structures and school culture and ethos. As Welner and Oakes (2008) concluded in a major review of curriculum structure: "the relationship between structures and instruction is loose; the former can facilitate the latter but cannot dictate it" (p. 91). The aim is not only to establish a fine balance between prescription and professional judgment, but for the technical form and parameters of the central prescription to facilitate rather than dictate classroom pedagogy and assessment (Welner & Oakes, 2008).

Part of the standarization debate has included the setting of standards for all manner of educational concepts. This trend is discussed more fully by Klenowski in this volume. Here, however, we wish to comment on one section of the standards debate that receives little air time and that we have discussed in other forums where our aim has been to reform policy (Luke, Weir & Woods, 2008). This additional consideration, when thinking about standards, concerns the delivery system's accountability and what we call delivery standards. The capacity of the system to provide requisite and optimal teaching and learning conditions is central to curriculum delivery. While currently the focus on content and performance standards alone places the burden of proof (and we would say access) "on teachers and students almost exclusively" (Ericsson, 2005, p. 239), we suggest that this trend should shift.

The establishment of baseline delivery standards within a system's curriculum and syllabus design process is a key foundation for an equitable system and part of the informed prescription of any system. Content and performance standards without delivery standards are necessary but not sufficient and perhaps indeed impossible to achieve. Delivery standards define the availability of programs, staff and other resources that schools, districts, states and systems should be accountable to provide so that students are able to meet content and performance standards (Ravitch, 1996). They are criteria for, and the basis of, assessing the sufficiency or quality of the resources, practices and conditions necessary to provide all students with an opportunity to learn, and teachers the best opportunity to teach. In other words they explain what systemic support – in terms of fiscal, human, material and curricular resources – is required to provide a high-quality, high equity education system and meet the documented goals of any education system.

The balance of informed prescription and informed professionalism relies not simply on the strength of central mandate, a top-down demand upon teachers, and by default, students. Instead it relies upon a total system commitment to the realization of professionalism. The compelling evidence after a decade of policy suggests that simple hard prescription, with incentives and disincentives will not yield improved quality or equity. Rather, the setting of learning expectations and standards needs to occur in the context where the system's resources converge on teacher professional capacity at curriculum, instruction and evaluation. This requires the setting of clear, aspirational and transparent standards for educational performance, but it also requires access to resources, relevant, useful professional development and other school support structures.

It should ultimately be our challenge as educators to create rigorous systems that employ professionals who are given the authority to act and the support, knowledge and responsibility to do so in ways that ensure equitable outcomes for all students (Schleicher, 2008). In systems that claim to have the educational goal of providing high quality and high equity education, there should be an assumption that the system's syllabi – its contents and technical form – can be part of achieving this goal. The syllabus has the important function of setting conditions for enhancing a knowledge-rich professionalism – but other policy settings also need to be in place. These include a clear and simplified message system about aims and priorities regarding quality and equity (see Levin in this volume) and delivery standards such as those described in Luke, Weir and Woods, (2008), which map out the professional infrastructure, workforce capacity, school governance and management structures that likewise are geared to enable instructional quality (Timperley et. al, 2007).

Curriculum, Equity and the Technical Form of Curriculum Documents

The technical form of the syllabus has been neglected in current curriculum debates. How the syllabus is shaped, how it is used in the context of system accountability around standards and how teacher use of the syllabus is resourced and supported sets conditions for a balance of prescription and professionalism. Establishing that balance in ways that are conducive to high quality with high equity teaching and learning is the task facing policy makers and teachers.

As detailed earlier, for those of us who begin from a normative view on education committed to equity and social justice, a principal concern has been over the politics of recognition. The broad assumption of such approaches is that the modification of curriculum to include the values, ideologies, histories and practices of linguistic and cultural minorities, indigenous peoples, women and others will set the grounds for a more inclusive educational environment – in ways that begin to achieve more equitable outcomes for all students, but these groups specifically.

But what part does the *form* of the curriculum take in the ideal of achieving a socially-just education system – one that provides both high quality but also high equity? The technical form of the curriculum was first described by Michael Apple (1978) in the landmark work *Ideology and Curriculum*. Apple's argument was elegantly simple: that the way that knowledge was shaped and defined in official curriculum documents, attendant textbooks and curriculum packages had potentially reproductive effects – shaping the kinds of skills, knowledges and competences that children and young people had access to. His example at the time was of a science textbook and, notably, an accompanying teachers' guide that narrowly circumscribed and limited the kinds of skills and practices, knowledges and discourses that children had access to. This example proved to be a telling one. Apple went on to argue, using Braverman's (1974) Marxist analysis of labour – that particular curricular forms had the effect of deskilling teachers, separating conception from execution, thereby turning teaching into a mechanical, cognitively shallow activity. Three decades later – after a decade of moves to legislate scripted approaches to literacy and numeracy instruction by the US and UK governments and more recently in Australia (with a particular focus on the education of students in remote indigenous communities) – Apple's analysis retains its theoretical and practical relevance.

A series of studies have explored Apple's model of teacher deskilling. Drawing from contemporary learning sciences, Darling-Hammond and Bransford's (2005) programmatic critique of those approaches to teaching that de-professionalize curriculum and pedagogy, in effect turning teachers' professionalism into displays of routine expertise that operationalize prescribed practices. Their point is that this approach may deter innovative and creative responses to new curriculum content, to emergent and heterogeneous student background knowledge and learning needs, and, indeed, to the professional challenges of new knowledge, new community and new technological conditions. But the effect does not stop with teachers. McCarty's (2008) study of the effects of scripted pedagogy on literacy teaching and learning in indigenous communities in Arizona shows how heavily managed and scripted teaching can reduce and silence cultural knowledge, linguistic diversity and, ultimately, stifle independent and autonomous thought.

How might we set the conditions for the technical form of syllabus to be organized in ways that support more equitable workings of the enacted curriculum? This is not a straightforward matter. The analytic and empirical question relates to what curriculum form can set the conditions for the more equitable and socially just patterns of achievement for students?

Throughout our own work as researchers and teacher educators, we have maintained a steadfast commitment to democratic education for equity and social justice. In curriculum theory, this has entailed a focus on the need to change the substantive content of curriculum to include those histories and cultural world views, experiences and epistemological standpoints of those communities and cultures that have been excluded from mainstream curriculum. And it has included a focus on the need to alter curriculum, pedagogy and assessment – the key message systems of schooling – in ways that enable the more equitable transmission and acquisition of conventionally defined educational outcomes, from standardized test scores to credential acquisition. Our aim, then, has been nothing less than to break, alter or, at least, ameliorate longstanding facts of the unequal processes of intergenerational social, cultural and economic reproduction in schooling.

But what does this approach – and the extensive curriculum research and scholarship, theory and analysis that curriculum researchers have developed – have to say to many of our professional colleagues who work at constructing and building the extensive curriculum documents that guide teachers? Here we refer not to those who work with and for publishers actually putting together units, lesson plans and the ubiquitous packages of textbooks and resource series – though their direct and indirect influence through official state textbook adoptions remains. Our focus here is on curriculum developers, bureaucrats and systems organizers – many of whom are former teachers, principals and teacher educators – who work in state departments, school districts and large schools actually writing and constructing official curriculum documents: the syllabus documents that set out to guide, shape and enable teachers' and students' work.

No doubt particular curriculum content or a particular pedagogical approach can contribute to these tasks. The significant modification of mainstream approaches to schooling can make a difference – and there is evidence that in specific contexts, approaches to critical literacy, culturally appropriate pedagogy, curriculum contents that are more inclusive can – and will – make a difference for those students who historically have not done well in mainstream schooling. We also acknowledge that models of direct instruction in basic skills, of traditional didactic, rote pedagogy also have shown demonstrable effects on specific cohorts of cultural and linguistic minority, economically marginalized students in specific contexts (Luke, 2008). Detailed ethnographic studies of schools and classrooms have shown that pedagogies, flexibly exercized in response to cohort and context, can make a difference. And indeed, any curriculum ultimately comes to ground in the classroom, in teachers' and students' lived and embodied exchanges. So while in this chapter we focus our conclusions on curriculum, we are well aware of the importance of pedagogic relay and of assessment – that is the daily interactions and playing out of relations of and between communities, teachers and students – in the lived experience and future translation of schooling for students.

Several factors influence the technical form of the official curriculum documents. The curriculum approach taken in a specific curriculum context has an influence. Outcomes-based syllabus documents (Spady, 1994) for example map out a technocratic model of education (Apple, 1990) that breaks subject areas into smaller constituent parts, thus leading to a technical form of enumerated categorical lists of outcomes for specific subjects and age/grades. The process-based model on the other hand, which is affiliated with the cognitive developmental work of Bruner in the post-Sputnik era, has always treated curriculum in terms of a developmental continuum of educational experiences and processes and as such the technical form of the curriculum tends to be more strongly developmental, stressing students' engagement with and experience of particular repertoires affiliated with subject areas and content. The traditional content model, based on a neoclassical model of curriculum from the work of Bloom, Hirsch and Ravitch, is based on the identification of canonical knowledges and texts in fields. Its technical form entails the enumeration and prescription of content knowledge, prescribed readings and topics. Differently, the critical model, affiliated with critical theory and cultural studies in the humanities and social sciences strongly with its emphasis on the need for competing, revisionist descriptions and models of the world and for critical, active and agentive student engagement with knowledge has had little impact on the technical form of the curriculum, but directly addresses content issues and tends to stress higher order or critical skills. As such curriculum theory has impacted upon the technical form of the curriculum, but there are other important factors, not always visible, that impact on the technical form of syllabus documents also. In the sections that follow we map out some of these factors.

Technical Form and the New Economy

Over the past decade there has been a shift toward defining educational goals and philosophy directly in relation to knowledge economies and the demands of changing technology, labour markets, cultural and economic globalization. During that time, many OECD ministries of education have moved their systems' philosophies and policies to address economic, cultural and social change. These include still-emergent foci on intercultural communications, new geopolitical conditions and relations, multiliteracies, digital and youth cultures – and varied curriculum responses to increased multiculturalism and multilingualism of the student cohorts (e.g., articles in Green & Luke, 2006; Kelly, Green & Luke, 2008). But the principal effect has been a call for curriculum that will ensure that new skills and knowledges for the new economies and technologies will be acquired (Australian Council of Deans, 2002; Cope & Kalantzis, 2007). This is a reframing of post war human capital theory, a focus on the production of skilled workers and, since 9/11, cultural cohesion. It marks both an extension of the generic skills models introduced through vocational education in the 1990s (in Australia these have been detailed in a suite of reports see for e.g., The Finn Report, Australian Education Council, 1991; and the Carmichael Report, Employment and Skills Formation Council, 1992) and a substantive shift in the perceived orientations of work in new economies (Gee, Hull & Lankshear, 1996). There is a robust debate over the nature of these skills, over their relevance and applicability in specialist domains and across the population and whether and how they can be integrated into mainstream curriculum (e.g., Reid, 2005). There is an ongoing debate over what these new knowledge economy skills mean for questions of equity (OECD, 2005).

The impact of these recurrent debates has seen many systems adopt an overlay of generic competences to be mapped against the traditional school subjects in each syllabus. This has been a common approach internationally, but there are examples of systems that have worked at a more integrated level. For example, the Ontario approach has been to embed the generic skills (e.g., higher order thinking) in the standards matrix that teachers use to report student performance in each subject.

There is little or no empirical data on the actual uptake of generic skills. As one example, the New Basics approach (Department of Education, Training and the Arts, 2004) was an innovative approach to rich curriculum trialled in Queensland in the early 2000s and its evaluation (Australian Council of Education Research, 2004) showed that innovative approaches to curriculum and pedagogy could yield improvement on key generic skills (multiliteracies, planning, collaborative work, cultural understandings, and intellectual depth) without basic skill test score decline. These results were achieved through the embedding of the new skill sets in mandated curricular tasks. The most thoroughly researched and documented work on generic skills teaching, learning and acquisition is in the vocational education areas (for a review, see Billet, Fenwick and Sommerville, 2006). Further, the reported results of the variety of systemic testing for accountability purposes across different contexts and systems provide data on skill acquisition in traditional areas of literacy and numeracy. But work on the actual uptake of other generic skills in classrooms and the effects upon students' longitudinal pathways and achievement patterns has yet to be undertaken (Luke, Weir, Land & Sanderson, 2007).

The generic skills for the new economy argument has had an impact on the technical form of the curriculum. Specifically, most systems now list in their official curriculum or syllabus documents these new skills for cross-curricular integration into teaching and learning. Yet their impacts on the enacted curriculum in specific subject areas have not been substantiated or documented. Further, other than basic literacy and numeracy performance, they are not tied to high stakes assessment and accountability systems (Luke, Weir, Sanderson & Land, 2007). As a result, those assessable generic skills tend to count in student evaluation, while those skills affiliated with the new economy that cannot yet be assessed or evaluated (e.g., multiliteracies, intercultural communication, collaborative group work) have been de-emphasized in work programs.

Technical Form and Standardized Testing

Comparative benchmarking of system testing data in literacy and numeracy at key junctures has been established in a variety of systems across OECD countries and contexts. It is axiomatic in curriculum theory and in educational policy studies that the higher the stakes of the external testing system, the higher the accountability pressure rating (Nichols, Glass & Berliner, 2005). That is, in the technocratic accountability model, the relationship between curriculum, pedadgogy and assessment is realigned. The higher the stakes in terms of the comparative aggregate and individual assessment of schools, teachers and students – especially when systemic incentives and disincentives are applied – the more the system moves towards hard prescription (Welner & Oakes, 2008). The US No Child Left Behind legislation has epitomized the model of hard prescription: with a systematic set of sanctions (e.g., public censure, replacement of staff, funding cutbacks, closure, outsourcing of students, issuing of vouchers) and incentives (e.g., public praise and rankings, merit pay) for schools meeting and not meeting test score targets. In high stakes systems, official formal assessment tends to mediate the enacted curriculum; teachers responding to punitive measures from systems can be driven to prepare students for the tests and this leads to narrowing the scope of the curriculum (Nichols & Berliner, 2007). Further, an over-reliance on testing to enforce prescription of the curriculum can have the collateral effect of constraining teacher professional capacity and judgement (Darling-Hammond & Bransford, 2005). This may limit rather than enable the school level reform of pedagogy (Newmann and Associates, 1996; Fullan, 2008) and serious questions have been raised about the sustainability of any test score gains achieved through heightened accountability pressure ratings (Nichols, Glass & Berliner, 2005).

What is crucial, then, is that the domains and constructs of the assessment instruments stand in a principled alignment with the curriculum (see Klenowski in this volume for further discussion). Most systemic testing systems have attempted this task of alignment. However, problems arise regarding outcomes that may be officially valued in the syllabus but are beyond the scientific description and measurement of psychometrics and available large-scale assessment instrumentation (see Moss, Girard & Haniford, 2006). These outcomes have tended to become less visible in the enacted curriculum of systems with strict accountability as testing policy driving their approach.

No matter how technically excellent, tests and examinations will tend to narrow or make a defacto selection from curriculum into what is describable within their testing format and technical parameters. There is an extensive international literature on the limits of conventional testing and examinations in assessing and describing student achievement in a broad range of domains – from traditional judgements (e.g., artistic taste), developmental claims (e.g., creativity) and new workplace competencies (e.g., collaborative work) to social outcomes (e.g., character, values) and new digital competencies (e.g., online communication, gaming) (e.g., Rochex, 2006; Baker, 2007). The crucial issues of adolescent identity raised by Alvermann and Marshall (in this volume) – central to the Middle Phase of schooling – and the challenges of assessing early years capacities (see Greishaber in this volume) also stand outside the ambit of conventional assessment. Furthermore, there is ongoing debate over how best to assess and capture a range of cognitive phenomena: higher order thinking, critical thinking and analysis and competence with new digital multiliteracies.

The expansion of accountability stakes around test and examination results have the potential effect of narrowing the curriculum, of increasing the teaching and learning of that which is assessable to assessment using conventional techniques. This fits well with the "outcomes-based" technical form, featuring a conceptual reductionism of learning and knowledge to assessable skills. Standardized testing can be an important part of informed prescription. It can help raise teacher and school expectations of children of identifiable equity groups and it can assist in developmental diagnostic decisions by teachers. But if the testing and examination system becomes too high stakes and too exhaustive, the risk is that the tests become a form of defacto curriculum, with teachers and schools ignoring or eliminating that which isn't tested and in this way the accountability context can deter informed professionalism in local curriculum and assessment practice, and therefore the achievement of improved quality and equity. Additionally there can be a constraining of the development and teaching of new capabilities that are emerging in civic, community and workplace life. To combat this narrowing of the curriculum there is an urgent need for the implementation of non-test-based assessment approaches and instruments at the system, school and classroom level. It is important to recognize the centrality of classroom-based, teacher-based assessment in improving and broadening the achievement of students from diverse learning backgrounds and histories, especially in a context where systems-based tests and assessments are so highly valued.

Technical Form and Teacher Professionalism

There has been public debate over issues of curriculum content, and issues of teacher quality as part of moves to improve outcomes in numerous systems over the past five years. The debates are usually founded on reanalysis of comparative historical data and claims that this data indicates that the overall quality of teachers, as represented in their prior achievement levels, had declined (see for example Leigh, 2005). Currently in systems such as the US and Australia there has been public criticism of admission of teacher education students with lower senior matriculation scores. This debate reinforces claims that problems with curriculum and overall achievement can be directly attributable to lack of teacher quality. These claims are often matched with claims about the disciplinary knowledge and capacity of teachers in the sciences and mathematics.

The response to these claims of teacher ineffectiveness and decline of standards can be constructed as a binary. Teachers' unions and professional organizations and many teacher educators have argued for increased pay, expanded professional development funding, smaller class sizes and teacher-based approaches to reform and the recognition of merit. The response from many government and systems personnel has been to call for or implement merit pay structures and to further increase accountability pressure through testing and public comparisons of school results.

There is a clear consensus in the school reform and improvement literature, and in curriculum development and implementation research that teacher quality counts. By this we mean that the pedagogic relay as it is expressed in teacher–student interaction in day-to-day schooling can impact student outcomes. But exactly what elements of teacher knowledge are required to improve quality and equity is the object of theoretical debate – and a paucity of empirical data. Our findings with colleagues as part of a recent large scale evaluation of school reform in Australia has been that in those schools where reform is not focused on pedagogy, the improvement to student outcomes on conventional measures is minimal regardless of shifts – however significant – on school ethos and student or community engagement.

The preferred strategy in the US, UK and more recently Australia and other similar contexts to solve the education quality problem has first entailed the development of teacher standards and statutory bodies to regulate teacher education programs (for a review, see Mayer, 2005 and also Little, Horn & Bartlett, 2000; Little, 2003). This includes a range of strategies including setting standards for program accreditation, and exit testing of teacher education graduates using standardized instruments. Additionally the US and UK have mandated scripted instructional approaches. In the UK national literacy program and US Reading First legislation, teachers are trained or accredited by textbook publisher trainers to teach mandated curriculum packages. These explicitly prescribe the pace, content and approach to teaching. Adherence is monitored via administrative observation at the school level and regular standardized testing. This has spurred the development of a multi-billion dollar textbook commodity industry (Larson, 2001), which continues to be the subject of intense legislative scrutiny in the US debates over NCLB.

The approach is not new, dating back to the first scientific reading series developed in 1913 in the United States. These evolved into teacher proof curricula, materials for teaching that could be taught by any teacher with variable levels of training

(Giroux, 1988; Allington & McGill-Franzen, 2000). Later in this volume Shannon's chapter details the mixed results of this approach.

The principle of scripted pedagogy is for the curriculum materials to standardize and, therefore, quality control classroom-based curriculum, instructional approach and assessment. This shifts the locus of authority for everyday instructional decisions, selection and use of curriculum materials away from teacher professionalism and towards the package. Reproductive expertise is the ability to deploy a scripted pedagogy with some degree of efficiency and effectiveness (Darling-Hammond & Bransford, 2005). Adaptive professionalism refers to the ability to interpret syllabi, engage with diverse learners and school contexts and to make relevant and effective decisions about how to modify, alter and adapt the curriculum in relation to evidence on learner background, ability, pace and approach to learning. This, they argue, is essential for addressing the needs of equity and at-risk groups, and for improving the overall quality of education. Hargreaves (2003) argues that this marks a shift in teachers' work from an industrial, Fordist production model to a new economy focus on teaching as a contextual, adaptive and problem-solving activity. He goes on to argue that it is contradictory to have schools aiming for the production of knowledge-economy workers, while at the same time setting conditions where teachers are not building and using new professional knowledge.

Prominent high quality and high equity systems have made pre and inservice teacher training, professionalism and local curriculum capacity high priorities. The cultural contexts of many prominent systems such as Korea, Ireland, Finland and Canada value teachers and teaching as a profession (cf. Alexander, 2001). The US-based literature on school reform has provided case-based evidence that effective teachers of minority and lower socio-economic students have high levels of professionalism and the capacity to adapt curriculum to specific cohorts of students' cultural background knowledge and cognitive strategies (Newmann & Associates, 1996; Ladson-Billings, 1997). So it is unlikely that teachers without adaptive professionalism characteristics will be successful teachers when judged on equity grounds, regardless of their success in a reproductive sense.

Debates around teacher quality have impacted on the technical form of the curriculum, leading to increases in the level of technical specification for syllabus content leading to an expansion of syllabus content and foundational explanation in an attempt to compensate for perceived lack of workforce expertise in specific fields. High quality and high equity systems have taken a different strategy: with tighter syllabi, rich professional development resources, stronger alignment of syllabi with preservice teacher education and structural incentives for ongoing professional development and teacher development. Systems that are high quality and high equity value and support adaptive teacher professionalism.

To reiterate our position, we argue here that the technical form of the syllabus or other official curriculum documents in any system is at least as important as the curriculum content, and that when properly supported, it is possible that the technical form of the curriculum can set the school and classroom conditions for improving outcomes and results for all students. Uniform or excessively hard prescription as the basis for curriculum documents can decrease the level of and possibility for professionalism, and as a consequence deter both quality and equity.

The Technical Form of the Curriculum and Improving Outcomes

Our view is that the informed prescription, informed professionalism balance cannot be achieved by incrementally more explicit and more detailed prescription within syllabus documents. Longer, more detailed and extensive syllabi are not the answer. Moves towards higher, more explicit definition have not provided better or more informed professional practice, or improved outcomes for students and their communities. Increased high-stakes testing can encourage teachers to begin to teach to the test, the risk being that the test will become the syllabus. Expansion of syllabus documents will not provide a solution to this risk. Instead what we suggest is the consideration of low definition syllabus documents and the expansion of support to identify, and where necessary build, the professionalism of teachers. This leads us to the point of stating our recommendations for syllabus design, which we do here in general terms, reiterating that all contexts are different and require locally-contextualized responses to educational problems and challenges.

We began this chapter with the claim that the syllabus is not the curriculum. The technical form we propose would stand as a map. It would aim towards low definition, parsimonious and economical statements – avoiding lengthy lists of outcomes, content or skills and long pre-service style introductions to foundational knowledges. The syllabus can guide and enhance professional expertise – but it cannot and should not act as a substitute for well-resourced and informed teacher pre- and inservice development. Furthermore, the combination of low definition syllabi and rich adjunct professional resources provides the system with more flexibility in responding to change in the field and to controversy over content.

To achieve informed professionalism, teachers would then turn to authorized professional development resources, approved and aligned textbook materials and programs, web resources and expertise gained and enhanced in pre and inservice training. The corpus of professional materials would be purpose-built for teachers' needs, vocabularies and technical expertise. It would be more readily modified and altered in response to new cohorts of students, cohort needs of teachers, change and innovation in pedagogy and field knowledge. These resources – the basis for what Schleicher (2008) refers to as knowledge rich professionalism – should and must be adaptable, flexible and continuously under expert professional review.

Syllabus documents should be as short as possible, the length determined by the task of mapping the subject. They must be written in teacher-accessible, professional language. They must follow the principles of low definition curriculum. They should refer teachers to adjunct online resources on materials selection, unit and lesson planning, classroom and school-based assessment, pedagogical strategies and the specific needs for identifiable student cohorts including indigenous students,

students with special needs, migrant, rural and socioeconomically marginalized students. Rather than jam-packing the syllabus with foundational understandings, resources, sample lessons and units, classroom assessment guidelines and special considerations for learners, the relegation of these materials to authorized and fully-vetted, teacher-accessible professional resources is one way of ensuring low definition documents.

Each syllabus should cover a designated school subject in its specific phase or year level. Wherever possible these should be collected into phase statements as this enhances opportunities for co-curricular planning between grades and supports the explicit opportunities to address questions of primary to secondary transition. The organization should also provide teachers with a synoptic view of developmental scope and sequence that is not strictly age or grade hierarchical, and which enables teachers to adopt the curriculum to accommodate a broader range of developmental capacities and backgrounds.

Syllabus documents should aim to identify domains of a subject (e.g., writing, reading) and identify for each domain, specific expected learnings. These statements of learnings should be as brief, accessible and minimal in number as possible, with only those deemed as essential for all students – not minima but a map of what is to be learned in the field – being included. These could be described in principled blends of various categories: ranging from traditional content statements, skills and behaviours to tasks and performances or processes and experiences. This would enable a flexibility to accommodate different school subject philosophies, different phase requirements and different curriculum models.

Syllabus documents must provide indicative standard statements of key domains and learnings to guide teacher judgement and provide a common vocabulary for teachers, students and parents. Such statements should be based on an agreed model of cross-curricular capabilities. The articulation of these standards in comparable judgments could be supported through moderation procedures appropriate to the subject and phase. The aim of the standards would be to establish a shared vocabulary for talking about the setting of assessable tasks, the judging and gauging of student performance and the translation of these into useful and comprehensible statements of achievement.

Syllabus documents necessarily indicate where systemic standardized instruments and mandated moderated assessment are linked to specific domains and learnings, but they should also provide suggested guidelines for school and teacher assessment practices. Technical details, exemplars and models would be available in adjunct materials, such as the proposed common task or project assessment bank.

These principles suggest a particular technical format of the syllabus with categories used to cut the school subject in ways that provide teachers with a productive means to do the curriculum work required. To achieve this, syllabus documents should include a statement of the philosophy and logic of the school subject it details, noting key developments and benchmarks in research on the subject and local contextual variables. This would enable curriculum developers to choose stronger alignments with disciplines and applied fields, or more loosely coupled and multi-disciplinary relationships as appropriate. The statement should be brief and defensible, and preclude an unprincipled collection of outcomes or contents that was not justifiable on foundational grounds or benchmarked against relevant fields. It would make transparent and accessible any paradigm selections from a particular discipline or field.

Of equal importance is a statement of the overall educational purposes and goals of the school subject, noting the benefits and value of mastery of the subject and its affiliated learnings. This would enable curriculum developers and teachers to consider how and where mastery of the school subject fits into the philosophy of the system and the overall goals for the development and pathways of students. It would require that curriculum writers engage with and state the overall goals of the subject (e.g., scientific literacy for all, the production of specialized scientific expertise, skills for active citizenship, values) and briefly state how these would have longitudinal educational benefit to the students, the community and society. It would require that subject content decisions be justified with reference to the overall educational development and benefit of the students in the system. It would preclude content inclusion on the grounds of past inclusion or disciplinary precedent without educational justification.

Additionally, syllabi should include a statement on the phase/age/developmental issues of the diverse communities of learners (e.g., by gender, language, Indigeneity, age, location, special needs) that the subject is to be taught to. This would enable curriculum developers and teachers to consider how to shape the interpretation and translation of syllabus content and select appropriate resources that match student background knowledge, cultural and linguistic diversity, approaches to learning, prior achievement and special learning needs. Curriculum developers need to consider the varied phase-specific cohorts of students likely to study the subject and their diverse resources, capabilities and potential challenges – the equity focus characteristic of high quality and high equity systems. Developing such a statement would require explicit consideration of the instructional and assessment variables impacting on a diverse cohort of students. It would enable curriculum developers and teachers to consider how to shape the delivery of the syllabus and select appropriate resources that match student age/phase, background knowledge, cultural and linguistic diversity, approaches to learning and prior achievement. It would enable curriculum developers and teachers to consider how to shape curriculum and instruction in relation to the distinctive resources and challenges of indigenous and ethnically diverse students. It would dovetail with policy foci on equity and provide the explicit equity focus that characterizes high quality, high equity systems. This approach would preclude statements of content within syllabi of official curriculum documents that were not based on due consideration of all the system's learners.

Of course all official curriculum documents need to include clear, simple and economical statements of expected learnings. These could be framed as any locally relevant combination of knowledges, skills, behaviours, performances, experiences, competences and capacities, in language technically accessible and useful for teachers. This would enable curriculum developers to focus and define the content of specific school subjects according to different curriculum models. It would enable teachers to select instructional approaches and assessment practices that fit the learners and the expected learnings. They should be essential and expected for all students, but would not be minimum competency statements. Each expected learning could be accompanied by a teacher prompt, several specific heuristic questions that would briefly clarify the expected learning as the teacher turns to consider which relevant lesson planning materials and resources they might consider. These resources would need to be available from relevant system and professional development providers.

Syllabus documents should also include a common nomenclature for describing student performance in the subject. These should be framed as aspirational goals for students and teachers to set as targets for achievement and used for reporting achievement. In this way they would provide the system, teachers, parents and students with a common, accessible vocabulary for gauging their learning. They must set high aspirational standards for all students, be consistent across subject, phase and student groups and clarify the goals of a system in relation to high quality and high equity and improved public opinion of education within the system.

Finally, syllabus documents must have notes of relevant assessment strategies to guide the development of systemic, school and classroom assessment and moderation that are linked closely to the standards statements. The documents would note alignments and misalignments with systemic testing programs and other assessment tasks as appropriate to the subject and phase. The syllabus should not provide explicit guidelines on how to assess per se, but instead refer to relevant documents and approaches provided elsewhere by the system and other relevant agencies and organizations.

The approach we suggest here is underpinned by a set of clear high quality, high equity goals about the articulation of high expectations and standards for all students; the goal of improved learning opportunities and outcomes for all children; and improved public trust in schools and relevant education system. This is a deliberate shift. We have aimed to reset and shift our policy answers with the aim of providing a new set of running rules for teachers, policy-makers, teacher educators, researchers and scholars, community and industry representatives who develop and write syllabi. We have argued here that changing the syllabus without aligning system and school conditions will not enhance informed professionalism, is unlikely to change the enacted curriculum and is unlikely to generate high quality and high equity achievement patterns.

The syllabus design process proposed here will set enabling conditions for informed professionalism in pedagogy and assessment aimed at high quality and high equity student achievement. But it can only set enabling conditions. It will not be successful without the delivery standards of other systemic policies and resources.

To begin with, high quality, high equity systems begin from reviews of current syllabi and involve practicing teachers, industry partners and community elders, disciplinary and educational researchers directly in the syllabus development process. They cannot be composed by curriculum experts and then presented in a consultative process after their development. They should involve a three-stage design process and this should be consistent across subjects and phases and transparent to all stakeholders. The three stages are:

- Technical and field analysis of current documents and of current best practice in the field;
- Syllabus writing; and
- A process of trial and release with appropriate mechanisms for feedback and revision.

In preservice teacher education, curriculum subjects need to be aligned to the current local syllabus, with student teachers working directly with syllabus documents and adjunct materials, while at the same time being prepared as curriculum workers to work with a variety of documents. High expectations of the teaching profession are built on raising qualification levels and not lowering entry levels and implementing subsequent exit tests in low-level basic skills as is the current policy drive in certain systems. High quality, high equity systems have either put in place or are moving towards the expectation of masters-level qualifications (in education and in relevant cognate fields) for all teachers. There should be an emphasis on qualification upgrades in classroom-based curriculum and assessment. This continued learning in inservice programs should include principals and school leaders because what is required is school leadership that focuses on curriculum and pedagogy. Inservice training should always be supported by a range of online and print materials as resources to assist school and cluster-based curriculum development. This will require systems to put in place a process of authorizing and validating resources and professional development used, so that their alignment with the curriculum is assured (see Levin in this volume for a discussion of the Ontario approach). This decreases the risk of textbook publishers leading and directing the curriculum.

The technical form of the curriculum constrains and specifies the delicate policy balance of what the OECD refers to as informed prescription and informed professionalism (Schleicher, 2008). This balance is central in the literature on different approaches to accountability and systems governance (Nichols, Glass & Berliner, 2005; Welner & Oakes, 2007), in the literature on sustainable school reform (e.g., Fullan, 2008), in the literature on teacher development and professionalism (Cochran-Smith, 2001; Timperley, Wilson, Barrar & Fung 2007) and in recent work on educational policy reform (Barber & Sebba, 1999; Levin, 2008). Further, the achievement of this balance is central to current educational policy debates over quality and equity.

There are currently strong curriculum policy bids to control what goes on in classrooms through prescription of approach and drives to enforce these measures through testing and accountability. These moves can generate inverse and unintended effects. As we and others have argued, and continue to argue here, high quality, high equity systems balance the central setting of expectations and standards, the careful and parsimonious use of a range of accountability measures, with coordinated systemic resourcing of professional development and training, appropriate technology and explicit policy and practical attention to students from socio-economically marginalized and minority backgrounds.

It is our view that the technical form of the syllabus is a neglected area of current curriculum debates that have largely been preoccupied with questions of curriculum content – variously construed as cultural values, ideologies, specific skills sets, competences and disciplinary knowledge. So while we recognize the important cultural, intellectual, cognitive, social and economic questions about which school subjects, which knowledges, skills, competences and capabilities should be included in the curriculum, here we have discussed a programmatic, principled and educationally defensible direction for the shape, structure and purposes of syllabi or official curriculum documents. We make the simple and yet multidimensional claim that low definition, clear, accessible and short syllabus documents, those that:

- specify core knowledges, skills and competences as aspirational targets;
- provide a common and transparent professional vocabulary for standards;
- are matched with a parsimonious and appropriately used testing and examination systems;
- have a system-wide emphasis on building teacher professional capacity to enhance local school and classroom-based curriculum planning and assessment practice; and
- include a strong equity focus on the specific learning needs and challenges for children from socioeconomically marginalized communities will provide the foundation of a high quality and high equity system.

Our suggestion in this chapter has been that redesigning the syllabus can set enabling conditions for high quality, high equity outcomes. It cannot "cause" change and progress in any direct or simple way. But it can be one of the key elements of an overall system strategy for enhancing teaching and learning. The syllabus must aim towards informed, parsimonious and comprehensible prescription that enhances rather than deters or discourages informed professionalism.

We conclude that the technical form of the syllabus matters. It must enhance professionalism at all levels to achieve equity. It must be accessible and economical. It should provide a map and not attempt to describe an entire curriculum field, relevant pedagogy and assessment strategies. These can be provided through adjunct resources for teachers to use as part of informed professionalism. The technical form selected for syllabi by systems must accommodate different curriculum models, different phases and different paradigmatic approaches to content, so that the documents have local relevance. Syllabi should be part of an aligned system, based on clearly articulated goals, aimed at achieving a high quality, high equity system.

As such review, design and implementation must be consistent, transparent and appropriately resourced.

Note

1 Different systems use different nomenclature to describe the official curriculum documents prepared by systems to direct the work of teachers and students across school subjects. In Australia the term used is usually syllabus, although there is a shift toward "curriculum" as an all encompassing term. Other names for these same documents include curriculum guidelines.

References

Abedi, J. (2002). Standardized achievement tests and English language learners: Psychometrics issues. *Educational Assessment, 8*(3), 231–57.

Alexander, R. (2001). *Culture and pedagogy*. Oxford: Blackwell.

Allington, R. L. and McGill-Franzen, A. (2000). Looking back, looking forward: A conversation about teaching reading in the 21st Century. *Reading Research Quarterly, 35*(1), 136–53.

Apple, M. (1978). *Ideology and curriculum*. New York: Routledge.

Apple, M. (1990). Is there a curriculum voice to reclaim? *Phi Delta Kappan, 71*(7), 526–30.

Ashcroft, B., Griffiths, G. and Tiffin, H. (1989). *The Empire writes back: Post-colonial literatures, theory and practice*. New York, NY: Routledge.

Australian Council for Education Research (2004). *Evaluation report of the New Basics Research Program*. Melbourne: Australian Council for Educational Research.

Australian Council of Deans (2002). *Top of the class: Report on the inquiry into teacher education*. Canberra: House of Representatives Standing Committee on Education and Vocational Training, Commonwealth Government.

Australian Education Council (1991). *Young people's participation in post-compulsory education and training: The Finn report*. Canberra, Australia: Department of Education Science and Training.

Baker, E. L. (2007). The end(s) of testing. *Educational Researcher, 36*(6) 309–17.

Barber, M. and Sebba, J. (1999). Reflections on progress towards a world-class education system. *Cambridge Journal of Education, 29*(2), 184–93.

Bernstein, B. (1990). *The structure of pedagogic discourse*. London: Routledge & Kegan Paul.

Billet, S., Fenwick, T. and Sommerville, M. (Eds) (2006). *Work, subjectivity and learning: Understanding learning through working life*. Dordrecht, The Netherlands: Springer.

Bowles, S. and Gintis, H. (1976). *Schooling in capitalist America: Education reform and the contradictions of economic life*. New York, NY: Basic Book.

Braverman, H. (1974). *Labor and monopoly capital*. New York, NY: Monthly Review Press.

Chall, J. (1967). *Learning to read: The great debate*. New York, NY: McGraw-Hill.

Cochran-Smith, M. (1999). Color blindness and basket making are not the answers: Confronting the dilemmas of race, culture and language diversity in teacher education. *American Educational Research Journal, 32*(3), 493–522.

Cochran-Smith, M. (2001). The outcomes question in teacher education. *Teaching and Teacher Education, 17*(5), 527–46.

Cole, M. (1996) *Cultural psychology*. Cambridge: Cambridge University Press.

Connelly, F. M., He, M. F. and Phillion, J. (Eds) (2008). *The Sage handbook of curriculum and instruction*. Thousand Oaks, CA: Sage.

Cope, B. and Kalantzis, M. (2007). *New learning*. Cambridge: Cambridge University Press.

Darling-Hammond, L. and Bransford, J. (Eds) (2005). *Preparing teachers for a changing world*. San Francisco: Josey Bass.

Deng, Z. (2007). Knowing the subject matter of a secondary school science subject. *Journal of Curriculum Studies, 39*(5), 503–35.

Deng, Z. and Luke, A. (2008). Subject matter: Defining and theorizing school subjects. In F. M. Connelly, M. F. He and J. Phillion (Eds) *The Sage handbook of curriculum and instruction* (pp. 66–87). Thousand Oaks, CA: Sage.

Department of Education, Training and the Arts (2004). *New Basics research report*. Brisbane: Author.

Dewey, J. (1902). *Child and the curriculum*. Chicago: University of Chicago Press.

Dewey, J. (1915). *The school and society*. Chicago: University of Chicago Press.

Dewey, J. (1938). *Experience and education*. New York, NY: Kappa Delta Pi.

Employment and Skills Formation Council (1992). *The Australian Certificate Training System: The Carmichael report*. Canberra, Australia: Department of Education Science and Training.

Ericsson, P. F. (2005). Raising the standards for standards: A call for definitions. *English Education, 37*(3), 223–43.

Feinman-Nemser, S. (2001). From preparation to professionalism: Designing a continuum to strengthen and sustain teaching. *Teachers College Record, 103*(6), 1013–55.

Foucault, M. (1972). *The archaeology of knowledge* (A. M. Sheridan Smith, Trans.). New York, NY: Pantheon Books.

Fraser, N. (1997). *Justice interruptus*. New York, NY: Routledge.

Fraser, N. (2003). Social justice in the age of identity politics: Redistribution, recognition and participation. In N. Fraser and A. Honneth (Eds) *Redistribution or recognition? A political-philosophical exchange* (pp. 7–88). London, UK: Verso.

Freebody, P. (2006). *Obedience, learning, virtue and arithmetic: Knowledge, skill and disposition in the organisation of senior schooling*. Brisbane, QLD: Queensland Studies Authority.

Freebody, P., Martin, J. and Maton, K. (2008). Talk, text and knowledge in cumulative, integrated learning: A response to "intellectual challenge." *Australian Journal of Language and Literacy, 31*(2), 188–201.

Fullan, M. (2008). Curriculum integration and sustainability. In F. M. Connelly, M. F. He and J. Phillion (Eds) *The Sage handbook of curriculum and instruction* (pp. 113–21). Thousand Oaks, CA: Sage.

Gale, T. and Densmore, K. (2000). *Just schooling*. Philadelphia: Open University Press.

Gee, J. P., Hull, G. and Lankshear, C. (1996). *The new work order*. Boulder, CO: Westview Press.

Giroux, H. (1988). *Teachers as intellectuals: Toward a critical pedagogy for learning*. Critical studies in education series. Granby, Mass.: Bergin & Garvey.

Gore, J., Williams, C. and Ladwig, J. (2006). *On the place of pedagogy in the induction of early career teachers*. Australian Association for Researchers in Education Conference, November 26–30, 2006.

Green, J. and Luke, A. (Eds) (2006). What counts as learning? *Review of Research in Education, Washington DC: American Educational Research Association, 30*(1) xi–xiv.

Hargreaves, A. (2003). *Teaching in the knowledge society*. NY: Teachers College Press.

Kelly, A. V. (2004). *The curriculum: Theory and practice* (5th edition). London & Thousand Oaks, CF: Sage Publications.

Kelly, G., Green, J. and Luke, A. (Eds) (2008). What counts as knowledge when knowledge counts. *Review of Research in Education, 32*, Washington, DC: American Educational Research Association.

Kuhn, T. (1962). *The structure of scientific revolutions*. Boston: MIT Press.

Ladson-Billings, G. (1997). *The dreamkeepers: Successful teachers of African-American children*. San Francisco: Jossey-Bass.

Ladson-Billings, G. and Brown, K. (2008). Curriculum and cultural diversity. In F. M. Connelly, M. F. He and J. Phillion (Eds) *The Sage handbook of curriculum and instruction* (pp. 153–75). Thousand Oaks, CA: Sage.

Ladwig, J. (2010). What NAPLAN doesn't address (but could and should). *Professional Voice*, *8*(1), 35–40.

Larson, J. (Ed.) (2001). *Literacy as snake oil: Beyond the quick fix*. New York: Peter Lang.

Lee, J. (2006). *Tracking achievement gaps and assessing the impact of NCLB on the gaps: An in-depth look into national and state reading and maths outcome trends*. Cambridge, MA: Harvard University Civil Rights Project.

Leigh, A. (2005). *Estimating teacher effectiveness from two-year changes in students' test scores*. Retrieved from http://rsss.anu.edu.au/documents/TQPanel.pdf

Lemke, J. (1990). *Talking science*. Westport, CT: Greenwood Publishing Group.

Levin, B. (2008). Curriculum policy and the politics of what should be learned in schools. In F. M. Connelly, M. F. He and J. Phillion (Eds) *The Sage handbook of curriculum and instruction* (pp. 7–24). Thousand Oaks, CA: Sage.

Little, J. W. (2003). Inside teacher community: Representations of classroom practice. *Teachers College Record*, *105*(6), 913–45.

Little, J. W., Horn, I. and Bartlett, L. (2000). *Teacher learning, professional community and accountability in the context of high school reform*. Washington, DC: Office of Educational Research and Development.

Luke, A. (1988). *Literacy, textbooks and ideology*. London & New York: Falmer Press.

Luke, A. (2006). Teaching after the market. In L. Weiss, C. McCarthy and G. Dimitriadis (Eds) *Ideology, curriculum and the new sociology of education*. New York, NY: Routledge.

Luke, A. (2008). Introduction essay. In F. M. Connelly, M. He and J. Phillion (Eds) *The SAGE handbook of curriculum and instruction*. Thousand Oaks, CA. Sage Publications.

Luke, A. and Woods, A. (2009). Policy and adolescent literacy. In L. Chritenbury, R. Bomer and P. Smagorinsky (Eds) *Handbook of adolescent literacy*. New York, NY: Guilford Press.

Luke, A., Weir, K., Land, R. and Sanderson, D. (2007). *A comparative review of systemic approaches to the assessment of capabilities*. Adelaide: Department of Education and Children's Services.

Luke, A., Weir, K. and Woods, A. (2008). *Development of a set of principles to guide a P-12 syllabus framework*. Brisbane, Queensland: Queensland Studies Authority.

Mayer, D. (2005). Reviving the policy bargain discussion: The status of professional accountability and the contribution of teacher performance assessment. *The Clearing House*, *78*(4), 177–81.

McCarty, T. (2008). *The impact of high-stakes accountability policies on Native American learners: Evidence from the research*. Unpublished Paper. Arizona: Arizona State University.

McGaw, B. (2006). *Education and social cohesion*. Dean's Lecture Series delivered at the Faculty of Education, Melbourne University.

McKeon, R., Owen, D. B. and McKeon, Z. K. (2001). *On knowing the natural sciences*. Chicago: University of Chicago Press.

Moss, P., Girard, B. J. and Haniford, L. (2006). Validity in educational research. *Review of Research in Education*, *30*, 109–62.

Newmann, F. and Associates. (1996). *Authentic achievement: Restructuring schools for intellectual quality*. San Francisco: Jossey Bass.

Nichols, S. and Berliner, D. (2007). *Collateral damage*. Cambridge, MA: Harvard Educational Press.

Nichols, S., Glass, G. and Berliner, D. (2005). *High stakes testing and student achievement: Problems for the No Child Left Behind Act*. Tempe, AZ: Educational Policy Research Unit.

Nieto, S. (1999). Critical multicultural education and students' perspectives. In S. May (Ed.) *Rethinking multicultural and antiracist education: Towards critical multiculturalism* (pp. 191–215). London: Falmer Press.

Nieto, S. (2010). *Language, culture and teaching: Critical perspectives*. New York, NY: Routledge.

Organisation for Economic Co-operation and Development (OECD) (2005). *School factors relating to quality and equity: Results from PISA 2000*. Paris: Author. Retrieved from www.pisa.oecd.org/dataoecd/15/20/34668095.pdf

Pinar, W. F. (2001). *The gender of racial politics and violence in America: Lynching, prison rape, and the crisis of masculinity*. New York: Peter Lang.

Pinar, W. F. (Ed.) (2005). *International handbook of curriculum research*. Mahwah, NJ: Lawrence Erlbaum.

Raudenbush, S. (2005) Learning from attempts to improve schooling: The contribution of methodological diversity. *Educational Researcher, 34*(5), 25–33.

Ravitch, D. (1996, April 11). 50 ways to teach them grammar. *The Washington Post.*

Reid, A. (2005). *Rethinking national curriculum collaboration: Towards an Australian curriculum*. Canberra: Department of Education, Science and Training.

Rochex, J-Y. (2006). Social, methodological and theoretical issues about assessment: Lessons form a secondary analysis of PISA 2000 literacy tests. *Review of Research in Education, 30*, 163–211.

Schleicher, A. (2008). Seeing school systems through the prism of PISA. In A. Luke, K. Weir and A. Woods (Eds) *Development of a set of principles to guide a P-12 syllabus framework*. Brisbane, Queensland: Queensland Studies Authority.

Schwartz, M. (2006). For whom do we write the curriculum? *Journal of Curriculum Studies, 38*(4), 449–57.

Shulman, L. S. (1986). Those who understand: Knowledge growth in teaching. *Educational Researcher, 15*(2), 4–14.

Smith, M. S. (2007). *NAEP 2007 – What about NCLB*. Keynote presented as Graduate School of Education, Berkeley University, October 10, 2007.

Spady, W. (1994). *Outcome-based education: Critical issues and answers*. Arlington, VA: American Association of School Administrators.

Spring, J. (2004). *American education*. New York, NY: McGraw Hill.

Stengel, B. S. (1997). "Academic discipline" and "school subject": Contestable curricular concepts. *Journal of Curriculum Studies, 29*(5), 585–602.

Syllabus. n.d. In Oxford English Dictionary, Web. Retrieved from http://oxforddictionaries. com/definition/syllabus?q=syllabus

Timperley, H., Wilson, A., Barrar, A. and Fung, I. (2007). *Teacher professional learning and development: Best evidence synthesis iteration*. Auckland: Ministry of Education. Retrieved from www. educationcounts.govt.nz/–data/assets/pdf_file/0017/16901/TPLandDBES entire.pdf

Tyler, R. W. (1949). *Basic principles of curriculum and instruction*. Chicago: University of Chicago Press.

Welner, K. G. and Oakes, J. (2008). Structuring curriculum: Technical, normative and political considerations. In F. M. Connelly, M. F. He and J. Phillion (Eds) *The Sage handbook of curriculum and instruction* (pp. 91–111). Thousand Oaks, CA: Sage.

Westbury, I. (2008). Making curricula: Why do states make curricula and how? In F. M. Connelly, M. F. He and J. Phillion, (Eds) *The Sage handbook of curriculum and instruction* (pp. 45–65). Thousand Oaks, CA: Sage.

Woods, A., Luke, A. and Weir, K. (2010). Curriculum planning and development: Curriculum and syllabus design. In P. Pearson, P. David and A. Luke (Eds) *Curriculum volume: International encyclopedia of education* (3rd edition). New York: Elsevier.

Young, M. F. D. (1971). *Knowledge and control: New directions for the sociology of education*. London: Collier-Macmillan

Young, M. F. D. (2008). *Bringing knowledge back in: From social constructivism to social realism in the sociology of education*. Abingdon: Routledge.

3

SCHOOL SUBJECTS AND ACADEMIC DISCIPLINES

The Differences

Zongyi Deng

Introduction

Disciplinarity has a grip on much of the discourse on curriculum policy and instructional practice. Schools are mandated to teach academic disciplines such as mathematics, chemistry, geography, history, and economics to the future generations. Teachers are supposed to work with and transform the content of the academic discipline for classroom teaching. Lurking beneath the surface of this discourse is a fundamental conceptual distinction that has not received sufficient attention from policymakers, researchers, and educators – the distinction between school subjects and academic disciplines (Stengel, 1997). Yet this distinction is crucial for a proper understanding of curriculum development and pedagogical practice.

The purpose of this chapter is to clarify the differences between school subjects and academic disciplines, and in so doing, to argue for the centrality of school subjects in curriculum development and pedagogical practice. By a school subject, I refer to an area of learning within the school curriculum that constitutes an institutionally defined field of knowledge and practice for teaching and learning. By an academic discipline, I refer to a field or branch of learning affiliated with an academic department within a university, formulated for the advancement of research and scholarship and the professional training of researchers, academics, and specialists. School subjects can be traditional academic subjects such as mathematics, history, and geography that could have direct affiliations with their parent academic disciplines. They can also be unconventional ones such as tourism and hospitality that have no or minimal connections with academic disciplines.

This chapter begins by looking at different conceptions of the central aim of schooling embedded in various curricular ideologies and discourses. It next analyzes and unpacks the differences and relationships between school subjects and academic disciplines. This is followed by a discussion of the formation of a school subject with reference to the curriculum-making processes involved, and then an analysis of the formation of liberal studies as a new school subject in the current context of curriculum reform in Hong Kong. The chapter ends by addressing what is involved in knowing the content of a school subject for teaching.

Aims of Schooling: Competing Curricular Ideologies and Discourses

Over the last century schooling has been asked to serve four different aims that are reflected in four curricular ideologies: *academic rationalism, humanism, social efficiency,* and *social reconstructionism.* Academic rationalists hold that the primary function of schooling is intellectual development through initiating students into specific bodies of knowledge, techniques, and ways of knowing embedded in academic disciplines. Humanists, on the other hand, define the central goal of schooling in terms of fostering students' potential, personal freedom, self-actualization, and all round development. For the advocates of social efficiency, the central purpose of schooling is to meet the current and future manpower needs of a society by training youth to become contributing members of society. For social reconstructionists, schooling is primarily an instrument for ameliorating social problems (inequalities, injustice, poverty, etc.) and engendering social reform and reconstruction (cf. Eisner & Vallance, 1974; McNeil, 1996; Schiro, 2008). These four competing ideologies have continued salience in ongoing curriculum policy debates, each of which embodies a distinct version of what schooling is for and what knowledge is of most worth.

In the 21st century three curricular discourses, *autonomous learners, participatory citizenship,* and *globalization,* have become rather influential in the debates, which can be viewed as "new" humanism, social efficiency and, to a certain extent, social reconstructionism. These discourses argue that contemporary schooling should allow individual learners to construct their own knowledge base and competences. It should prepare young people for their future role as active, responsible, and productive citizens in a democratic society. Furthermore, schools are expected to be instrumental in equipping individuals for the challenges created by economic and cultural globalization. These discourses have been employed by governments across the globe as the rationales for changing curriculum content (cf. Rosenmund, 2006).

The above diverse aims and expectations of schooling entail different implications for how school subjects should relate to academic disciplines. There are three possible juxtapositions in which the above curricular ideologies and discourses find their respective locations.

School Subjects and Academic Disciplines: Three Juxtapositions

School subjects can have different and variable relationships to academic disciplines, depending on their aims, contents, and developmental phases. According to Stengel

(1997), there are three broad juxtapositions between school subjects and academic disciplines:

- school subjects and academic disciplines are essentially continuous;
- school subjects and academic disciplines are basically discontinuous;
- school subjects and academic disciplines are different but related.

Each of the juxtapositions implies a particular curricular position concerning how school subjects are constructed with respect to academic disciplines.

1. Continuous

The continuous position is embedded in academic rationalism – an ideology that underscores the importance of transmitting disciplinary knowledge for the development of the intellectual capacity of students and for the maintenance or reproduction of academic culture. This is epitomized in what is called the *doctrine of disciplinarity*, according to which school subjects are derived from and organized according to the "structure" of academic disciplines (Tanner & Tanner, 1995). For academic rationalists, the central purpose of a school subject, like that of a discipline, is to initiate the young into the academic community of scholars. School subjects, therefore, are supposed to "derive their life, their viability, from their related intellectual disciplines" (Davis, 1998, p. 207). They constitute a faithful and valid introduction to the academic disciplines whose names they bear. While students are admittedly dealing with relatively simple ideas and methods, they nonetheless study the same ideas and methods known by experts in the academic disciplines. Disciplinarity is alive and well in contemporary discourse on curriculum policy and teachers' professional development, albeit in different forms. (For a detailed discussion, see Deng & Luke, 2008.)

This curricular position is fraught with problems. Its exclusive reliance on academic disciplines in defining and delineating school subjects leaves out other kinds of knowledge (e.g., practical knowledge, technical knowledge, tacit knowledge, local community knowledge, etc.) that could be potential curriculum content. Curriculum development framed by this approach ignores the interests, attitudes, and feelings of learners. Furthermore, this curricular position shows little concern about meeting social, economic, and political needs, and is silent on issues about social reform and reconstruction. According to Tanner and Tanner (1995), the world of knowledge, the needs of learners, and the needs and demands of society are three essential factors that determine and shape what should count as curriculum content – factors that set school subjects apart from academic disciplines.

2. Discontinuous

One could reject the continuous position by arguing that school subjects and academic disciplines are essentially discontinuous in purpose and substance, and thereby allow for opportunities of the construction of school subjects that could get beyond the narrow academic or disciplinary concern (Stengel, 1997). The discontinuous position finds support in humanism, social efficiency, and social reconstructionism. Humanist educators argue that school subjects are created to provide students with "intrinsically rewarding experiences" that contribute to the pursuit of self actualization, personal growth, and individual freedom (McNeil, 1996). School subjects, therefore, need to be formulated according to the interest, attitudes, and developmental stages of individual students. They need to derive content from a wide range of sources – such as personal experiences, human activities, and community cultures and wisdoms. Disciplinary knowledge might (or might not) be useful for the formation of school subjects.

From the perspective of social efficiency, school subjects are constructed for the primary purpose of maintaining and enhancing economic and social productivity by equipping future citizens with the requisite knowledge, skills, and capital. The formation of school subjects, therefore, is justified with close reference to the needs of occupation, profession, and vocation. Specialized and applied fields (e.g., engineering, accounting, and marketing, among others), therefore, are the primary sources from which the contents of school subjects are derived. Academic disciplines are drawn upon only when they demonstrate their efficacy in promoting those skills and knowledge actually needed in occupations.

For social reconstructionists, school subjects are created to provide students with meaningful learning experiences that might lead to emancipation and engender social agency. To this end, the formation of school subjects is based upon an examination of social contexts, social issues, and futures, with the intention of helping individuals reconstruct their own analyses, standpoints, and actions. Like humanistic educators, social reconstructionists believe that school subjects derive contents from a wide range of sources. Academic disciplines are used only as they relate to the contexts and issues examined.

The three contemporary curricular discourses – autonomous learners, participatory citizenship, and globalization – further set school subjects apart from academic disciplines. These discourses call for a learner-oriented (rather than discipline-centered) approach to the construction of a school subject that allows learners to construct their own knowledge according to their individual needs and interests. They require the school subject to be formulated in ways that help students cultivate certain kinds of sensitivity, disposition, and awareness needed for responsible civic participation in an increasingly globalized society. They call attention to the need of equipping students with generic competences and lifelong learning abilities considered to be essential for facing the challenges of globalization and the knowledge-based economy (cf. McEneaney & Meyer, 2000; Rosenmund, 2006). This is illustrated in the section below using the case of liberal studies as a core secondary-school subject in current curriculum reforms in Hong Kong.

3. Different but Related

The third juxtaposition has three possible permutations that demonstrate the relationship between school subjects and academic disciplines can exist in one of the three ways: (a) that academic disciplines precede school subjects, (b) that school subjects precede academic disciplines, or (c) that the relation between the two is dialectic (Stengel, 1997). Position (a) holds that a school subject results from the transformation of an academic discipline. This taken-for-granted view is always employed in conjunction with the continuous position, viewing the purpose of education as the acquisition of disciplinary knowledge. The two other positions are of more theoretical than practical interest. Position (b) is reflected in Herbartian theory of recapitulation, according to which parallels exist between the stages in the historical development of disciplinary knowledge and the stages through which the individual passes on the way to maturity, and therefore, school subjects are formulated to reflect those parallels (Kliebard, 1992). School subjects come first and academic disciplines later in one's learning journey from school to university. Position (c) can be viewed as a combination of positions (a) and (b), which is epitomized in Dewey's (1902/1990) classic text, *The child and the curriculum*. For Dewey, an academic discipline provides the endpoint for the formation of a school subject and the school subject furnishes the avenue for getting to know the academic discipline. (For a detailed discussion, see Stengel, 1997 and Deng, 2007.)

So far our discussion is primarily at the societal or institutional level, with a focus on curricular ideologies and discourses that distinguish and relate school subjects and academic disciplines. The discussion supports that school subjects are distinctive, purpose-built enterprises, constructed in response to different social, cultural, and political demands and challenges, and toward educational aims. The discussion now examines how particular curricular ideologies and discourses are translated into a school subject by looking at the curriculum-making processes involved.

The Formation of a School Subject

The formation of a school subject, broadly construed, involves three levels of curriculum making; the *societal*, the *programmatic*, and the *classroom*, each of which yields a distinct kind of curriculum. The societal curriculum, also called the *ideal* or *abstract* curriculum, embodies a conception of what schooling should be with respect to the society and culture. Curriculum making at this level is characterized by ideologies and discourses on curriculum policy at the intersection between schooling, culture, and society. Thus the societal curriculum "typifies" what is desirable in social and cultural orders, what is to be valued and sought after by members of a society or nation (Doyle, 1992a, 1992b, 2008).

The programmatic curriculum, or the *technical* or *official* curriculum, is contained in curriculum documents (e.g., syllabus) and materials for use in schools and class-rooms. Curriculum making at this level translates the societal curriculum into school subjects, programs, or courses of study provided to a school or system of schools (Doyle, 1992a, 1992b; Westbury, 2000). The process of constructing a school subject or a course of study entails the selection and arrangement of content (knowledge, skills, and dispositions) and the transformation of that content for school and classroom use. It involves a "theory of content" with respect to both the societal expectations and the activities of teaching (Doyle, 1992b).

The classroom curriculum – i.e., the *enacted* curriculum – is characterized by a cluster of events jointly developed by a teacher and a group of students within a particular instructional context (Doyle, 1992a, 1992b). Curriculum making at this level involves transforming the programmatic curriculum embodied in curriculum documents and materials into "educative" experiences for students. It requires further elaboration of the programmatic curriculum, making it connect with the experiences, interests, and the capacities of students (Westbury, 2000).

Taken as a whole, the societal and programmatic curricula together form the institutional curriculum, which concerns the provision of teaching and learning experiences for an educational or school system, the responsibility of which is always the province of national ministries or state departments of education. From the above perspective, a school subject is formed as the result of institutional selection, organization, and framing content for social, economic, cultural, curricular, and pedagogical purposes. Many important decisions concerning content are therefore made prior to the actual instructional activities and the content actually taught in the classroom, and are independent in many respects from classroom teachers. A school subject (rather than an academic discipline) constitutes an organizing framework that gives meaning and shape to curriculum content, teaching, and learning activities (Karmon, 2007).

The above claims can be illustrated by the formation of liberal studies in the current context of curriculum reforms in Hong Kong.

Liberal Studies as a School Subject[1]

Since the turn of the 21st century, Hong Kong has embarked on significant curriculum reforms in response to the changing social, economic, and political contexts – characterized by globalization, knowledge-based economy, and an increasingly close tie with the Mainland (Education and Manpower Bureau [EMB], 2004). In 2000 the government introduced the new "3+3+4" academic structure – according to which there would be three years lower secondary, three years senior secondary, and four years normal undergraduate education.[2] This new structure was fully implemented in September 2009. Aligned with it is the new senior secondary (NSS) curriculum that consists of four core subjects (Chinese, English, mathematics, and liberal studies), elective subjects (e.g., physics, chemistry, and humanities) and other learning experiences (moral and civic education, community service, aesthetic and physical activities). The NSS curriculum is believed to be more "flexible," "coherent," and "diversified," allowing students to develop a broader knowledge base and a more solid foundation for whole-person development and the pursuit of life-long learning (Education Commission [EC], 2000; EMB, 2004).

Liberal studies has become a compulsory school subject for all senior secondary-school students. At the societal level, the subject is conceived as a curriculum innovation in response to the changing social, economic, and political contexts. The central purpose of this subject is to broaden students' knowledge bases, enhance their social awareness, cultivate positive attitudes and values, and develop critical thinking, adaptability, and lifelong learning capacities – qualities believed to be important for facing the challenges of the 21st century. Its specific curriculum aims are stated as:

- to enhance students' understanding of themselves, their society, their nation, the human world and the physical environment;
- to enable students to develop multiple perspectives on perennial and contemporary issues in different contexts (e.g., cultural, social, economic, political, and technological contexts);
- to help students become independent thinkers so that they can construct knowledge appropriate to changing personal and social circumstances;
- to develop in students a range of skills for life-long learning, including critical thinking skills, creativity, problem-solving skills, communication skills, and information technology skills;
- to help students appreciate and respect diversity in cultures and views in a pluralistic society and handle conflicting values; and
- to help students develop positive values and attitude towards life, so that they can become informed and responsible citizens of society, the country and the world (Curriculum Development Council [CDC] & Hong Kong Examination and Assessment Authority [HKEAA], 2007, p. 5).

At the programmatic level, liberal studies takes the form of a curriculum framework and related instructional and assessment guidelines contained in an official document to be used by schools and teachers (i.e., CDC & HKEAA, 2007). Underlying the curriculum framework is a special way of selecting, organizing, and framing content that is intended to serve the central purpose of the subject, thus constituting the *theory of content* in liberal studies. Content is selected and organized via a "student-oriented approach" with the intention to "help students understand themselves, and their relations with others and the environment in which they live" (p. 4). Accordingly, three broad areas of concern are identified, namely "Self and Personal Development," "Society and Culture," and "Science, Technology and the Environment." These three areas are further divided into six learning modules including: (1) personal development and interpersonal relationships; (2) contemporary Hong Kong society; (3) modern China; (4) globalization; (5) public health; and (6) energy technology and the environment.

Each module starts with a *prologue*, which lays out related concepts for teaching and learning, and is organized around a few *themes*, each of which is framed in terms of *key issues* and *related issues* for inquiry. For each theme, the framework suggests *related values and attitudes* that teachers are supposed to help students develop as well. Table 3.1 illustrates how content is arranged and framed concerning the module *Public Health*.

TABLE 3.1 Content Selection, Organization, and Framing in the Module *Public Health*

Prologue	Public health is an ongoing concern. The outbreak of new infectious diseases poses a real threat to us. Public health issues are not only matters of health and lifestyle, but also touch on how public resources are allocated. Our understanding of public health and disease has been enhanced in many ways by advances in science and technology, and has also been influenced by various cultural factors. Advancement in biotechnology and medicine has improved diagnosis, disease prevention, and control, but it has also raised economic, moral, and legal concerns about, for example, the patenting and economic efficiency of new drugs, moral considerations about genetic screening, and the regulation of research in embryonic stem cell technology.

Theme 1: Understanding of Public Health

Key issue	How are people's understandings of disease and public health affected by different factors?
Related issues	How did people understand the causes of diseases in the past? Was their understanding scientific? How are people's understandings of health affected by economic, social, and other factors? How are people's understandings of public health affected by the development of science and technology? In what ways are people's understandings of public health affected by health information, social expectations, personal values, and beliefs in different cultures?
Related values and attitudes	Valuing the suggestions of others; respect for evidence; respect for different ways of life, beliefs, and opinions; cultural heritage.

Theme 2: Science, Technology and Public Health

Key issue	To what extent do science and technology enhance the development of public health?
Related issues	Can science and technology provide new solutions in the prevention and control of diseases? In the area of public health, how is the development of science and technology affected by various factors, and what issues are triggered by this development? How can the fruits of scientific and technological research be respected and protected? What challenges do different sectors of society, the government, and international organizations have in maintaining and promoting public health?
Related values and attitudes	Betterment of humankind; human rights and responsibilities; cooperation; moral considerations.

The above way of arranging and framing the content is intended to facilitate issue-inquiry and cross-curricular approaches to teaching and learning. The key and related issues are purported to be controversial so as to encourage students' critical thinking. Most of the issues are intended to be cross-curricular or interdisciplinary, the examination of which requires drawing on differing perspectives, ways of thinking, and values from various school subjects and other learning experiences. In exploring these issues students are expected to "apply the knowledge and perspectives they have developed from different subjects, to make connections across different disciplines of knowledge" (CDC & HKEAA, 2007, p. 3). In addition, the subject provides students with opportunities to shape their own learning trajectory by introducing an Independent Enquiry Study (IES), a research project in which students apply knowledge and perspectives gained from the three areas of study to explore selected curricular themes (e.g., media, education, and religion) that cater to their interests and aspirations.

Classroom teachers are supposed to develop school-based curriculum on the basis of the liberal studies curriculum framework and related instructional and assessment guidelines. They are expected to interpret and translate the content embodied in the framework into instructional events and activities, with close reference to students' existing knowledge and experiences. They are expected to build and expand upon what students already know, engaging them in the process of constructing their own knowledge and competences.

The above discussion foregrounds the notion that a school subject is the end product of a creative development process. It is introduced into schools and classrooms as a distinct representation of content, entailing a theory of content – a special way of selecting, organizing, and framing content for social, cultural, educational, curricular, and pedagogical purposes. The content of a school subject, in other words, is an embodiment of the designers' intentions, containing educational potential (see Deng, 2011). The assumption of curriculum designers of liberal studies is that the content, once students have explored it in a way that is consistent with their intentions, could broaden students' perspectives, develop positive attitudes and values, and enhance their social awareness and critical thinking skills. Of course, the notion of curriculum potential is rather complex, encompassing both intended and unintended educational opportunities (see Ben-Peretz, 1975, 1990). I underscore the importance of disclosing the *intended* curriculum potential (associated with the theory of content) on the grounds that a school subject is a purposeful creation, with an inherent curricular design embodied in curriculum materials. This, nevertheless, does not exclude the need for uncovering the unintended educational opportunities in actual classroom practices. To disclose the intended potential, teachers need to pay attention to the theory of content involved. It requires teachers' specialized understanding of the content centered upon a school subject, to which I now turn.

Knowing the Content of a School Subject

In educational circles there is a strong tendency to emphasize the necessity of teachers' understanding of the content of an academic discipline – rather than the content of a school subject. This tendency finds support in the influential theoretical framework developed by Shulman and associates at Stanford (see for example, Shulman, 1986, 1987; Grossman, Wilson & Shulman, 1989; Wilson, Shulman, & Richert, 1987). The fundamental premise of this group of researchers is that, as far as teachers' specialized understanding of content is concerned, teachers need to have three kinds of subject matter knowledge: content knowledge, pedagogical content knowledge, and curricular knowledge.[3] Content knowledge includes knowledge of the substance and structure of the academic discipline. Pedagogical content knowledge involves an understanding of pedagogical representations and instructional strategies, and of students' pre-conceptions with respect to particular curriculum topics at particular grade levels. By means of this knowledge, the teacher *transforms* his or her disciplinary content into "forms that are pedagogically powerful and yet adaptive to the variations in ability and background presented by students" (Shulman, 1987, p. 15). Curricular knowledge involves an understanding of the curriculum and the instructional materials available for teaching a subject at various grade levels, which can be an aid to the transformation process. Underlying their framework are two assumptions: (1) that school subjects and academic disciplines are essentially continuous in substance and practice; and (2) that classroom teachers necessarily work with and transform the content of an academic discipline into the content of a school subject (Deng, 2007).

The underlying assumptions of the Shulman and associates' framework index a commitment to the doctrine of disciplinarity (Deng, 2007; Deng & Luke, 2008). It is inevitably fraught with problems inherent in the continuous juxtaposition of school subjects and academic disciplines discussed earlier. As far as teachers' specialized understanding of content is concerned, Shulman and associates' unproblematic reliance on the academic discipline as an essential frame of reference for defining and delineating teachers' specialized understanding of content tends to overlook what is involved in knowing the content of a school subject for teaching.

The argument proposed here is that teachers do need basic knowledge of related academic disciplines, but knowing the content of a school subject lies at the heart of their professional understanding. School subjects, not academic disciplines, constitute the "locus" of classroom teaching; they frame classroom teachers' practice and perspectives on curriculum and instruction (Grossman & Stodolsky, 1995). Knowing the content of a school subject involves knowing more than the content per se; it entails knowing the theory of content – i.e., knowing how the content is selected, formulated, framed, and transformed in ways that render meaningful and educative experiences for students. This knowing is crucial for disclosing the educational potential inherent in the content (Deng, 2009, 2011). As illustrations, it is possible to look at knowing the content of a secondary-school science subject (e.g., physics, chemistry, and biology) and knowing the content of liberal studies.

Knowing the content of a secondary-school science subject involves knowing five intersecting aspects or dimensions; *logical, epistemological, psychological, pedagogical,* and *sociocultural.* The logical is represented by a body of concepts and principles embodied in the school curriculum that constitute the "landscape" of the subject. There is an underlying "geology" that accounts for how this landscape can be developed, formulated, organized, and connected with the landscapes of other secondary-school subjects, characterized by ways of linking the logical with the psychological, epistemological, and socio-cultural planes. Knowing the content involves knowing the psychological (concerning how the concepts and principles to be taught can be developed out of the interest, experience, and prior knowledge of students); the epistemological (concerning how we know these concepts and principles and how they come to reach their present refined form); the pedagogical (concerning the effective ways of representing and reformulating the concepts and principles); and the socio-cultural (concerning how knowledge relates to and interacts with society, technology, and culture). In other words, the teacher needs to know how the logical can be formulated and transformed on the psychological, epistemological, pedagogical, and socio-cultural planes, so as to render meaningful and educative experiences to students (Deng, 2007).

Similarly, knowing the content of liberal studies entails knowing how content can be organized, framed, and transformed into learning experiences in order to broaden students' perspectives, enhance their social awareness, develop positive attitudes and values, and foster problem-solving and critical thinking skills. With respect to a particular module (e.g., public health) in liberal studies, four aspects are essential for knowing the content: namely *inquiry framing* (framing content for cross-curricular and issue-based inquiry), *socio-cultural framing* (framing content with reference to socio-cultural contexts), *psycho-epistemological framing* (framing content with reference to the curricular or knowledge context of students), and *pedagogic translation* (translating content into teaching and learning activities and selecting instructional resources). Each of these aspects can be characterized by a set of probing questions.

Inquiry Framing

What are the themes and key issues (i.e., questions for inquiry) pertaining to the module?
What are the key concepts that underlie each of the themes? How are these concepts related to the concepts in other modules?
What are the related issues for exploration?

Socio-cultural Framing

What significance do the key issues and related issues have for students, the society, and the world?
How might these issues arise from various socio-cultural contexts?
What different perspectives can be brought to bear on addressing these issues?
What kinds of critical thinking can be encouraged? What attitudes and values are worthy of cultivation?

Psycho-epistemological Framing

What prerequisite knowledge and skills are needed for learning the issues and concepts?
How might the key issues and concepts connect with what students learn in other school subjects or from other learning experiences in the curriculum?

What have students already known and experienced in relation to these issues and concepts?

How might their existing knowledge and experience be drawn upon for learning the issues and concepts?

Pedagogic Translation

On the basis of the above considerations, what could be teaching and learning activities (e.g., group discussion, debate, role-play, project work, and independent inquiry) that could broaden students' perspectives and provide them with opportunities for problem-solving, independent learning, and cross-curricular and critical thinking?

What resources (e.g., the media, IT software, and the internet) could be employed for achieving the instructional purposes? What tools are most useful for assessing student learning? How could the results of assessment be used to inform instruction?

These four aspects are interrelated, and together constitute teachers' specialized understanding of the content of liberal studies. Asking these questions allows teachers to interpret and reinvent the meanings of the content of a particular module in specific instructional contexts. Teachers assume the role of curriculum developer at the school or classroom level (see Deng, 2009).

Conclusion

School subjects are not given, nor are they direct translations of academic disciplines. They can have different and variable relationships to academic disciplines and applied fields. School subjects are human constructions in response to social, economic, cultural, political, and educational realities and needs. They are "uniquely purpose-built educational enterprises, designed with and through educational imagination towards educative ends" (Deng & Luke, 2008, p. 83). The formation of a school subject entails a theory of content – a special way of selecting, framing, and translating content for educational purposes. Knowing the content of a school subject thus entails knowing more than the content per se; it entails an understanding of the theory of content that is crucial for disclosing the educational potential embodied in the content.

Notes

1 For a fuller, more comprehensive discussion of liberal studies, see Deng (2009).
2 The previous system was comprised of three years of junior secondary, four years of senior secondary, and three years of normal undergraduate education.
3 In addition to these three categories of subject matter knowledge, Shulman and associates believe that teachers need to have knowledge of general pedagogy, of learners, of contexts, and of educational purposes.

References

Ben-Peretz, M. (1975). The concept of curriculum potential. *Curriculum Theory Network, 5*(2), 151–59.

Ben-Peretz, M. (1990). *The teacher-curriculum encounter: Freeing teachers from the tyranny of texts.* Albany: State University Press.

Curriculum Development Council & Hong Kong Examination and Assessment Authority (CDC & HKEAA). (2007). *Liberal studies: Curriculum and assessment guide.* Hong Kong: Education Bureau.

Davis, O. L., Jr. (1998). Editorial: Thinking in the school subjects: Toward improved teaching and learning. *Journal of Curriculum and Supervision, 13,* 205–9.

Deng, Z. (2007). Knowing the subject matter of a secondary-school science subject. *Journal of Curriculum Studies, 39*(5), 503–35.

Deng, Z. (2009). The formation of a school subject and the nature of curriculum content: An analysis of liberal studies in Hong Kong. *Journal of Curriculum Studies, 41*(5), 585–604.

Deng, Z. (2011). Revisiting curriculum potential. *Curriculum Inquiry, 41*(5), 538–59.

Deng, Z. and Luke, A. (2008). Subject matter: Defining and theorizing school subjects. In F. M. Connelly, M. F. He and J. Phillion (Eds) *The Sage handbook of curriculum and instruction* (pp. 66–87). Thousand Oaks, CA: Sage.

Dewey, J. (1902/1990). *The school and society & the child and the curriculum.* Chicago: The University of Chicago Press (Original work published in 1902).

Doyle, W. (1992a). Curriculum and pedagogy. In P. W. Jackson (Ed.) *Handbook of research on curriculum* (pp. 486–516). New York: Macmillan.

Doyle, W. (1992b). Constructing curriculum in the classroom. In F. K. Oser, A. Dick and J. Patry (Eds) *Effective and responsible teaching: The new syntheses* (pp. 66–79). San Francisco: Jossey-Bass.

Doyle, W. (2008). *Competence as a blurred category in curriculum theory.* Paper presented at the conference "Research on vocational education and training for international comparison and as international comparison." Georg-August-Universität, Göttingen, Germany.

Education Commission (EC) (2000). *Learning for life, learning through life: Reform proposals for the educational system in Hong Kong.* Hong Kong: Education Commission.

Education and Manpower Bureau (EMB) (2004). *Reforming the academic structure for senior secondary education and higher education: Actions for investing in the future.* Hong Kong: Education and Manpower Bureau.

Eisner, E. W. and Vallance, E. (Eds) (1974). *Conflicting conceptions of the curriculum.* National Society for the Study of Education Series on Contemporary Educational Issues. Berkeley, CA: McCutchan.

Grossman, P. L., Wilson, S. M. and Shulman, L. S. (1989). Teachers of substance: Subject matter knowledge for teaching. In M. Reynolds (Ed.) *Knowledge base for the beginning teacher* (pp. 23–36). New York: Pergamon.

Grossman, P. L. and Stodolsky, S. S. (1995). Content as context: The role of school subjects in secondary school teaching. *Educational Researcher, 24*(8), 5–11.

Karmon, A. (2007). "Institutional organization of knowledge": The missing link in educational discourse. *Teachers College Record, 109*(3), 603–34.

Kliebard, H. M. (1992). *Forging the American curriculum: Essays in curriculum history and theory.* New York: Routledge.

McEneaney, E. H. and Meyer, J. W. (2000). The content of the curriculum: An institutionalist perspective. In M. T. Hallinan (Ed.) *Handbook of the sociology of education* (pp. 189–211). New York: Kluwer.

McNeil, J. (1996). *Curriculum: A comprehensive introduction* (5th edition). New York: Harper Collins.

Rosenmund, M. (2006). The current discourse on curriculum change: A comparative analysis of national reports on education. In A. Benavot and C. Braslavsky (Eds) *School knowledge in comparative and historical perspective: Changing curricula in primary and secondary education* (pp. 173–94). CERC Studies in Comparative Education, No 19. Hong Kong: University of Hong Kong, Comparative Education Research Centre.

Schiro, M. S. (2008). *Curriculum theory: Conflicting visions and enduring concerns.* CA: SAGE Publications.

Shulman, L. S. (1986). Those who understand: Knowledge growth in teaching. *Educational Researcher, 15*(2), 4–14.

Shulman, L. S. (1987). Knowledge and teaching: Foundations of the new reform. *Harvard Educational Review, 57*(1), 1–22.

Stengel, B. S. (1997). "Academic discipline" and "school subject": Contestable curricular concepts. *Journal of Curriculum Studies, 29*(5), 585–602.

Tanner, D., and Tanner, L. N. (1995). *Curriculum development: Theory into practice* (3rd edition). Englewood Cliffs, NJ: Merrill.

Westbury, I. (2000). Teaching as a reflective practice: What might didaktik teach curriculum. In I. Westbury, S. Hopmann and K. Riquarts (Eds) *Teaching as a reflective practice: The German didaktik tradition* (pp. 15–39). Mahwah, NJ: Lawrence Erlbaum Associates.

Wilson, S. M., Shulman, L. S. and Richert, A. E. (1987). "150 different ways" of knowing: Representations of knowledge in teaching. In J. Calderhead (Ed.) *Exploring teachers' thinking* (pp. 104–24). London: Cassell.

4

CURRICULUM POLICY GUIDELINES

Context, Structures and Functions

F. Michael Connelly and Gerry Connelly

This chapter on curriculum policy guidelines is an outgrowth of our background paper on curriculum guidelines (Connelly & Connelly, 2008), prepared at Allan Luke's request, for a project on the design of curriculum syllabi in Queensland, Australia (Luke, Weir & Woods, 2008) initiated by the Queensland Studies Authority. In that paper we made the point that curriculum guidelines are policy documents that perform two sets of functions, one set political and one set practical. They are documents that play an important role in political, public discourse over the aims, purposes and accomplishments of education, and they specify what is to be taught in schools, in what order and in what relationship. In this chapter we repeat and expand this point.

It happened that shortly after completing the Queensland paper we wrote the section on curriculum policy for the Encyclopedia of Curriculum Studies (Connelly & Connelly, 2010). We found that there is little literature on curriculum policy per se. Literature summaries emphasize curriculum policy input (politics and context) and curriculum policy output (implementation), while curriculum policy per se remains mostly a black box. The juxtaposition of those two related writing tasks brought us face to face with additional curriculum policy questions, which we address in this chapter. In addition to the political and practical functions of guidelines, two key things to note at the outset are that: curriculum guidelines are a form of curriculum policy that need to be developed and understood in terms of other forms of curriculum policy; and curriculum guidelines are at the center of a complex, holistic, public, political, professional and practical network of educational discourse.

Our perspective in the Queensland background paper was based primarily on our experience with relevant processes in the Canadian Province of Ontario. One of us, Gerry Connelly, was former Director of the Ontario Ministry of Education's Curriculum Policy Branch and was responsible for the development, revision and implementation of Ontario curriculum policy. Currently she is Director of Education for the Toronto District School Board (TDSB) and is administratively responsible for TDSB implementation of government curriculum policy. She is also responsible for the development, revision and implementation of TDSB curriculum policy and for ensuring board policy is congruent with Ministry of Education policy. This insider perspective shifted to a more outside-in perspective as we undertook the encyclopedia task. We bring these two perspectives together in this chapter.

Part I: Curriculum Policy in Context

Curriculum considerations are at the center of public education. What students study, and do, under the auspices of formal schooling defines both the purpose of public education and defines curriculum. Public discourse over education inevitably comes down to curriculum. Public discourse may be explicitly curricular, as in discussions over literacy, numeracy and equity, or it may be implicitly curricular, as in discussions over such matters as teacher standards, classroom environment and the like. The latter are curricular because they matter only to the extent that it may be shown that teacher standards and classroom environment enhance the quality of the student learning experience. Moreover, broader public discourse on social values, social status, equity, the economy, labor needs, immigration and international competition often turns to education and thence to curriculum as root cause and/or solution. The economic and skilled labor discussions in the West in the 1980s and again in the 2000s as we write are illustrative.

The centrality of curriculum discourse and curriculum policy may seem obvious to those with a classroom perspective on education and may also appear obvious in jurisdictions such as Great Britain, which have a national curriculum policy (Qualifications and Curriculum Authority, 2009). But the reality is that, while there is a burgeoning educational policy literature, the literature on curriculum policy is all but non-existent. There are encyclopedia, handbooks and other sources with curriculum policy in the title (e.g., Kirst & Walker, 1971; Elmore & Sykes, 1992; Walker, 1992; Levin, 2008; Short, 2008). But none of these reviews deal directly with curriculum policy per se. Instead, the focus is on the political, social and practical context of curriculum policy and how this contributes to a political understanding of these policies. There is extensive literature on the implementation of curriculum policy showing that there is little fidelity to curriculum policy in school curriculum practice. Moreover, what review literature there is, is overwhelmingly focused on the United States. Short (2008) observed that Elmore and Sykes' review "marked the birth ... of curriculum policy research" (p. 920). But these authors say that their review is on "public policy studies that have some bearing on curriculum" (p. 185). They are clear that they are not reviewing curriculum policy per se. If Short is right, this may partially account for the lack of curriculum policy research. What is implied about the state of the curriculum policy literature in these "curriculum policy" reviews is visible in the *International Handbook of Educational Policy* (Bascia, Cumming, Datnow,

Leithwood & Livingstone, 2005) and the *Handbook of Education Policy Research* (Sykes, Plank, & Schneider, 2009). The term *curriculum policy* appears in neither the table of contents nor the index of these comprehensive documents.

Another reason for the omission of curriculum policy analysis in these major policy reviews may be that those working in policy research are administrative scholars. Their interest is with overall administration and system processes rather than with the concrete realities of the curriculum world. An administrative focus of interest, and the fact that administrative and curriculum scholars are normally former school people with experience of the hierarchy of authority in the relationship of teachers and administrators in school is, no doubt, reflected in this policy curiosity. The positions tend to shape the direction of thought, teachers looking inwards toward their classrooms and students and administrators looking outwards towards system and context.

Gidney (1999) tells a revealing curriculum policy development story on the 1968 transition of the Ontario secondary school curriculum policy, called HS1, from a system of compulsory sequential credits and fixed student course selection pathways to an open credit system with multiple possible student pathways. The rewriting of HS1 was the responsibility of the program branch and was in response to a widely discussed position paper titled Living and Learning (Ontario Department of Education, 1968) aimed at integrating elementary education and secondary education in the provinces which were, traditionally, separately organized and administered. The program branch contained a curriculum section and a supervision section. According to Gidney, the two sections formed two camps, "progressive" (curriculum) and "traditional" (administrative), with sharp disagreements over proposed reforms. The dramatic progressive curriculum changes that eventually occurred came about because the Deputy Minister of Education appointed a committee consisting of seven members from the curriculum section and only three members from the supervision section. This historian's account of the development of a curriculum policy sheds light on the nature of the educational policy literature, and why it is that actual curriculum policy and policy analysis are mostly invisible in the policy literature. Apart from the ideological question embedded in the Ontario story, it is clear that administration and curriculum provided different vantage points for viewing education and for considering HS1 curriculum policy changes.

There are few studies like Placier, Walker and Foster's (2002) detailed study of the Missouri curriculum standards document, Cornbleth and Waugh's (1995) study of equity policies in two US states and Levin's (2008) detailed political account of the Ontario mathematics curriculum. The important thing about these studies is that they are analyses of actual, specific, curriculum policies. It is also worth noting, however, that these studies are preoccupied with the context and politics of curriculum policy making rather than with the structure and function of curriculum policy. Taken side by side with the reviews noted above, the overall effect is as if a biologist set out to describe an organism by focusing on its habitat, neglecting to tell us anything about the organism other than that it was a hapless product of its environment.

There is, we believe, a little-noticed curriculum policy literature that resides in the shadows unseen by the administratively and politically oriented policy review search light. One such example is a special issue of the *International Journal of Science Education* (Fensham, 1995) on science curriculum policy.

Westbury's (2008) analysis of curriculum policy in seven countries warrants special mention. He, too, focuses on the political/social context of curriculum policy. But instead of looking into curriculum from this context and concluding that curriculum policy is the outcome of external political forces, he looks out to context from the vantage point of curriculum. From this perspective he sees curriculum policy as serving a number of narrative functions for governments, for instance, demonstrating government accountability. With Westbury, we see legitimate functions where others see political influences. We use this idea to structure our presentation of curriculum policy guideline functions.

Curriculum Policy and the Web of Educational Discourse and Action

From the point of view of curriculum policy, the most important point emerging from the reviews discussed above is how embedded curriculum policy is in a web of state, national and other educational policies and initiatives, as well as being embedded in a plethora of educational organizations and voices with political and policy agendas. In the United States, for example, there have been a series of influential Acts since the 1950s: the National Defense Education Act (NDEA) of 1958, the Elementary and Secondary Education Act of 1965, Improving America's Schools Act of 1994, No Child Left Behind Act of 2001 (NCLB) and the education appropriation in the American Recovery and Investment Act of 2009. Locally, regionally and nationally there are a wide variety of teacher, administrator and school board professional organizations, accrediting associations, national professional organizations, colleges and universities, textbook publishers, teacher education institutions, philanthropic organizations, foundations, the media and many other NGOs with an education interest. Moreover, as these reviews make clear, this multidimensional context is set within a global context and is influenced by such matters as international competition, technology, transnational migration, trade and the economy.

It is important to note that for a curriculum policy initiative any, or all, or even perhaps none, of these influences may be relevant. An influence may be so relevant that it is the primary motivation for the curriculum reform as, for example, is the case with the Missouri Show Me Standards (Placier et al., 2002) document, which is a direct response to Missouri state law and which, in turn, is in direct response to the NCLB Act. The NCLB Act is a response to social inequities and achievement gaps in the US public education system. Curriculum policy is created and/or modified within this network of influence. Thus, curriculum policy is always fluid and subject to change in response to the fluidity and changes in its context.

Curriculum Policy Implementation and Practical Use

The reviews make it clear that curriculum policy in democratic systems is implemented in various ways, with little practical fidelity to curriculum policy. Spillane (2008) remarks that the "United States post-Sputnik era national reforms ... had limited influence on curricular content" (p. 641). The most recent review on this matter is found in seven chapters (Levin, Apple, Westbury, Deng & Luke) under the heading Making Curriculum (Welner & Oakes, Fullan & Means), Managing Curriculum and in Short's review of curriculum policy research under the heading Inquiring into Curriculum in the *Sage Handbook of Curriculum and Instruction* (Connelly with He & Phillion, 2008). The net conclusion of this literature is that the attempt to shape practice through the writing of curriculum policy is mostly unsuccessful. In the above mentioned volume, Apple argues that social movements drive educational change and sweep aside intentional policy efforts to bring about change. Fullan and Means review the curriculum implementation literature and also conclude that there is little relationship between curriculum reforms and curriculum practice. Unlike Apple, Fullan and Means believe that with the right systemic approach, curriculum policy implementation with fidelity remains a possibility. Westbury's focus is on national reform and, while he also concludes that national reforms do not direct practical change, he argues that there are positive, useful, political, narrative functions of curriculum policy.

Following Westbury (2008), policy makers need to be aware that there are complex reasons for drafting curriculum policy in addition to the aim of improving practice. If the literature is accurate, curriculum policy makers are, in general, as likely to influence public opinion of government as they are to influence school practice.

Formal, Implicit and Prudential Curriculum Policy

An adequate account of curriculum policy guidelines needs to account for guideline input (political/social discourse and action) and guideline output (implementation and practical use). Our solution to the puzzle of how to bring these matters together – formal, written curriculum policy, contextual matters influencing that policy and implementation of curriculum policy in practice – is to name three broad types of curriculum policy: formal, implicit and prudential. We define *formal curriculum policy* as "the official, mandatory, written statement of what is to be taught to students." (Connelly & Connelly, 2010). *Implicit curriculum policy* refers to policy at various government levels and in different influential organizations, that either directly influences curriculum practices or is influential in the writing of formal curriculum policy. It is common for governments to accompany formal curriculum policy documents with resource materials, approved textbooks and advisory memoranda. School system users of such documents, for the most part, do not make a distinction between what is *required* by policy and what is *recommended*, with the result that these documents also constitute *implicit curriculum policy*. *Prudential curriculum policy* is a term designed to account for the lack of practical fidelity to curriculum policy documents. The term recognizes that schools and school people have local and personal curriculum policies that drive what actually happens in the curriculum. We define *prudential curriculum policy* as "the prudence, practical wisdom and practical knowledge used by teachers, school administrators, school board staff, and elected trustees as they adapt formal and implicit curriculum policy for local situations".

Curriculum Policy and Curriculum Textbooks

At certain times, and places, curriculum policy may be little other than an official list of approved textbooks and other materials for classroom use. In Canada and the United States, gaining textbook approval province by province and state by state provides greater control of the implementation of curriculum policy. In such a situation, without the intervention of curriculum policy, textbooks become courses of study and define both curriculum policy and practice. Ironically, having no written curriculum policy is a way of gaining fidelity. When textbooks are both curriculum policy and course outline, fidelity is maximized. A version of this is the practice followed in Canada of having a list of approved textbooks and other curriculum materials called, in Ontario, the Trillium List (Ontario Ministry of Education, 2009a). Approval is granted mainly in terms of official curriculum policy (Ontario Ministry of Education, 2008). Thus, in Ontario, there is a policy for textbook approval, but textbooks are not considered to be curriculum policy. In this situation, the official curriculum policy is a document and the working policy includes textbooks chosen by a teacher, school or school board from the approved list. For this chapter, important as textbooks are and remain in curriculum policy implementation, we restrict our attention to policies written by government bodies.

Names for Curriculum Policy

In Canada, it is common for professional educators to refer to curriculum policy as *curriculum guidelines* or *curriculum guide*. But curriculum policy goes by other names and is rarely named *curriculum guidelines* per se. Ontario refers to its curriculum policy simply as *curriculum documents*. The province of Saskatchewan uses the term *core curriculum*, Alberta refers to *program of studies* and British Columbia variously refers to *provincially prescribed curriculum*, *curriculum document* and *curriculum guides*. The language used tends to reflect popular and professional usage. Terms such as curriculum framework (Michigan), national curriculum (Great Britain), core subjects (Great Britain), syllabus (Australia) and curriculum standards (Missouri) name curriculum policy documents.

For purposes of this chapter, we call *formal curriculum policy* "curriculum guidelines". We use the term *curriculum guidelines* because the idea of a *guideline* acknowledges the prudential quality of curriculum policy as it is implemented in practice. The risk in this term, something that needs to be assessed by policy makers, is that the door may be opened too wide with little legal recourse if local jurisdictions and/or local teachers deviate from the formal curriculum in ways judged to be unacceptable. The term *curriculum syllabus* is widely used in Australia and we considered using this term. However, in North America the connotation of a syllabus is that of detailed course outline. We believe that the notion of *curriculum guidelines* opens the door to statements of philosophy, purpose and framework and permits consideration of the place of a subject or topic across the curriculum and sequentially through the grades. The idea of syllabus, at least in North America as being limited to course outline, tends to suggest a narrower notion of curriculum policy than we wish to discuss.

Part II: Writing Curriculum Guidelines: Structures and Functions

This section synthesizes the preceding discussion of curriculum policy in a form that might be thought of as guidelines for the art and craft of writing curriculum policy guidelines. Each point in our discussion should be thought of as a decision point for a curriculum policy maker rather than as a necessary criterion of good policy writing. For instance, we suggest that one of the principle structural decisions is whether to have an overall general curriculum policy guideline for a government jurisdiction or whether it is sufficient to have independent separate guidelines for various topics and subjects. Ontario, for example, has no overall curriculum guideline though it has curriculum guidelines for elementary school and secondary school topics and subjects. Currently, the Minister of Education considers this policy structure limiting and is in the process of crafting an overall provincial curriculum guideline within which the various elementary and secondary guidelines will take their place. The reverse situation is seen in Sweden, which has a broad general curriculum policy guideline. This guideline has been judged to be insufficiently detailed to provide meaningful guidance for teachers and Sweden is undergoing a process of creating more detailed topic and subject guidelines (Government Offices of Sweden, 2008/09). Our purpose is not to take sides on this matter (though we do favor overall guidelines), but to suggest that policy makers need to make a decision on the matter of whether or not to write an encompassing curriculum policy guideline for a government jurisdiction.

Writing Curriculum Guidelines

Writing curriculum guidelines involves two broad overall sets of considerations associated with what we call the structures and functions of curriculum guidelines. *Structural decisions* need to be made on six matters discussed below: whether to have system wide guidelines in addition to topic and subject guidelines; general language used to construct guidelines; content specific language for topic and subject guidelines; degree of guideline specificity and associated teacher autonomy; integration of curriculum policy horizontally across the curriculum and vertically through the curriculum over ages and grades and the role, and level of detail, of support documents. Traditionally, structural decisions are guided by academic, professional and civil service literature reviews and expertise.

Functional decisions are somewhat more complex and less technical. Guidelines are poised between what we call *implicit curriculum policy* in the form of contextual pressures on the matter of what should be taught in schools, and *prudential curriculum policy* in the form of practical adaptations, modifications and interpretations of guidelines. This positioning presents those responsible for curriculum policy making – heads of government curriculum departments, deputy ministers of education, ministers of education, guideline committee chairs – with the complicated task of keeping a watchful eye on the implicit curriculum policy context and the need to make ongoing judgments about what to build into curriculum policy guidelines. A watchful eye must also be kept on prudential curriculum policy in the form of professional, practical competencies and capabilities, as well as on political/policy positions adopted by administrator, school board and teacher organizations. Guidelines need to be written in harmony with the educational level of teacher users, with professional teacher association standards and expectations and with public expectations. Guidelines need to be both useful as a guide to practice and stimulating professionally. Those responsible for the development of curriculum policy guidelines need to keep a watchful eye on curriculum guidelines as they are written to ensure that the writing process remains consistent with what is wanted. Writing committees can shift priorities and directions under the influence of their members.

It is common in Canada for curriculum policy guideline writing teams to be composed primarily of teachers. The idea is that this will lead to greater usability. This process fosters teacher professionalism and collegial relationships between government and teacher organizations and is, on balance, a highly successful writing strategy. The possible limitation of such a process, without consideration of other factors noted above, is that the guideline writing process may lose touch with public/political matters in implicit curriculum policy and, perhaps, even lose touch with practical/professional matters in prudential curriculum policy. On the latter point, it is often ironically said that the only teachers capable of teaching a new curriculum guideline are those who wrote it. The story of HS1 reported above illustrates the complicated set of considerations that must necessarily enter into the writing of curriculum guidelines. It will be recalled that in the HS1 case the Deputy Minister juggled committee composition in order to achieve government aims.

Structural Decisions for Writing Curriculum Guidelines

System Wide Curriculum Policy Guidelines

We have already noted that some jurisdictions, such as Ontario, have no overall curriculum policy guideline, while others such as Sweden and Great Britain have national system wide curriculum guidelines. A system-wide guideline creates a policy context for the system as a whole and creates a framework for the more detailed topic and subject guidelines at the pre-school, elementary and secondary levels. One of the virtues of a system-wide curriculum policy guideline is that overview statements are more readily amenable to the non-technical writing of inspirational, philosophical statements reflecting public hopes, dreams and ambitions. The following from the British curriculum guideline policy is illustrative: "Education should also reaffirm our commitment to the virtues of truth, justice, honesty, trust and a sense of duty" (Qualifications and Curriculum Authority, 2009).

Constitutionally, education is a provincial responsibility in Canada and all curriculum policy is written provincially. Nevertheless, there are non policy Canadian initiatives that recognize the possible value in comprehensive system-wide curriculum policy statements. The Council of Ministers of Education (2008) joint provincial and territorial declaration, Learn Canada 2020, lists four pillars of lifelong learning e.g., Early Childhood Learning and Development and eight key activity areas e.g., literacy. The document is said to reflect the educational priorities of Canadians and, while it is not a curriculum policy document, it is clearly intended to influence curriculum policy. An earlier Council of Ministers' effort along the same lines was the development of the Pan-Canadian Protocol for Collaboration on School Curriculum (Council of Ministers of Education, 1997). Providing a sense of a harmonious whole is one way of thinking about the writing of a jurisdiction's overall curriculum policy guideline.

Language Decisions: General Considerations

There is no theory, nor proven practice, that yields curriculum policy guideline language and structure for all places and times. Language varies with what is publicly and professionally current and popular. The objectives movement, structure of knowledge movement, student achievement movement, student activity movement, standards movement, accountability movement and so on all give rise to different terms for organizing curriculum policy guidelines. In general, four things need to be considered:

1. Guideline language needs to be current and needs to reflect widespread public and professional discourse;
2. Guideline language needs to reflect overall government intentions;
3. Guideline language needs to be recognizable by public and professional leaders and users; and
4. Guideline language needs to be clear, easily understood and readable.

Ontario, for example, uses, among others, the following terms in its curriculum guideline documents: overall expectations, specific expectations, subject by grade, strand, knowledge categories, achievement level, what students can do and provincial standard. Missouri uses a language of standards: what students should know and be able to do, goals, subject areas, knowledge and skills. A review of other jurisdictions would reveal a long list of reasonably closely related terms tied together by the current international preoccupation with achievement, standards and accountability. Curriculum policy guideline language connected to popular public and professional language can enhance relevance and readability.

Language Decisions: Content Specific Considerations

In addition to the language used to describe and structure system-wide curriculum policy guidelines, specific topics and subject matters have their own traditions with their own languages that need to be taken into account. Moreover, like the general language discussed above, content language is not fixed. There is a widely accepted disciplinary language used in school curriculum subject matters, but the language of the disciplines is only one among several ways in which curriculum topics and subject matters may be described. Consider, for example, social studies curriculum guidelines oriented to social life rather than to history and geography, science curriculum guidelines oriented to interdisciplinary science or possibly to the relationship of science and society rather than to the disciplines of chemistry, physics and biology, or literature guidelines oriented to a traditional canon vs guidelines oriented to critical literacy. Roberts (1995), for example, describes a language shift in Alberta science curriculum guidelines. Science guidelines moved from a "layer-cake" structure in which subject matter areas were treated sequentially through the years with biology in Grade 10, chemistry in Grade 11, physics in Grade 12, to a "coordinated" approach in which students studied each subject each year in an integrated science format. Each topic and curriculum subject matter area has a variety of such terms available for curriculum guideline structure. Curriculum guideline writers need to be aware of these alternative possibilities and need to consider how the variable resulting structures relate to, and support, the overall system-wide curriculum guideline, if such exists.

They need also to be aware that terms are seldom neutral. Their use may tap into passionately held ideological positions e.g. "critical literacy" in discussions over Australian curriculum policy reforms (Thomson, 2008).

Specificity and Curriculum Policy Guidelines

The level of detail determines the range of possible interpretations of the written document and the flexibility by which it may be used by teachers and others. At one extreme, curriculum guidelines may be so specific that the same thing is taught at the same time in every appropriate classroom in a jurisdiction. Little interpretation is possible. Textbook and syllabus-style curriculum policy guidelines may run towards this extreme. At the other extreme, statements may be so broad that almost anything might be shown to be consistent with policy. Considerable interpretation is possible. The Swedish example discussed above exhibits, in the eyes of Swedish policy makers, this latter possibility. In Ontario, following the HS1 revisions associated with the document Living and Learning, a high degree of independent curriculum content decision making was expected of secondary school teachers. Many teachers were uncomfortable with the level of professional freedom provided and efforts were made through the Ontario Secondary School Teachers Federation to have government curriculum policy specified in more detail. One of the arguments given was that policy should specify what is to be taught while teachers should decide how it is to be taught. Thus, the level of specificity (or prescription as discussed in Chapter 2 in this volume) in which curriculum guidelines are written is both a matter of what is desired by way of required knowledge and skills as well as a matter of encouraging and supporting teacher professionalism. Too much detail may reduce teacher professionalism while too little detail may swamp teachers with extra curriculum planning work. There is no standard or formula by which the golden mean may be established. Jurisdictions, and topics and subjects within jurisdictions, vary in teacher qualifications and teacher association professionalism. Moreover, each jurisdiction has a particular history that determines what is possible for any guideline at any point in time.

In principle, guidelines may range from lesson-by-lesson plans of study to broad philosophical goal statements with minimum content specification. An open democratic process leads to variability in level of specification from curriculum guideline to curriculum guideline. Efforts to maintain consistency across guidelines need to be balanced with democratic sensitivity. In general, in democratic systems balance has been established over time under the influence of stakeholders representing both the policy instrument function *and* the practical guideline function. In summary, policy makers need to aim for a degree of appropriate specificity to enhance professionalism and with due regard for differences across the topics and subject areas.

Horizontal and Vertical Structure of Curriculum Guidelines

A decision to have a system-wide curriculum guideline highlights the need to consider guideline horizontal and vertical structure. *Horizontal structure* refers to relationships across the curriculum at any one point in time; *vertical structure* refers to relationships throughout the curriculum across the ages and grades. It is possible, for example, for an elementary school science curriculum guideline writing committee for the intermediate years, Grades 7 and 8, to do their work without reference to science policy for Grades 1 to 6 or for the high school years (*vertical*). Moreover, they may do their work without reference to language arts, physical education and the various other topics and subject areas in the curriculum (*horizontal*).

Curriculum policy guideline writers need to make organizational decisions on the vertical sequence through the age/grade years for topics and subjects. They also need to make horizontal decisions over time allocated to the various topics and subjects and over possible connections and overlaps among these topics and subjects, including how these relate to the curriculum as a whole. Without consideration of horizontal and vertical structure, curriculum guidelines stand in isolation.

Support Documents and Curriculum Policy Guidelines

One way of dealing with the degree of specificity decision is to make a distinction between policy guidelines and support documents. For instance, in Ontario, "Policy documents outline mandatory requirements and standards. Resource documents support implementation of policy and their use is a local decision" (Ontario Ministry of Education, 2009b). A wide range of detailed support documents are available to supplement curriculum policy guidelines. For instance, Language, Grades 1–8 is a 160 page curriculum policy guideline document supplemented by a 122 page support document, The Ontario Curriculum, Grades 1–8: English as a Second Language and English Literacy Development – A Resource Guide. Support documents are a useful way of providing practical guidance for teachers who feel they need it, while allowing teachers the flexibility to exercise professionalism.

Functional Decisions for Writing Curriculum Guidelines

Curriculum guidelines are best thought of as the pivot point or fulcrum between the two sets of contextual policy influences: the influence of political/public discourse on curriculum guidelines, *and* the influence of adaptation and reinterpretation of guidelines during implementation. Curriculum guidelines stand between implicit curriculum policy and prudential curriculum policy. From the literature it is clear that many think curriculum policy guidelines per se are inconsequential. On the one side, they are seen as buffeted by political forces with little independent life of their own. On the other side, they are seen as documents that are mostly ignored in practice. But, as noted above, Westbury makes the case that guidelines have important functions that serve government needs. We adopt this stance in the following and describe policy instrument functions and practical guideline functions corresponding to what we previously referred to as the contextual input of political/public influences on curriculum policy (implicit curriculum policy) and contextual output of adaptations and interpretations of curriculum policy during implementation (prudential curriculum policy). In our view, curriculum policy guidelines are at the heart of the enterprise, balancing implicit and prudential curriculum policy matters. Guidelines have important curriculum functions re public/political discourse *and* practical/professional use. We believe that curriculum policy makers need to be aware of these two broad functions as curriculum guidelines are drafted. In practice these functions vary from subject to subject, topic to topic, time to time and government to government.

The policy instrument and practical functions noted below follow from our discussion above and are provided in point form.

Policy Instrument Function

- Curriculum guidelines are vehicles to implement public educational change.
- Taken as a whole, curriculum guidelines reflect the political allocation and distribution of knowledge in society. Social/political attitudes, social equity,

economic ambitions and the like are reflected in the content, and balance, among guidelines.

- In curriculum settings, such as Ontario, with policy instrument and practical guideline functions and where there is a tapestry of curriculum development ranging from commercial publishers, school boards with expansive curriculum functions and highly professional teacher associations with teacher standards, professional development and resources, the curriculum guideline functions as a locus around which this curricular web operates. Everything comes back to curriculum guidelines.
- In tension with this focal role of guidelines in the curriculum web is the fact that none of the links between any element in the web and the guideline are firm nor fixed. Linkages between curriculum guideline standards and public expectations depend on the expertise, beliefs and values of specific individuals making the link; they depend on local norms, values and politics which, in some jurisdictions, vary from place to place and from community to community. It is not possible, nor desirable, to attempt to put in place mechanisms to reduce this natural system of flexibility between curriculum guidelines and the curricular system.
- Curriculum guidelines may become the target, and outcome, of special interest advocacy groups.
- Curriculum guidelines are policy instruments for the ideological steering of school systems.
- Curriculum guidelines have narrative functions as elected politicians and political parties point to guidelines as representing their ideology; for example, curriculum guidelines on equity.
- Curriculum guidelines have narrative functions as governments point to guidelines, and the flurry of development activity that goes into their making, and re-making, as evidence of government action on political promises made.

Practical Guideline Function

- Curriculum guidelines, taken as a whole, foster continuity throughout (*vertical*) and across (*horizontal*) the curriculum.
- Curriculum guidelines foster grade-to-grade and division-to-division transitions (*vertical*).
- Curriculum guidelines encourage teacher professionalism. This emerges from the concept of *prudential curriculum policy* and the flexibility teachers have to interpret curriculum guidelines and to utilize special classroom resources appropriate to local situations and particular student needs.
- Curriculum guidelines may specify student expectations and contribute to students' realizing their potential.
- Standards, student expectations and curriculum guidelines combine to create a system in which the government may claim competitive advantage with other governments. Government competition and ranking on international comparative

measures is often used to justify particular curriculum guidelines, e.g., a country's ranking in an international mathematics assessment.

- The idea of standards associated with curriculum guidelines allows for the development of assessment standards (content standards) and benchmarks for instruction and evaluation, thereby publicly relating government intentions to expectations.
- Curriculum guidelines are central reference documents for approved curriculum material and textbook lists, for the development of assessment standards and strategies and for preservice teacher education programs and inservice professional development programs.
- Curriculum guidelines inform the delivery of educational services in classrooms. For teachers, curriculum guidelines provide a framework of what is to be done from among the infinite range of possibilities.
- Curriculum guidelines, in their development and implementation, have a community building function. All those with science expertise or interest may, for instance, orient themselves politically, possibly in working teams, around the development and interpretation of a science curriculum guideline.
- In jurisdictions such as Ontario, curriculum guidelines have an administrative agenda-setting function (Pierre, 2000). School board administrators, committees and board groups orient themselves around particular guidelines to develop local board guidelines and classroom curricula.

To conclude this chapter we shift to detailing principles and considerations related to the writing of curriculum guidelines.

Part III: Additional Issues in the Development and Use of Guidelines

Autonomy of the Ministry/Department of Education Civil Service

Government systems vary in the degree of autonomy assigned to education civil servants responsible for curriculum guideline development. With high levels of autonomy, some curriculum development may be more academic and professional in character, and planning teams may be relatively small in size. A more open democratic model and process such as is used in Ontario means that the guideline development process becomes *less* traditionally academic and professional. A broader array of public and political concerns informs the process. Ongoing collaboration, tension and tradeoffs between political/public and professional/academic concerns occur. Moreover, the planning process becomes a representative one with a wide array of stakeholders beyond the more traditional academic professional membership. Draft versions of guidelines are circulated not only to professionals and academics but to representative public/political organizations for feedback. In Ontario, with a history of both a policy instrument function and a practical guideline function, there is minimal professional and academic tension with public political concerns. But, in jurisdictions where this process is relatively new, government efforts need to be made to explain and rationalize the process to all stakeholders.

Factors affecting the success of the curriculum guideline development process are: (1) the array of representative stakeholder groups on curriculum guideline committees; (2) actual and perceived control and authority in committees; (3) strategies for balancing academic and professional content criteria with political and public concerns and (4) the process of vetting interim documents with the profession on the one side and political and public interest groups on the other. A widely representative and transparent process may tend to be contentious and time consuming but may be expected to yield higher legitimacy.

Support Documents

Support Documents at the Government Level

In Ontario, curriculum guidelines are supplemented by an array of support documents. For instance, for Ontario's Grade One guideline, for the topic Matter and Materials: Cleaning up Skills, there is:

- A chart of *task rubrics* organized by level of achievement. "Rubric" is defined as achievement criteria and descriptions of four levels of achievement for each task;
- A set of student samples. These are actual student responses organized by the rubrics; and
- A teacher package. A detailed breakdown, by time, including description of task, instructions for students, curriculum expectations, teacher instructions, directions on use of the rubrics, tasks that might be followed, a detailed exemplar task, and an Appendix of work sheets that might be used with students.

Support Documents at the Board of Education Level

Boards of education may take on an important role in the development of curriculum support documents to augment government guidelines. Boards of education may even develop curriculum guidelines and courses of study independently, though these normally need government approval. The Toronto District School Board, the largest school board in Ontario with 266,000 students in 560 schools, representing over 13% of Ontario students, has a vast array of guidelines and professional support documents that rival government efforts in breadth and detail. Smaller boards of education may have little role in the development of support documents. In the current age of electronic information availability, almost all boards of education provide electronic resource leads. Sharing of resources from different jurisdictions is widely used.

Built-in Links among Curriculum Content, Curriculum Standards and Achievement

Curriculum content, curriculum standards and student achievement need to be related to one another in guidelines framed in terms of standards (called "expectations" in Ontario) and achievement. The curriculum guideline for Grades 1 to 8 in Ontario, for example, contains a conceptual/content grid for the science curriculum along with student expectations at each of four achievement levels.

Boards of Education, Curriculum Guidelines and Local Curriculum Politics

Because the system of curriculum policy making ranges from the public to the local school level, the system is only loosely coupled. This means that, notwithstanding efforts at government implementation of curriculum guidelines, a wide diversity of local board of education and school development occurs and, in Ontario, is encouraged. One of the political consequences of this loosely coupled system is that support documents developed at a board level may generate heated public/political discourse and reflect directly back on the political party in power. For this reason, in democratic systems and certainly in Ontario, the Minister of Education maintains close political contact with elected school board trustees, maintaining a watchful eye on possible political consequences of local curriculum activity.

Level of Professional Teaching Expertise in a Curriculum Guideline Area

In general, as noted above, one of the functions of a good curriculum guideline is to enhance teacher professionalism. In general, this will tend to occur where there is relatively low guideline specificity combined with high levels of guideline resource documents and opportunities for teacher professional development. But the relationship of expertise to content varies from subject to subject and from grade level to grade level. For example, for many jurisdictions, elementary school teachers have minimal science background. Such a situation may warrant more detailed guidelines, freeing teachers for the broad educational mandates of the elementary school.

Teacher Organizations and the Democratic Process

Teacher organizations in democracies normally have dual professional and union roles. In Canada, these roles are well developed at the provincial level and teacher associations and federations are internally structured along professional and union lines. On the professional side, teacher federations are involved in professional development, the provision of resource materials and liaisons with government on curriculum policy guidelines. Salary and working conditions are the main concerns of the union role. The two roles may come together in curriculum policy if the teacher organization has strong views on a curriculum guideline matter and/or believes that teacher professionalism as defined by the organization is threatened.

Teacher Professionalism and the Democratic Process

There may be tension between teacher professionalism and the democratic political process of involving non-professional stakeholders in the curriculum guideline development process. The professional role of teachers, academics and other professionals is muted in a democratic curriculum guideline development process. A balance needs to be struck between encouraging professionalism and academic expertise while responding to a democratic process open to the voices of many stakeholders.

Teacher Unions and the Democratic Process

In jurisdictions where teacher unions are strong, highly public disputes may develop between teacher organizations and government and/or local boards of education. Disputes may escalate through provincial labor relations and human rights boards and commissions and culminate in strike action. Teacher strikes have serious repercussions for governments in power. Thus, at least in Canada, though there are many stakeholders whose voices play a role in curriculum guideline development and implementation, the teacher's voice is ultimately the one most carefully watched by policy makers.

Relationship of Curriculum Guideline Topic to Political/Public Discourse

Because of the *policy instrument function* of curriculum guidelines, guidelines vary widely in their political sensitivity at any point in time. If, for instance, equity is an important political topic, curriculum guideline development will be filtered through the lens of equity. Curriculum guidelines reflect public, political discourse and decisions over guideline process and content must necessarily reflect the topic's public status.

Urgency and Curriculum Guidelines

Under normal circumstances, jurisdictions using a cyclic guideline review process set a leisurely review, development and implementation pace. Time is taken to review the literature and the work of other jurisdictions. It is not uncommon to have media "leaks" of politically sensitive matters aimed at judging public reaction for the purpose of making appropriate adjustments during the guideline writing process. But, occasionally, which probably feels like "often" to a Minister of Education, hot button public topics arise that require swift curriculum guideline action by government.

A racial or sexual school yard incident or an in-school stabbing or shooting, for example, may trigger urgent discussion over social justice, equity or anti-bullying in the curriculum. In response, the Minister may issue a memorandum with the force of a curriculum policy guideline.

The Implementation Process

New and revised curriculum guidelines normally enter a government-driven implementation process. This process reflects the dual functions of guidelines: *policy instrument* and *practical guideline function.* While almost all implementation efforts are publicly justified in terms of their practical aims, the process may be highly political. In effect, the implementation process is an extension of the political/public discourse associated with guideline development. If, for example, there are disputes over traditional and postmodern notions of literacy in the language arts curriculum, they are unlikely to subside upon the release of a new curriculum guideline. New curriculum guidelines may meet with resistance and/or approval from teacher groups, academics, parents and other school community groups. As a result, in democratic systems curriculum guideline implementation has a political/public side in addition to its academic content side of trying to align practice with policy.

Governments may financially lever guideline implementation. As part of the Ontario implementation process, low achieving schools, based on curriculum guideline standards, receive extra resources. Other jurisdictions may withdraw resources from low-achieving schools.

Guidelines for the Writing of Curriculum Policy Guidelines

The final matter we wish to consider is government policy on the writing of curriculum guideline policy. In democratic systems, curriculum guidelines are always under scrutiny and subject to revision. At one time, particularly in the sciences, it was said that the "explosion of knowledge" drove the need for policy revision. But, as our review of the curriculum policy landscape shows, implicit and prudential curriculum policy considerations drive reform agendas. Political/public discourse and practical/professional interpretation continually change the configuration of contextual forces acting on curriculum guidelines. The result is that some systems have developed a policy for the revision of policy.

The Ontario Curriculum (Ontario Ministry of Education, 2009c) website describes a cyclic process for writing and revising formal curriculum policy. There is wide consultation with the profession, subject area academics, other ministries, parents, students, non-government organizations (NGOs), businesses and others in the public as well as reviews of trends and developments in the specific guideline topic or subject, and reviews of curriculum policies and policy development practices in other jurisdictions. Writing teams composed mostly or entirely of teachers drawn from school boards, sometimes with education and/or subject area professors and with a Ministry of Education advisor, are appointed. A similar process is followed by the British Columbia Ministry of Education (2008) with the added formal separation of the process into an internal Ministry review process and an external process.

References

Bascia, N., Cumming, A., Datnow, A., Leithwood, K. and Livingstone, D. (Eds) (2005). *International handbook of educational policy*. Dordrecht, The Netherlands: Springer.

British Columbia Ministry of Education (2008). Draft curriculum review process. Retrieved from www.bced.gov.bc.ca/irp/draftcurriculum_process.htm

Connelly, F. M. and Connelly, G. (2008). The curriculum guideline: Policy instrument and practical curriculum guide. In A. Luke, K. Weir and A. Woods (Eds) *Development of principles to guide a P-12 syllabus framework* (pp. 128–39). Brisbane: Queensland Studies Authority.

Connelly, F. M., & Connelly, G. (2010). Curriculum policy. In C. Kridel (Ed.) *Encyclopedia of curriculum studies* (pp. 224–27). Thousand Oaks, CA: Sage.

Connelly, F. M. (Ed.) with M. F. He and J. Phillion (Assoc. Eds) (2008). *The Sage handbook of curriculum and instruction*. Thousand Oaks, CA: Sage.

Cornbleth, C. and Waugh, D. (1995). *The great speckled bird: Multicultural politics and education policymaking*. New York: St. Martin's Press.

Council of Ministers of Education (1997). Pan-Canadian protocol for collaboration on school curriculum. Retrieved from www.cmec.ca/protocol-eng.htm

Council of Ministers of Education (2008). Joint declaration provincial and territorial ministers of education. Learn Canada 2020. Retrieved from www.cmec.ca/2008declaration.en.stm

Elmore, R. and Sykes, G. (1992). Curriculum policy. In P. W. Jackson (Ed.) *Handbook of research on curriculum* (pp. 185–215). New York: MacMillan.

Fensham, P. (1995). Editorial: Policy and science education. *International Journal of Science Education*, *17*(4), 411–12.

Gidney, R. D. (1999). *From hope to Harris: The reshaping of Ontario's schools*. Toronto: University of Toronto Press.

Government Offices of Sweden (2008/09). Summary of the government bill: Clearer goals and knowledge requirements – new school curricula. Retrieved from www.sweden.gov.se/sb/d/11304/a/117694

Kirst, M. W. and Walker, D. F. (1971). An analysis of curriculum policy-making. *Review of Educational Research*, *41*(5), 479–509.

Levin, B. (2008). Curriculum policy and the politics of what should be learned in schools (Chap. 1). In F. M. Connelly (Ed.) with M. F. He and J. Phillion (Assoc. Eds) *The Sage handbook of curriculum and instruction* (pp. 7–24). Thousand Oaks, CA: Sage.

Luke, A., Weir, K. and Woods, A. (2008). *Development of a set of principles to guide a P-12 syllabus framework*. Queensland, Australia: Queensland Studies Authority.

Ontario Department of Education (1968). *Living and learning: The report of the provincial committee on aims and objectives of education in the schools of Ontario*. Toronto: Ontario Department of Education.

Ontario Ministry of Education (2008). Guidelines for approval of textbooks. Retrieved from www.curriculum.org/occ/trillium/Textbook_Guide_English_2008.pdf

Ontario Ministry of Education (2009a). *The trillium list*. Retrieved from www.curriculum.org/occ/trillium/index_dev.shtml

Ontario Ministry of Education (2009b). *Frequently asked questions. What are policy and resource documents?* Retrieved from www.edu.gov.on.ca/eng/curriculum/secondary/#policy

Ontario Ministry of Education (2009c). *The Ontario curriculum*. Retrieved from www.edu.gov.on.ca/eng/curriculum/elementary/subjects.html

Pierre, J. (2000). Introduction: Understanding governance. In J. Pierre (Ed.) *Debating governance: Authority, steering, and democracy* (pp. 1–10). Oxford, UK: Oxford University Press.

Placier, M., Walker, M. and Foster, B. (2002). Writing the "show-me" standards: Teacher professionalism and political control in U.S. State curriculum policy. *Curriculum Inquiry*, *32*(3), 281–310.

Qualifications and Curriculum Authority (2009). *Values aims and purposes. National curriculum.* Retrieved from http://curriculum.qcda.gov.uk/key-stages-1-and-2/Values-aims-and-purposes/index.aspx

Roberts, D. (1995). Junior high school science transformed: Analyzing a science curriculum policy change. *International Journal of Science Education*, *17*(4), 493–504.

Short, E. (2008). Curriculum policy research (Chap. 20). In F. M. Connelly (Ed.) with M. F. He and J. Phillion (Assoc. Eds) *The Sage handbook of curriculum and instruction* (pp. 420–30). Thousand Oaks, CA: Sage.

Spillane, J. P. (2008). Policy, politics, and the national mathematics advisory panel report: Topology, functions and limits. *Educational Researcher*, *37*(9), 638–44.

Sykes, G., Plank, D. N. and Schneider, B. (2009). *Handbook of education policy research.* New York: Routledge.

Thomson, J. (2008). Philosophical attack draws fire. *The Australian*. Retrieved from www.theaustralian.news.com.au/story/0,24741258–21682,00.html

Walker, D. (1992). Curriculum policymaking. In M. C. Alkin (Ed.) *Encyclopedia of educational research* (6th edition, pp. 280–86). New York: Macmillan.

Westbury, I. (2008). Making curricula: Why do states make curricula, and how? (Chap. 3). In F. M. Connelly (Ed.) with M. F. He and J. Phillion (Assoc. Eds) *The Sage handbook of curriculum and instruction* (pp. 45–65). Thousand Oaks, CA: Sage.

5

THE TECHNOLOGICAL SOLUTION TO READING EDUCATION

A Century of Frustration

Patrick Shannon

Introduction

The century-long quest for certainty in school outcomes promises personal and social benefits. If governments could make the outcomes of public education more predictable through the manipulation and control of instructional inputs, individuals would be able to educate themselves continuously in order to meet the changing and increasing skill demands of fluid global economies. A predictably schooled workforce would enable businesses to enter labor into the calculus of their current plans with confidence of increased productivity and profits. Without this predictability, many individuals fail to keep pace with rising skill levels of employees in other countries and national economies struggle. Or so the modern economic narrative is told (Chang, 2010).

In order to act on this quest, government officials have turned to scientific findings and business practices to determine the one best method to teach all subjects. Somewhat ironically, these acts seem to curtail teachers' and students' development, positioning teachers as one element within the method and students as consumers of information. After a century of trying, the results have been disappointing at best and apparently detrimental to both business and individuals in general. Yet to date, attempts to move beyond this quest and the social forces that make the quest seem right and appropriate have proven to be elusive (Shannon, 2007).

All nations seeking to participate in the global economy embrace this quest to some degree. Consider the increasing popularity of audit culture within public institutions around the world in which performance indicators and calculation replace human judgment in the evaluations of practices and benefits (Caulkins, 2002; Shore, 2008; Trnavcevic & Logaj, 2008). The contributors to the *Review of Research in Education* (Kelly, Luke & Green, 2008) summarize recent research developments and compare them to the narrowing of curriculum and increases in testing across all subjects and borders. In more pointed discussions, the contributors to *Neoliberalism and Education Reform* (Ross & Gibson, 2007) name the instrumentalism of the quests directly and call for alternatives.

In what follows, I limit my remarks to reading education in the United States because it provides a detailed record of this quest for certainty across nine decades. I describe the development of scientific, business, and government discourses within the reading instruction field and discuss how they became the normal ways of thinking about teaching reading, rendering alternatives as quaint, odd, or injurious. This American example corresponds to current policies and reactions in other English speaking countries as well (e.g., Soler & Openshaw, 2007; Goouch & Lambirth, 2008; Stockard, 2010). Renewed emphasis on decoding, explicit instruction, specified curricula, and testing cut across borders and educational systems.

Across the 20th century, American educational scientists, commercial publishers, and government officials worked in order to develop a system of instruction that would teach all students to read. Using reliable, replicable, and objective methods, scientists sought to identify, measure, and then order the behavioral and cognitive variables of reading and compared instructional methods in order to isolate the one most effective in inducing children to read. Publishers translated those scientific findings into technologies (teachers' manuals, elaborate anthologies and practices, and tests) for teachers to follow in order to produce predictable outcomes. The state and federal officials enacted policies to ensure that those scientific technologies were available to all and that the teachers use them. According to federally funded reports throughout the century, all three groups performed well, and we now have consensus on what reading is and how to teach it (Horn, 1919; Austin & Morrison, 1963; National Reading Panel [NRP] Report, 2000). Elaborate and detailed technologies are used in over 95% of elementary classrooms (Barton & Wilder, 1964; Smith, 1934/2002; Brownstein & Hicks, 2005), and the federal government now insists that these technologies be employed in order to qualify for federal funding (Manzo, 2005). Yet, reading achievement lags well below expected levels, particularly for targeted populations, and business continues to worry about the literacy levels of current and prospective managers and workers (Gray, 1919; Chall, 1965; Berliner, 2006).

A First Attempt

At the turn of the 19th century, individuals and businesses faced challenges similar to those they face today. The United States was changing rapidly from agrarian communities to industrialized cities, requiring a new skills set. Time honored ways of production were considered too slow and unreliable to meet the demands for new goods. In order to compete, businesses needed workers who could hone their productive behaviors according to the new criteria of time and precision in order to produce uniform goods in greater quantities. Using these criteria, industrial experts examined the productive actions of master craftsmen in order to define the best method for production of each good. Labeled "scientific management," newly created work experts divided the labor of the craftsmen into elementary movements, eliminated the useless ones, standardized the remaining ones, and then wrote the rules and procedures for that behavior on instructional cards in order to make them easily replicated across settings (Taylor, 1912). If workers followed these instructions, cost of production decreased, worker productivity increased, and profits rose accordingly. To monitor the fidelity of the work, foreman and managerial positions were created in a similar way.

At the same time, efforts to bring scientific methods to the traditional philosophic study of people's minds and thinking created a new set of experts; educational psychologists, who sought to redefine reading, learning, and teaching according to scientific principles (Venezky, 1984). The psychology of reading was forged analytically from the assumption that reading involved three stages: perception, translation, and then, thinking. Studies of cues for letter and word recognition, eye voice span, and sub-vocalization led to the development of tests that could pinpoint the route of reading step by step from perception of print to its translation to phonemes and words. Different tests were invented in order to probe readers' thinking about those words. Perceptual and translation tests considered letters, letter strings, words, and sentences; and thinking tests were short passages to be read silently with several questions to follow.

Learning was redefined as sequential mastery of sub-skills leading to the summation of a complex behavior (Thorndike, 1906). Learning the three stages of reading began with connections between letter stimuli and production of corresponding phonemes. Teaching reading, then, became the application of the scientific laws of learning – learning followed one order from simple skills to complex behaviors; practice increased the likelihood of connections between stimuli and responses; positive feelings associated with connections enhanced these bonds and increased the likelihood that new skills would be connected to those already mastered. Testing of each skill in isolation would determine if students should progress to the next skill in the sequence.

These movements merged in the work of the National Society for the Study of Education (NSSE) between 1915 and 1919 (Horn, 1919). Educational experts were charged with applying principles of scientific management to eliminate the waste in and improve the productivity of schools. In *Principles of Methods in Teaching Reading as Derived from Scientific Investigation*, William S. Gray induced 48 principles of teaching reading after reviewing 35 experiments and observational studies (1919). As Frederick Taylor found in steel mills, Gray noted that schools had master teachers working beside novices who had little idea of how to teach reading. The NSSE addressed this issue not by engaging the neophyte teachers in discussions about reading, children, and teaching, but by evaluating more closely the existing school textbooks according to the results of scientific management committees. In reading instruction, the organization's recommendations were to standardize practice through the equivalent of instructional cards – adoption of a single textbook series throughout a school with a detailed teachers' manual at each grade level.

Reading textbook publishers hired Gray and other members of the NSSE committees in order to produce the manuals for their series (Smith, 1934/2002). Within three years, each textbook company increased its directions for teachers from the traditional one- or two-paged preface in its previous editions to hundreds of pages of didactic instructions on how to use the materials at each grade level correctly. Lessons were organized around the three-stage model of reading according to Thorndike's laws of learning. Perception and translation skills were identified, defined explicitly, and sequenced by difficulty; skill practices were developed and packaged in disposable workbook forms; simple scripts were written to direct teacher and student interchanges; and eventually special tests were created for each skill in order to measure mastery. Publishers and reading experts offered these technological innovations to administrators and teachers as scientific facts to be followed, regardless of the social context of the instructions or the abilities and attitudes of the students and teachers. All assumed that, if the directions were followed explicitly, all students would learn to read efficiently and effectively. In 1955, however, TIME magazine editors used the title of Flesch's book, *Why Johnny Can't Read*, to complain that, despite the pre-eminent position of the US economy among nations, the science and business of reading education were not producing many readers in American schools.

A Second Attempt

By the late 1920s, the logic and technology were in place to direct the quest for certainty in reading instruction. Standardization of scientific inputs was expected to bring predictable outcomes, enabling students to succeed at school and later at work. With the authority of science, business, and the state behind it, the project was nearly complete by the 1960s. Surveys demonstrated that over 95% of teachers acknowledged that they used the technologies during their instruction, leading the researchers to quip that teachers used the manuals "slavishly" (Austin & Morrison, 1963, p. 224) and "teachers think they are professionals – but want to rely on basal readers, graded workbooks, and teachers' manuals, and other materials prefabricated by the experts" (Barton & Wilder, 1964, p. 382). Despite the implementation of the project, experts, business, and the state were not satisfied with the results because significant percentages of American students, particularly the poor and minority students, were not scoring high enough on national achievement tests (House, 1978).

Through philanthropic and federal funding, the National Conference on Research in English engaged in what became known as the First Grade Studies (Pearson, 1997) in order to find the one best method among the commercial technologies available (see Bond & Dykstra, 1967; and the 30th anniversary printing and commentary in *Reading Research Quarterly*, 1997). Although a combination of perceptual and translation approaches brought higher test scores than perceptual approaches alone, the 27 researchers involved in the project concluded that no method or combination of methods was effective with all students. There was as much variation of students' test scores within a method as there was between methods. In other words, differences in teacher knowledge and practices accounted for the successes and failures of students' learning to read regardless of which technologies they used.

In response to the First Grade Studies, reading experts and publishers reemployed the fundamentals of scientific management and the laws of learning (Rosenshine & Stevens, 1984). With federal funding, the experts designed new studies and experiments in order to isolate the salient practices of effective teachers and effective schools with the intent to strengthen the directions in teachers' manuals for teachers. Time on task, explicit instruction on comprehension, and content coverage were highlighted. Effective teachers provided more direct instruction because they prioritized their lessons and eliminated transition times; they recognized that the thinking stage of reading required direct intervention to improve; and they pushed their students at a rapid pace through the lengthy scope and sequence of skills provided in the manuals. Publishers were quick to make these modest adjustments to their manuals.

Publishers championed tests for each skill in the scope and sequence and promoted those outcomes as a way to measure student learning (Johnston, 1984). They argued that an accumulation of successful series skill test scores was an equivalent, perhaps preferable, representation of students' reading when compared to paragraph and question formats for reading achievement tests. Such skill tests enabled administrators to monitor students' learning and teachers' instruction more closely by tracking student scores during a school year as well as across school years. If scores were low, teachers and administrators knew which skills to reteach and retest. If the scores remained low, however, administrators knew which teachers needed support in using the technology correctly. At some point, students would become capable of demonstrating their reading abilities on national achievement tests as well as the commercial skill tests. Yet, in 1983, the National Commission on Excellence in Education report *A Nation At Risk* claimed that for the first time public school graduates were less literate than their parents and grandparents.

A Third Attempt

Following a series of reports from business and government organizations that cited the inability of public schools to produce workers with sufficient skills to handle the new literacy demands of shifting national and global employment, the official governmental solution was to set national standards, testing, and policies that would prepare workers to enable American business to compete internationally. Flexibility, problem solving, and entrepreneurship were to replace the decades-old skills of time and precision within a singular publically funded, state controlled, open, and forgiving system (Marshall & Tucker, 1992; Goldin, 2003). Although tensions arose among groups of experts over the causes of problems in public schools, all agreed that a technological solution was still the best approach to reach expected outcomes.

Since the 1980s, the federal government has become more assertive in public schools matters. America 2000, Goals 2000, Educate America, and the No Child Left Behind legislation became progressively more insistent on the employment of a tight accountability system that begins with scripted lessons from commercial publishers and ends with test scores that demonstrate a nation of proficient readers (Allington, 2002; Coles, 2003). Although state education departments continue to operate the checks and balances of that system, the federal government controls compliance with the federal plans through funding incentives (and disincentives) (Hess, 2003). To gain scientific legitimacy for its position, the federal government brokered consensus among reading experts through a series of experimental studies and reports.

The Centers for the Study of Reading, the National Institute of Child Health and Human Development, and Center for the Improvement of Early Reading Achievement provided a steady stream of research affirming and shaping the reality of the three stage model of reading and the laws of learning that were summarized in a series of state-of-the-art of teaching reading reports – *Becoming a Nation of Readers* (1985), *Beginning to Read: Thinking and Learning about Print* (1990), *Preventing Reading Difficulties in Young Children* (1998), and *National Reading Panel Report* (2000). At present, the federal government defines reading as the deployment of alphabetics, phonics, fluency, vocabulary, and comprehension; and teaching as direct instruction of each component from perception through translation to thinking about text en route to federally mandated proficiency scores on state reading tests.

Members of the Business Roundtable partnered with the federal government throughout the third attempt to find the one best system for teaching reading (see www.businessroundtable.org/initiatives/education). Its involvement began by co-sponsoring the Educational Summit during the National Governors' Conference in 1988 and continues to its current efforts to provide common core national standards in all subjects (www.corestandards.org), a digital curriculum to deliver those standards (www.edweek.org/media/pearsonfoundationreleasegates.pdf), and national tests for each subject at multiple grade levels (www.parcconline.org/). Intending to accelerate the rate of school improvement, the Business Roundtable promoted somewhat contradictory proposals to increase federal regulation of public schools, while increasing private competition through individual educational vouchers and unregulated publicly funded charter schools.

With each educational policy, educational publishers and entrepreneurs moved swiftly to produce state required instructional and testing technologies (Miner, 2004). The No Child Left Behind legislation proved to be a boon to publishers. Beyond the textbooks and tests, corporations supply test preparation materials, information management systems, primary and supplemental curricula, professional development, and other elements of the required accountability systems. In the early 2000s, financial analysts labeled school publishing and testing corporations "Bush stocks" because their markets appeared guaranteed under the federal legislation (Metcalf, 2004).

Former President of the International Reading Association, Richard Allington, characterizes the third attempt:

> For the past forty years, beginning with Title I, the federal model for education in America has been: "Buy new stuff." Under NCLB, the model shifted slightly, to "Buy new stuff that markets itself as research based."
>
> *(as quoted in Collier, 2008, p. 24)*

These research based materials continue the century-long quest for certainty of outcome by substituting technology (new commercial highly scripted lessons, programmed practices, and objective skill tests) for teachers' judgment in the name of fidelity to the one best method to produce proficient readers. Reading coaches perform the roles of shop foremen in scientific management, keeping teachers and students close to the plans articulated in the teachers' manuals. In order to increase school accountability, test scores are made available to the public, and in many states, are tied directly to school and teacher evaluations. Replicated in every grade from kindergarten to senior year in high school, the science of the National Reading Panel, the published technologies, and the NCLB policy promises that every child will read proficiently by 2014. Yet, calculated results of the new and enhanced one best system have not arrived.

In the 2007 State of the Union Address, President George W. Bush called on Congress to reauthorize No Child Left Behind (NCLB) legislation "because it's working." His claim had only modest support within the test score data collected in each school district across America. Although a 2006 Education Trust report concluded that modest gains in state reading test scores have been made at the elementary levels (Hall & Kennedy, 2006) and African American and Latino students narrowed slightly the achievement gaps on these tests at the elementary level as well, the results were less encouraging at the middle school and high school levels. Some states even demonstrated declines on the tests during the first three years of NCLB. Adding further caution, the Education Trust noted that National Assessment of Education Progress (NAEP) (the national report card according to NCLB) results did not corroborate state test gains. Only six states demonstrated comparable results at both levels, while the remainder reported state proficiency rates two and sometimes three times higher than the national test produced. For example, Alabama demonstrated 83% proficiency on the state test, but only 22% on the NAEP; New Jersey's proficiency scores were 82% for state and 37% for national; and Oregon's were 81% and 29%. The Civil Rights Project examined the same data as the Education Trust and drew four less optimistic conclusions:

1. NCLB had not had a significant general impact on reading achievement across the nation. At current rate of growth, only 34% of American students will be proficient by 2014 (not the 100% required by NCLB).
2. NCLB is not closing the racial gaps, although slightly more minority students are reaching proficiency. At current rates, only 24% of poor or minority students will reach proficiency by 2014.

3. The model states for NCLB (Texas, Florida, and North Carolina) did not show significant gains before NCLB and have not improved since the legislation was passed. Trends over longer periods of time, then, are not promising.
4. Finally, the state test data are most misleading for poor and minority students. Although state tests overestimate white students' reading proficiency by a factor of two, the state tests inflate African American students' proficiency by a factor of four (Lee, 2006, p. 47).

In the introduction to the report, Project Director Gary Orfield did not mince words:

> The goals of raising achievement and lowering the gaps are very good ones, and the data provided by NCLB is (sic) essential, but policy makers must be ready to critically examine why so little has been accomplished, why officials are making misleading and inaccurate claims, and what can be done to use the invaluable data and focus created by the Act to begin to actually accelerate progress toward those objectives.
>
> *(p. 8)*

In April 2009, the federal Institute of Education Sciences finally released the results of its Reading First Impact Study (the reading program of NCLB) (NCEE, 2008). After spending six billion dollars on new technologies of reading instruction "on average, across the 18 participating sites, estimated impacts on student reading comprehension test scores were not statistically significant" when compared to sites that were not participating in the Reading First Program (Institute of Education Sciences, 2009, p. 5). Despite increased time on task and emphasis on the National Reading Panel's "five essential components of reading instruction" within participating schools, the expected goal of increased understanding through rapid decoding had not been reached – even for schools that had served as pilot projects two years before the three year study began.

Moreover, reports from the US Department of Education Inspector General (2006) and US Senate Health, Education, Labor and Pensions Committee (2007) charged Reading First officials with conflict of interest concerning the distribution of technologies required in the programs. In order to staff leadership positions for the implementation of the Reading First Initiative, Department of Education administrators selected researchers who publishers employed in order to translate research findings into commercial technologies. The Inspector General's report names Reading First Director, Chris Doherty, and the National Institute of Child Health and Human Development (NICHD) head of research, Reid Lyon, as responsible for directing the program toward a single set of findings and technologies, and the Kennedy report details the financial rewards to four regional Reading First directors (Edward Kameenui, Douglas Carnine, Joseph Torgesen, and Sharon Vaughn) for their associations with Pearson/Scott Foresman, Voyager, Houghton

Mifflin, SRA/McGraw Hill, and The Dynamic Indicators of Basic Early Literacy Skills (DIBELS) publishers during their tenures in federal positions. In the face of the lack of success and conflict of interest, the US Congress voted to eliminate funding for the Reading First Initiative.

Orfield's statement, the International Education Services (IES) interim report, and reports on conflict of interest challenge the roles of science, business, and government in the pursuit of certainty in educational outcomes. If evidence and history are the best indicators of the future, then perhaps they question the pursuit of certainty in reading education altogether. At each opportunity in the 1920s, '60s, and '80s when empirical data suggested that teachers' knowledge made the difference in students' achievement, experts have opted to pursue technological solutions that diminished teachers' roles and required students to follow directions in order to read, rather than to invest in teacher knowledge and practices that would harness students' abilities to read in and out of school classrooms. When the technology solutions have failed each time to develop a nation of readers, government officials, business leaders, and reading experts blamed teachers' lack of devotion to their work and sought tighter systems of control of teachers' and students' efforts. Although No Child Left Behind increased the oversight and tightened regulations remarkably, the values embedded in that policy are similar to those of earlier attempts to find certainty of outcomes in reading instruction. Under increased pressure to raise test scores, schools pressure teachers to devote more time to reading instruction, curtailing music, art, social studies, and science within the curriculum and there appears to be widespread cheating among teachers, schools, and districts in order to meet mandated achievement targets toward complete proficiency by 2014 (Huffington Post, 2011).

Challenged on theoretical, empirical, and political grounds in the United States, a group of experts, the US government, and business entrepreneurs moved to export the technologies of the third attempt throughout Asia, Africa, and Central and South America (Gove & Cvelich, 2010). Working primarily through the World Bank, Research Triangle Institute has renamed DIBELS as Early Grade Reading Assessment, translated Reading First materials to French and Spanish, and led a world-wide testing program to show that "millions of children in low income countries around the world, whose prospects of academic, and with it – economic success are dimmed because [they] cannot read" (ii). To address this problem, UNESCO, the World Bank, and a host of nongovernment agencies distribute these materials, train teachers in their application, and encourage fidelity to the system through testing programs.

Hope and Change

During his campaign for the US Presidency, Barack Obama consulted with Linda Darling-Hammond, a well-known advocate for public schools and the intellectual enhancement of the educational labor force through certification programs and continuous professional development. Obama's educational platform pointed toward teachers and teaching as the solutions for troubled schools, and it described technology as tools useful only within the hands of knowledgeable teachers and administrators. Shortly after being elected, however, President Obama selected his friend Arne Duncan for Secretary of Education. Duncan had served as the Chief Executive Officer for Chicago Public Schools for seven years, after the Chicago Mayor "took over" the city's school system and laid a centralized accountability scheme of standardization over the city's decentralized administrative structure. Having closed many schools and consolidated others as charter schools while the CEO in Chicago, Duncan has pursued a somewhat contradictory combination of paths toward and away from the one best system for schooling.

Although NCLB was scheduled for reauthorization in 2009, the Obama administration allowed it to stand, issuing an executive order called Race to the Top. Using earmarked funds from the 2009 American Recovery and Reinvestment Act as incentives, the Race to the Top organized a competition among states to reform their schools according to specific federal criteria – adherence to national standards, reconstitution of their weakest schools, easier authorization of charter schools, and teacher and administrator assessments based on student test scores. In the Race to the Top, states would choose to enter the competition, avoiding charges of federal interference in state governance of public schools. The Obama Administration worked through the National Governor's Association and the Council of Chief State School Officers to broker sets of the Common Core Standards, and it withdrew the NCLB mandates for reading instruction, recharacterizing teaching to read as value added to text scores annually rather than students' Adequate Yearly Progress leading to universal proficiency by 2014. Many of the state proposals were aided by grants from the Gates Foundation. Forty-eight states chose to participate in the first round of competition, which Delaware and Tennessee won; and nine states and the District of Columbia were awarded less funding in the second round. Although only 11 states received extra funding because of the Race to the Top, 42 states have adopted the Common Core standards and committed to the other criteria as well.

Focusing primarily upon urban elementary and secondary schools, the federal government has been selective in its appeals to scientific research. On the one hand, they embrace the findings from the multi-year analyses of successes and failures during the Chicago Public School experiment with local control (Bryk, Sebring, Allensworth, Luppescu & Easton, 2010), which concluded that successes in improving reading test scores were dependent on the presence of five "essential supports" regardless of the teaching methods employed. "Schools strong in [Teachers' knowledge and development, learning climate in the school and classrooms, parent/teacher/community ties, curricular alignment within and across grades, and effective leadership] were at least ten times more likely than schools weak in [those] supports to show significant gains in both reading and mathematics" (p. 93). In this way, the Obama Administration apparently rejects the century-long one best method project for lack of hard evidence. On the other hand, contrary to research findings, Secretary Duncan continues to advocate for annual high stakes testing on national standards, charter schools, corporate administrative structures, merit pay, and test scores as the primary basis for teacher evaluation (Ravitch, 2010).

Moreover, rather than avoiding the appearance of conflict of interest between business and reading education policies that plagued the NCLB Reading First Initiative, Obama's Department of Education administrators brokered several federal collaborations of venture philanthropists (Gates and others), Achieve (nonprofit education arm of the Business Roundtable), and commercial publishing conglomerates (Pearson) in order to ensure that young adults graduate from high school "career or college ready." After a decade into NCLB and three years of Race to the Top, US high school graduation rates hold steady at around 70%; three quarters of adolescents who attempt to enlist in the military are deemed unfit and academically unprepared for service, and Scholastic Achievement Test (SAT) scores have dropped significantly over the last five years. The quest for the one best system of schooling in the United States has failed.

Many Good Methods of Reform

To be good citizens, we must engage school reform in order to become aware of its possible meaning in our everyday and working lives. These engagements make us more socially competent as voters, taxpayers, parents, and workers (Lemert, 2008). During the last century, we were told that school reform was essential for any nation to win the future economically. At first in the United States, reform was needed to build an institution based on a factory metaphor in which scientific management would yield the one best method of teaching in order to provide a knowledgeable workforce for local and national economies. For the last 30 years, US reformers have told us to reform that institution, rendering it flexible enough to match the rapid changes in a global economy. Adopting a market metaphor, reformers assume that the one best system will emerge through processes of creative destruction in which competitions among alternatives identify the most productive, efficient model for all rational educators and nations to adopt. Both of these representations stem from an economic frame for schooling that has focused and continues to focus science and state policy on the identification, production, and employment of a technological fix to teachers' lack of productivity in the production of the appropriate human capital in public schools.

This frame and these representations of school reform promise a particular future and assign students, school personnel, and all citizens to places within that future. Debates about school reform, then, tie us to other political, social, and economic debates and agendas across time, place, and people. Using our sociological imaginations (Mills, 1959), we can read those ties, asking why certain futures and assignments are offered to citizens as obvious, real, and desperately urgent, and others are not. As Mills wrote, the sociological imagination is "a quality of mind to help [us] to use information and to develop reason in order to achieve lucid summations of what is going on in the world and what may be happening within [our] selves" (p. 5). By pushing our engagements with school reform past competence to imagination, we can identify frames, analyze representations, and move our assigned position from consumers of expert and official positions to become producers of alternatives inside and outside the accepted economic frames (Shannon, 2011 and the other chapters in this book).

There are many groups and individuals to help us imagine more inclusive democratic human alternatives for school reform. For example, Baynham and Prinsloo (2010) provide discussions of the changing nature of the education project, pointing to new literacies, toward new content, and beyond the classroom door. Moss and others (2008) question the sophistication of our understandings of students' opportunities to learn and the evidence of learning in schools, suggesting that government education and social policies limit those opportunities for many. Saltman (2010) articulates the social, economic, and political agendas behind new philanthropists' interest in schooling, connecting business's concerns about organized labor with the assault on teachers' competence and their market interests with global educational projects. Of course, there are other helpful texts that point in different directions, and these authors do not necessarily agree with one another on the scope and direction of school reform. However, they all seek to expand the parameters of the discussion of how science, business, and the state could be involved in the education of citizens. They seek to refocus research and policy toward inclusion, enabling more democracy in more aspects of our lives. They question the business metaphor of the market for schooling, reducing the status of technology from the realm of solution to the utility of mediating tools in human hands. They allow us to imagine different frames and representations for school reform and different lives for ourselves.

References

Adams, M. J. (1990). *Beginning to read: Thinking and learning about print*. Cambridge, Mass: MIT Press.

Allington, R. (Ed.) (2002). *Big brother and the National Reading Curriculum*. Portsmouth, NH: Heinemann.

Anderson, R. C., Hiebert, E. H., Scott, J. A. and Wilkinson, I. I. J. (1985). *Becoming a nation of readers: The report of the Commission on Reading*. Washington DC: National Academy of Education.

Austin, M. and Morrison, C. (1963). *The first R*. New York: Wiley.

Barton, A. and Wilder, D. (1964). Research and practice in the teaching of reading. In M. Miles (Ed.) *Innovations in education*. New York: Teachers College Press.

Baynham, M. and Prinsloo, M. (Eds) (2010). *The future of literacy studies*. New York: Palgrave.

Berliner, D. (2006). Our impoverished view on educational reform. *Teachers College Record*, *107*, 56–87.

Bond, G. and Dykstra, R. (1967). The cooperative research program in first grade reading instruction. *Reading Research Quarterly*, *2*(4), 351–425.

Brownstein, A. and Hicks, T. (2005, August). When research goes to market. Retrieved from www.title1online.com/librairies/title1online/news

Bryk, A., Sebring, P., Allensworth, E., Luppescu, S. and Easton, J. (2010). *Organizing schools for improvement*. Chicago, IL: University of Chicago.

Business Roundtable (2009). Retrieved from www.businessroundtable.org/initiatives/education

Caulkins, S. (2002, May 12). Too many sums don't add up: An exploding audit culture drains the public coffer. *Observer*. www.guardian.co.uk/money/2002/may/12/madeleine bunting.business

Chall, J. (1965). *Leading to read: The great debate*. New York, NY: McGraw Hill.

Chang, H. (2010). *23 things they don't tell you about capitalism*. New York: Bloomsbury.

Coles, G. (2003). *Reading the naked truth: Literacy, legislation & lies*. Portsmouth, NH: Heinemann.

Collier, L. (2008, November). Fighting for scientifically valid reading strategies that work. *Council Chronicle, 14*, 22–24.

Editorial (1955, March 14). Why Johnny can't read. *TIME, 4*.

Goldin, C. (2003). The human capital century. *Education Next, 3*(1), 73–78. Retrieved from www.educationnext.org/20031/73.html

Goouch, K. and Lambirth, A. (2008). *Understanding phonics and the teaching of reading*. London, UK: Open University Press.

Gove, A. and Cvelich, P. (2010). *Igniting education for all: A report by the early grade learning community of practice*. Research Triangle Park, NC: Research Triangle Institute International.

Gray, W. S. (1919). Principles of method in teaching reading as derived from scientific investigation. In E. Horn (Ed.) *Fourth report of the Committee on the Economy of Time in Education. 18th yearbook of the National Society for the Study of Education* (pp. 26–51). Bloomington, IL: Public School.

Hall, D., and Kennedy, S. (2006). *Primary progress, secondary challenge*. Washington DC: Education Trust.

Hess, F. M. (2003). Refining or retreating? High stakes accountability in the States. In P. Peterson and M. West (Eds) *No child left behind?* (pp. 55–79). Washington, D.C.: Brookings Institution.

Horn, E. (Ed.) (1919). *Fourth report of the Committee on Economy of Time in Education. 18th yearbook of the National Society for the Study of Education*. Bloomington, IL: Public School Press.

House, E. (1978). Evaluation as scientific management of achievement in reading. *Comparative Educational Review, 22*, 388–401.

Huffington Post (July 26, 2011). *The five most shocking public school cheating scandals*. Retrieved from www.huffingtonpost.com/2011/07/26/the-5-most-shocking-publi_n_909593.html

Institute for Education Sciences (2009). *Reading First Impact Study - Final Report*. Retrieved from http://ies.ed.gov/ncee/pubsd/20094038/summ-b.asp

Kelly, G., Luke, A. and Green, J. (Eds) (2008). What counts as knowledge in educational settings: Disciplinary knowledge, assessment, and curriculum. *Review of Research in Education, 32*(1), 1–369.

Johnston, P. (1984). Assessment in reading. In P. D. Pearson (Ed.) *Handbook of reading research* (pp. 147–84). New York: Longman.

Lee, J. (June 2006). *Tracking achievement gaps and assessing the impact of NCLB on the gaps*. Cambridge MA: Civil Rights Project Harvard University.

Lemert, C. (2008). *Social things*. Lanham, MD: Rowman & Littlefield.

Manzo, K. K. (2005, September 7). States pressed to refashion reading first grant designs. *Education Week*. Retrieved from www.educationweek.org/articles/2005/09/07/02read

Marshall, R. and Tucker, M. (1992). *Thinking for a living: Education and the wealth of nations*. New. York: Basic Books.

Metcalf, S. (2004). Reading between the lines. In A. Kohn & P. Shannon (Eds) *Education, Inc.* (pp. 49–57). Portsmouth, NH: Heinemann.

Mills, C. W. (1959). *Sociological imagination*. Chicago, IL: University of Chicago.

Miner, B. (2004, Winter). Testing companies mine for gold. *Rethinking Schools, 19*, 49–57.

Moss, P., Pullin, D., Gee, J., Haertel, E. and Young, L. (Eds) (2008). *Assessment, equity, and opportunity to learn*. New York, NY: Cambridge.

National Center for Education Evaluation and Regional Assistance (NCEE). (April 2008). *Reading first impact study: Interim report.* Institute of Education Sciences, U.S. Department of Education, NCEE 2008–4016.

National Commission on Excellence in Education (1983). A nation at risk report. Retrieved from www.ed.gov/pubs/NatAtRisk/risk.htm

National Reading Panel (NRP). (2000, April 13). National reading panel report: Teaching children to read. Retrieved from www.nationalreadingpanel.org

National Research Council (1998). *Preventing reading difficulties in young children.* Washington DC: The National Academies Press.

Orfield, G. (2006). Foreword. In J. Lee *Tracking the achievement gaps and assessing the impact of NCLB on those gaps.* Cambridge, MA: Harvard University Civil Rights Project.

Pearson, P. D. (1997). The first-grade studies: A personal reflection. *Reading Research Quarterly, 32*(4), 428–32.

Ravitch, D. (2010). *The death and life of the great American school system.* New York, NY: Basic.

Rosenshine, B. and Stevens, R. (1984). Classroom instruction in reading. In P. D. Pearson (Ed.) *Handbook of reading research* (pp. 745–98). New York: Longman.

Ross, E. W. and Gibson, R. (Eds) (2007). *Neoliberalism and education reform.* Cresskill, NJ: Hampton.

Saltman, K. (2010). *The gift of education: Public education and venture philanthropy.* New York: Palgrave.

Shannon, P. (2007). *Reading against democracy.* Portsmouth, NH: Heinemann.

Shannon, P. (2011). *Reading wide awake: Politics, pedagogies & possibilities.* New York: Teachers College Press.

Shore, C. (2008). Audit culture and illiberal governance. *Anthropological Theory, 8,* 278–98.

Smith, N. (1934/2002). *American reading instruction.* Newark, DE: International Reading Association.

Soler, J. and Openshaw, R. (2007). To be or not to be? The politics of teaching phonics in England and New Zealand. *Journal of Early Childhood Literacy, 7,* 333–52.

Stockard, J. (2010). *Direct instruction and reading in Africa.* National Institute for Direct Instruction. Tech. Report #1, Eugene, OR.

Taylor, F. W. (1912, December). The present state of the art of industrial management. *The American Magazine, 71,* 18–31.

Thorndike, E. L. (1906). *Principles of teaching based on psychology.* New York: A. G. Seeler.

The 30th anniversary printing and commentaries on the First Grade Studies. (1997). *Reading Research Quarterly, 32*(4), 334–445.

Trnavcevic, A. and Logaj, V. (2008). *From quality to audit culture: Who dares to say no.* Unpublished paper. Retrieved from http://74.125.47.132/search?q=cache:kdtbdOLtrwkJ:www.pef. uni-lj.si/tepe2008/papers/Trnavcevic_Logaj.pdf+Trnavcevic+%26+Logaj+audit+culture& hl=en&ct=clnk&cd=1&gl=us&client=safari

U.S. Department of Education Inspector General. (2006, September). *The reading first program's grant application process: The final report.* Washington D.C. Retrieved from www.ed.gov/ about/offices/list/oig/aireports/i13f0017.pdf

U.S. Senate Health, Education, Labor and Pensions Committee. (2007, May 9). *The chairman's report on the conflicts of interest in the implementation of the Reading First Initiative.* Washington D.C. http://kennedy.senate.gov/imo/media/doc/Final%20Reading%20First%20Report% 202.pdf.

Venezky, R. (1984). The history of reading research. In P. D. Pearson (Ed.) *Handbook of reading research* (pp. 3–38). New York: Longman.

6

SUSTAINING TEACHER PROFESSIONALISM IN THE CONTEXT OF STANDARDS REFERENCED ASSESSMENT REFORM

Val Klenowski

Introduction

Standards referenced reform, tied to reporting, engages directly with assessment issues related to accountability. Assessment is the key to good education and is inseparable from curriculum. In an accountability context, standards are used as a lever to improve the reliability and consistency of teacher judgement, and classroom evidence is used by education systems for reporting and tracking achievement over time. Assessment is thus a powerful driver for change and is at the heart of the teaching-learning dynamic. The relationship between the learner, learning and assessment needs to be kept central and the idea of teacher empowerment is fundamental. This chapter is a call to honor and sustain teacher professionalism through educative forms of school-based and teacher-led evaluation, assessment and communities of judgement practice. It supports the argument for a central place for classroom assessment in the role of assessment in educational accountability.

Given the current international quest for countries to seek "national consistency in education" through the use of standards referenced assessment systems, involving student assessment and reporting against national standards and benchmarks, it is important to make explicit the intended and unintended consequences of such strategies. At the outset it is beneficial to acknowledge the inexorable existence of the pressures to pervert. In a context that is standards-driven and that values standardization, there is a great danger that technical, rationalist approaches that generalize and encourage the development of superficial assessment tasks and practices, will emerge. Attaining coherence between classroom assessment and system level accountability that includes system interest in transparency of outcomes has been much debated (Frederiksen & White, 2004; Wilson, 2004). It is teachers' judgements and interpretations of assessment data in the context of social moderation that is key, for it is teachers who have direct access to the information needed for any accountability system. Yet it cannot be presumed that teacher assessment is unproblematic. It is internationally acknowledged that the development of teachers' assessment capacity is not a strength of teacher education training.

To help understand the tensions that are involved in this issue, a framework, representing important dimensions, is introduced in the first section of this chapter. The next move is to define terms and concepts such as accountability and standards as they are used in this chapter. The chapter then outlines the different assessment regimes and associated practices for achieving accountability in the context of standards referenced reform and in so doing highlights their value and limitations. What is apparent in this analysis is the central role of teacher empowerment and professionalism in the case for intelligent accountability and more generative and educative forms of assessment, pedagogy and curriculum to enhance quality and improve equity of educational provision.

Framework

A framework for understanding how schools develop and improve has been described by MacBeath (1999). It is relevant in a context of accountability and standards referenced assessment reform. According to this framework, the three pertinent dimensions of school evaluation and development are: an internal–external continuum from self-evaluation at one extreme to evaluation from an outside source at the other; pressure–support continuum with a high level of support from the system at one end and strong pressure at the other and the bottom-up–top-down dimension that represents how a system sees and implements change.

For the purpose of this chapter the latter dimension requires further description. At one end of this continuum the change is delivered from above by legislation or by national structures, and at the other end the change can come from below, that is, from teachers, from students and parents, building on day-to-day school and classroom experience. MacBeath (1999) explains that neither extreme is ideal but the best kind of system is one in which bottom-up development is supported and endorsed from the top down.

To assist schools to grow it is now accepted that an optimum blend of all three dimensions – internal and external evaluation, support and pressure, bottom-up and top-down change – is required. The key factor that determines whether schools will flourish, or not, is the right combination across all of these dimensions, the ideal being that the direction of change is from internal to external evaluation, from pressure to support and from bottom-up development to top-down implementation of change. However, the optimum combination is dependent on the history, context and culture and the individual school's state of "psychological health" as this will differ from state to state, from district to district, from school to school (MacBeath, 1999). The importance of bottom-up development acknowledges the key role of the teacher at the local professional level of the school.

Accountability

Schools are accountable for what they do for students. In the 1980s the discourse of markets emerged in education and the place and purpose of accountability was made explicit. At that time, particularly in England, the dangers of "raw" exam or test results for accountability purposes were identified. Inspection of schools and standardized testing dominated accountability. These were used as the main criteria for judging school performance and measuring success in terms of student achievement. Using assessment results in this way can lead to schools being rewarded for the "quality" of the students they can attract and enrol rather than what they actually do for students to help them achieve. For it is students, their teachers and their parents who know and work with them in different settings, who are the primary sources of information to ascertain what schools do for students (MacBeath, 1999).

Intelligent accountability policies (O'Neill, 2002) involve trust-based professionalism or professional responsibility that grows over time from an ethos of respect within an education system that values teachers' and principals' professionalism in judging what is best for students and in reporting their achievements. In Finland, intelligent accountability enhances trust among teachers, students and education authorities in the accountability processes. What is more, they are all involved in the process so they develop a strong sense of professional responsibility and initiative (Fullan, 2005; Sahlberg, 2006, 2007). The impact on teaching and student learning has been positive. Assessment of student learning is based on teacher-led assessment rather than standardized external tests. Numerical grades are not used after Grade Five so that students are not compared with another. The law prohibits grades. Descriptive assessments and feedback are used, which is intended to impact positively on student performance and engagement in their learning (Assessment Reform Group, 1999). Teacher-made classroom assessment is a dominant practice and is used by teachers as an opportunity for learning as much as for assessing student achievement. As identified at the outset, teacher assessment is not without its limitations.

The shortcomings of such a system that relies on teachers' and schools' abilities to judge and report on students' achievement are that there are differences among criteria that teachers use to evaluate their students, even within the same school. Issues arise when students move to a new school and experience assessment that may involve different expectations than those of their previous school. Despite these shortcomings, the concept of intelligent accountability is preferred as it enables schools to keep the focus on learning and allows more freedom in curriculum planning compared with external standardized testing contexts. This freedom enables schools to address important equity issues that arise given the different sociocultural circumstances identified at the local level.

Standards

The term "standards" is ubiquitous and in the context of educational attainment it needs to be emphasized that there are no simple measuring instruments that can be used to determine an appropriate value for a student's achievement or, for that matter, of a school. There is no natural unit of measurement as there is for some physical quantities, such as weight or height. Standards are used in educational assessment and it is important to understand that the term can be used in a variety of ways. The definition of standards that is most appropriate in the context of standards referenced assessment systems for accountability include: "quality benchmarks" (expected practice or performance), "arbiters of quality" (relative success or merit) and "standards as milestones" (progressive or developmental targets) (Maxwell, 2002a, p. 1).

Standards as "quality benchmarks" define "an expected or typical outcome" and require representation on a continuum that defines a minimum acceptable level (Maxwell, 2008, p. 2). Both standards, as "arbiters of quality" and "standards as milestones," represent differentiated levels of performance. These two types of standards differ in focus and time frame so that the former may focus on a single assessment event while the latter provides for judgements over time along a continuum of learning (Maxwell, 2008).

The functions of standards as defined in these ways are first to provide a common frame of reference and a shared language for communicating student achievement. They are also intended to promote teachers' professional learning, focused on good assessment practices and judgement of the quality of student achievement against system level benchmarks or referents. In addition it is expected that they present more meaningful reports and engagement with assessment as a learning process.

Standards as descriptors of student achievement are used to monitor growth in student learning and provide information about the quality of student achievement. It is important to emphasize that examination or assessment standards cannot be objective in the same sense in which standards relating to physical measurements are objective. Assessment in education is intrinsically inexact and should be treated as such (Harlen, 1994). Standards need to be described in such a way that schools can relate to them. Student work needs to be used to substantiate meaning and then the standard descriptors need to be piloted, thereby grounding them in practice. They should encompass minimum and aspirational performances and be written in positive terms in language suitable for the intended audience so that moderation can occur.

Defining examination or assessment standards requires interpretation and inference. They are thus fundamentally subjective. The interpretation of assessment results should be about getting an indication of what students can do but not an exact specification (Cresswell, 2000). What should be assessed and the levels of attainment that are comparable to those represented by each grade in other examinations or assessments in the same family (Cresswell, 2000, pp. 71–72) should be defined by the standards as used in examination and assessment systems for public reporting. However, to compare attainment in different subjects we can only use indirect bases for comparison and for this we rely on statistics and expert judgement (Cresswell, 2000). Once again the role of the teacher is significant and in this context teachers have an important role in a community of judgement practice.

Teachers' Use of Standards

To develop this concept the current moves by the Australian Curriculum, Assessment and Reporting Authority (ACARA) who are developing a national curriculum and achievement standards will be used as an example. This example is relevant for a variety of reasons not least of which is the fact that this national curriculum is a first for Australian teachers. The national curriculum in English, Mathematics, Science and History was released in 2010. This Australian curriculum specifies content to be taught and the achievement standard expected for each year level and each discipline. In 2008 the National Curriculum Board issued a proposal for discussion regarding the use of achievement standards as follows:

> Achievement standards indicate the quality of achievement that is expected and provide the basis for judgements about the quality of students' work.
>
> *(National Curriculum Board, 2008)*

The purposes that the achievement standards must fulfil were outlined. The first purpose expressed was to make clear the expected quality of learning (knowledge, understanding and skills). Second, achievement standards were expected to

> provide helpful language with which teachers can discuss with students and their parents the students' current achievement level, progress to date and what should come next and finally they are expected to help identify students whose rate of progress puts them at risk of being unable to reach satisfactory achievement levels in later years.
>
> *(National Curriculum Board, 2008)*

In 2011 the Australian Curriculum achievement standards have been described as providing an expectation of the quality of learning students should typically demonstrate by a particular point in their schooling. This expectation includes the extent of their knowledge, the depth of their understanding and the sophistication of their skills. Currently ACARA is in the process of developing a sequence of achievement standards from Foundation to Year 10 to describe and illustrate progress in the particular learning areas. It is intended that this sequence for each learning area will provide teachers with a framework of growth and development and help teachers plan for and monitor learning during the course of a semester or year. The other purpose of the achievement standards is to assist teachers to make judgements about the extent and quality of learning. In this recent description of the achievement standards, emphasis is given to the skills and understandings that students are expected to demonstrate rather than the mode by which they do this. Teachers will still be required to adopt the assessment and reporting requirements of the relevant state, territory or sector that they work within while using the Australian Curriculum achievement standards as the reference point for their assessment practices.

Providing teachers with standards together with annotated examples of student work to assessment tasks will not be sufficient to achieve consistent use of the achievement standards by teachers (Klenowski & Wyatt-Smith, 2008). For as is evident both from theory (Sadler, 1987) and practice (Klenowski & Adie, 2009), verbal descriptors of standards that are abstract mental constructs can have their "interpretation, circumscribed, more or less adequately, *only by usage in context*. The concrete existential referents that make up the context are essential to its proper interpretation" (Sadler, 1987, p. 206, my emphasis). To assess student work using standards in the form of verbal descriptors, teachers will need to find the "best fit" rather than the perfect match. In making such a judgement teachers will need to draw on their professional knowledge, which will require contact with professional communities to create and maintain their understanding of the standards. The interactions at moderation meetings provide the means by which teachers justify and negotiate their award of the grade or level with reference to the standards (verbal descriptors) on the students' assessed work. Teachers also draw on their subject and tacit knowledge in moderation practice as they progress towards becoming an experienced assessor in a standards referenced context.

This relationship between classroom assessment and system level accountability that is focused on transparency of outcomes will be reliant on teachers' judgements and interpretations of assessment data in the context of social moderation. For it is teachers who have direct access to the information needed for an accountability system. Students, their teachers and their parents who know and work with them in different settings are the primary sources of information to determine what schools do for students (MacBeath, 1999).

Quantitative Assessments

The 1990s saw increased international dissatisfaction with the more quantitative, measurement forms of assessment. Much of this aversion stemmed from the view of learning on which these assessments were designed and their impacts on teaching and learning. Assessment approaches from this quantitative tradition have been challenged and alternative approaches have emerged.

The major criticisms of quantitative approaches to assessment include that: teachers teach to the test; external assessment for accountability purposes impacts detrimentally on pedagogy and inhibits educational assessment; tests drive and narrow the curriculum; standardized tests assess lower-level thinking skills to the neglect of the higher order thinking and learning skills; emphasis on test results and standards focus on products and academic purposes to the detriment of the social, affective and physical educational purposes; summative test results provide teachers with inadequate information for teaching purposes and meaningful feedback for student development is often lacking.

The changing emphases in assessment reform include a move away from assessing knowledge and products to assessing skills, understandings and processes. Also rather than assessment occurring at the end of a course through external means, assessment has been taking place throughout the course or unit of study. A greater variety of methods and evidence has been sought to demonstrate learning instead of relying only on written methods and this has been accompanied by a shift from norm referencing to criterion referencing with less reliance on pass or fail, summative assessments and more attention on identifying strengths and weaknesses formatively and recording positive achievement (Torrance, 1997).

Teacher Assessment

Teacher assessment is defined as:

> The process by which teachers gather evidence in a planned and systematic way in order to draw inferences about their students' learning, based on their professional judgement, and to report at a particular time on their students' achievements.
>
> *(Harlen, 2005, p. 247)*

With the recent shifts in assessment practice (Assessment Reform Group, 1999), the teacher assumes an important role and requires an understanding of the fundamental issues in assessment design that include "fitness for purpose" and the need for the mode of assessment to impact positively on teaching and learning. Other characteristics of "good" assessment include that they be: reliable and consistent outcomes; comparable judgements across assessors; freedom from bias; valid assessment in that it is true to what is taught and learned; rigorous practices; support of learning and reflection; open and connected to criteria rather than to comparative performance of others; inclusive of formative assessment and a range of assessment strategies so that all learners have a chance to perform well.

Assessment tasks therefore need to involve a variety of contexts, range of modes within the assessment and a range of response formats and styles. To achieve equity there is also a need to expand the range of indicators used to provide an opportunity for those who might be disadvantaged by one form of assessment and to offer alternative evidence of their expertise. To achieve this form of assessment practice requires teacher assessment and communities of judgement practice.

One testing method does not fit all circumstances. Therefore teacher assessment offers an important alternative because in this context locally developed indicators can prove to be more effective educationally than examinations or tests administered from the center. The teacher is able to attend to the student's needs that emerge from a particular context, sociocultural or historical background. Multiple judges are recommended and Queensland's Senior Secondary System is one such example. Students' work is assessed at the local level and forms part of the state system of assessment of student performance. Assessment data is collected both formally and informally and used by teachers and administrators to set learning goals and priorities to build on what students already know.

Standard-setting and assessment are linked as teachers design assessments that are intellectually challenging for their students. Teachers set standards as they identify the tasks that they want students to complete for assessment and they provide various opportunities for students to display thoughtful control over ideas.

Alternative Authentic Assessments

Alternative assessment methods have emerged in response to the dissatisfaction with quantitative systems. A catalyst for such change has been the realization that the type of assessment impacts profoundly on the learning dispositions, attitudes, strategies adopted and learning ability. Developments in both learning theories and the theory of educational assessment (Gipps, 1994) have supported the move towards authentic, alternative assessments.

Critique of the utility of tests in measuring what students actually know inspired a move towards "alternative, authentic assessment approaches" (Wiggins, 1989, 1991; Newmann, 1991). Authentic assessment includes tasks that challenge the student's intellect and test intellectual ability in a manner that reflects probable experience for the individual in the field. Authentic assessment: connects to the curriculum; engages students, teachers and others in assessing performance; looks beyond the school for models and sites of action; promotes complex thinking and problem-solving; encourages student "performance" of their learning and engages with issues of equity.

Alternative authentic assessments are varied and comprehensive, encouraging multiple methods for demonstrating learning. Problem-solving in this assessment context requires students to think analytically and demonstrate their proficiency as they would in situations beyond the classroom. Such assessments encourage students to develop skills, understandings and insights relevant to their particular needs and contexts.

These approaches attend to equity issues by making assessment fairer by reducing the dependence on performance in a single terminal examination as the only determinant of student achievement and by giving individuals the opportunity to demonstrate attainment over time and in a variety of contexts. This type of assessment is claimed to be more accurate, and reflective of an individual's learning and development, by identifying the abilities being examined. This helps to encompass a wider range of abilities and facilitates the recording of achievement. However, as indicated there are limitations and therefore external scrutiny of teacher judgements and quality assurance systems are required.

Addressing the Limitations of Teacher Assessment in Standards Driven Reform

Teachers need the freedom to make definitive evidence-based judgements on their students' work according to established standards and a quality framework that guarantees the dependability of teacher-led assessments. The key is to use external scrutiny to maintain the quality and professionalism of teachers' own judgements.

At the upper secondary level the assessment regime needs to reflect finer distinctions between student performance to fulfil the role of assessment for selection purposes for a wider range of destinations and progression opportunities than other levels of schooling. This is where effective and widespread use of the professional judgement of teachers is required more than ever and needs to be supported by rigorous quality assurance systems. Moderation is one such system that serves both accountability and improvement purposes. Moderation allows for comparability of standards both within andbetween schools and an audit of range and balance in curriculum coverage is part of the process. The teacher's role is fundamental in this process as from an analysis of the assessment data teachers develop their curriculum plans and base their teaching on the learning needs of their students.

Moderation

Moderation assists in developing coherence across the educational system. Consistency, comparability and equity are three principles relevant to moderation practice (Maxwell, 2002b). Consistency involves constancy of judgement by the individual teacher with respect to the same evidence judged at different times and involves the equivalent application of standards across different types of evidence and opportunities for assessment. Comparability is a within-subject comparison against the performance standards for the subject. Identical aspects of knowledge, understanding and skill are not required, but equivalence of standards in terms of knowledge, understanding and skill is expected for that level of achievement. Students can be set different tasks but demonstrate a common standard of performance revealing equivalent levels of knowledge, understanding and skill.

Equity involves the opportunity for every student to reach and demonstrate their current capability. Students may demonstrate their knowledge, skills and understanding in a variety of ways so the concern should be whether they have had suitable opportunities to demonstrate what they know and can do. Moderation practice helps to ensure that these characteristics have been addressed in making judgements and that students' performances have been appropriately interpreted with reference to the standard.

Moderation for accountability provides official confirmation of assessments used to report on individual students, or for cohorts of students, and involves validation (Maxwell, 2002b). Validation presumes that, if teachers make appropriate judgements about a selected cross-section of student demonstrations, they will make appropriate judgements about other student demonstrations. Moderation for accountability is designed to ensure fairness by adjusting results where there seems to be inconsistency or differences (Harlen, 1994). The moderation procedures monitor and assure comparability of the grades that are determined by this process. Important assessment data and advice are provided to teachers and schools concerning their judgements and such feedback fulfils an important quality assurance role.

Moderation for improvement involves collaborative processes promoting the professional development of teachers to undertake appropriate assessments, and to make consistent and comparable judgements (Maxwell, 2002b). It is ongoing and provides feedback for further development of comparability and may focus on both procedures and outcomes.

Research indicates that teachers who engage consistently in the moderation process are able to assess student performance more consistently, effectively, confidently and fairly (Curry, Gearhart, Kafka & Little, 2003). Teachers can also build common knowledge about curriculum expectations and levels of achievement and in so doing identify strengths and areas for growth based on evidence of student learning. By engaging in such practice teachers can also adjust and acquire new learning by comparing their thinking about student work and achievements to that of another teacher and to that of other students. They also share effective practices to meet the needs of all students, monitor progress and celebrate growth (Curry, Gearhart, Kafka & Little, 2003).

The Queensland Studies Authority (QSA) uses moderation as a quality assurance process for senior secondary studies. Moderation processes are directed at supporting and confirming understandings about judgements and performance. Teachers use assessment criteria and explicit standards to make professional judgements about performance levels demonstrated by students in the completion of assessed tasks. Teachers and assessors reach agreement about assessments through discussion, critique and debate. They use evidence of student work to develop common understandings of the curriculum and levels of achievement to inform teaching and learning, monitoring and assessing, reporting and evaluation (Ralston & Newman, 1999).

This approach to moderation at a system level serves as a vital accountability check and balances on efforts to achieve, and demonstrate, reliability of teacher judgement in high-stakes assessment. Beyond this, however, the process of system facilitated and supported moderation provides professional development opportunities for teachers in planning teaching and learning programs, designing suitably challenging assessment tasks with accompanying statements of criteria and standards, as well as making judgements of student performance. Essentially, it is moderation that ensures that common standards are being achieved and also helps to provide comparability against benchmarks expressed as desirable features.

Increased Professional Responsibility

Professional development occurs naturalistically through the agency of the teachers themselves as they share their knowledge and experience about working with standards in diverse school contexts and institutional settings. It is the important teacher talk and interactions during moderation meetings that impact positively on assessment practices, task design, student learning and teaching. Teacher moderation is most effective when there is "productive conflict" embedded in the school's culture and teachers are confident to express their thinking, asking questions about the assessment data or learning after listening to others (Curriculum Services Canada, 2007). Professional learning extends beyond the time and site of the moderation meeting.

Increased professionalism, richer learning for teachers and students and more professional conversations are some of the professional benefits achievable from moderation practice.

To further investigate the importance of moderation practice in building teacher assessment capacity and professional teacher judgments, the New Basics project in Queensland, Australia stands as an excellent example. In this project students were required to complete "rich tasks" that were carefully designed to be intellectually challenging and to have real-world value. These assessments were considered authentic. Performance on such tasks provides an informed and elaborate portrait of a student's achievement (see http://education.qld.gov.au/corporate/newbasics/html/richtasks/richtasks.html). The evaluation of the Consensus Based Standards Validation Process of moderation used in these primary and lower secondary levels (Klenowski, 2007) found that teacher professionalism had grown in terms of teacher confidence, building knowledge of strategies, procedures and systems to assess student work. Teacher professional development is inherent in the process of moderation as teachers engage in rich learning conversations focused on student work and learning. The level of professional conversations increased over time with a focus on improvement of teaching and learning classroom practices. The teachers gained creative ideas from a broader view of strategies that other teachers used to achieve success and they benefited from working and planning the assessment task together because of the richness in the learning experience. A collegial atmosphere developed with teams of teachers planning, sharing ideas and demonstrating accountability. Teachers have the most direct impact on student achievement and their role during moderation practice is fundamental.

Addressing Equity

Teachers assess students' learning to identify what they have learned, what they have not learned and where they are having difficulty. Assessment, because of its concern with what students have learned, is also based on a conception of the nature of learning and learners. When considering the fairness of the assessments there is a need then to be clear about these conceptions underlying the specific assessments (Gipps & Murphy, 1994). In addition to these conceptions of the nature of learning and learners, it is important in terms of equity to consider the choice of knowledge and skills selected for the assessments. To achieve equity, the curriculum needs to include valued knowledge and skills consisting of different kinds of cultural knowledge and experience, reflective of all groups, not privileging one group to the exclusion of others.

In 1989 it was Michael Apple who expressed how important it was for curricular questions to be addressed for equity purposes. In 1994 Gipps and Murphy included

TABLE 6.1 Curriculum, Assessment and Access Questions

Curricular Questions	Assessment Questions	Access Questions
Whose knowledge is taught?	What knowledge is assessed and equated with achievement?	Who gets taught and by whom?
Why is it taught in a particular way to this particular group?	Are the form, content and mode of assessment appropriate for different groups and individuals?	Are there differences in the resources available for different groups?
How do we enable the histories and cultures of people of colour, and of women, to be taught in responsible ways? (Apple, 1989)	Is this range of cultural knowledge reflected in definitions of achievement? How does cultural knowledge mediate individuals' responses to assessment in ways that alter the construct being assessed? (Gipps & Murphy, 1994)	What is incorporated from the cultures of those attending?

Source: Adapted from Stobart (2005: 279).

assessment questions, to which, most recently, Stobart (2005) has added access questions (See Table 6.1). These questions relate to the concepts of "cultural capital" and "social capital" (Bourdieu, 1986; Bourdieu & Passeron, 1977). "Cultural capital" can take the form of knowledge, skills, education or values that can give an individual an advantage or disadvantage, or a higher or lower status in society. For instance, if students have not developed certain skills, or have not had access to certain knowledge because of their background, gender or culture, then they are at a disadvantage when those skills or that knowledge is valued and assessed in high-stakes tests. Such examinations for selection purposes can favor those who have access to the "cultural capital" that is considered of value and in this way privileges the dominant group. Bourdieu's work, for example, illustrates how internal processes of schooling, including assessment for selection purposes and the attainment of formal qualifications, provide for the reproduction of the elite rather than being genuinely meritocratic. His work showed how such processes favored bourgeois "cultural capital" and experience such that working class students had to have more persistence and ability than those from a favored background to reach the same level in the education system (Broadfoot, 1996). These insights have implications for our assessment systems and the need for culture-responsive assessment that does not require one group (socio economic, cultural, gender) to have greater resilience, perseverance and competence than another to succeed.

The focus on these curricular and assessment questions has increased awareness regarding the need for strategies to develop assessment practices to address equity issues more effectively. To illustrate, the Australian Curriculum, Assessment and Certification Authorities (ACACA) guidelines recommend that assessment agencies:

> evaluate the occurrence in assessment instruments of reproductions of gender, socioeconomic, ethnic or other cultural stereotypes; conduct equity scanning of assessment instruments before use; promote research into the validity and fairness of assessment items for which the agency is responsible and employ specialist editors to examine the language of assessment instruments in terms of possible barriers to equal opportunity for all students.
>
> *(ACACA, 1995, p. 1)*

It is further recommended that each set of assessment instruments used to assess a student's achievement in a subject should: involve the use of a range and balance of background contexts in which assessment items are presented; include a range and balance of types of assessment instruments and modes of response, including a balance and range of visual and linguistic material, and involve a range and balance of conditions.

So equity does not mean treating students all the same or equality of outcomes. As is apparent from the guidelines above there is a need to positively support cultural and social diversity in policy, practice and principles. A fairer educational and assessment environment is required and teachers need to have a sense of social, legal and ethical responsibility to promote equity.

Conclusion

Policy can result in unintended consequences and unhelpful pressures on the development of assessment systems. The intended learning benefits of more productive assessment approaches are not always brought to fruition. Assessment has the potential to develop and sustain the teacher's engagement in judgement practice and curriculum planning only if the teacher's role remains central. It is school-based and teacher-led assessment that has the potential to address learning success for all by addressing equity issues if supported from the political center.

References

Apple, M. W. (1989). How equality has been redefined in the conservative restoration. In W. G. Secada (Ed.) *Equity in education* (pp. 7–35). London: Falmer Press.

Assessment Reform Group (1999). *Assessment for learning: Beyond the black box.* Cambridge: University of Cambridge, School of Education.

Australian Curriculum, Assessment and Certification Authorities (1995). *Guidelines for assessment quality and equity.* Brisbane: Queensland Board of Senior Secondary School Studies.

Bourdieu, P. (1986). The forms of capital. In J. G. Richardson (Ed.) *Handbook of theory and research for the sociology of education* (pp. 241–58). New York: Greenwood Press.

Bourdieu, P. and Passeron, J. C. (1977). *Reproduction in education, society and culture.* London: Sage.

Broadfoot, P. (1996). *Education, assessment and society.* Buckingham: Open University Press.

Cresswell, M. (2000). The role of public examinations in defining and monitoring standards. In H. Goldstein and A. Heath (Eds) *Educational standards* (pp. 69–104). Oxford: Oxford University Press.

Curriculum Services Canada (2007). Teacher moderation: Collaborative assessment of student work. *The Literacy and Numeracy Secretariat Capacity Building Series.* Ontario: Curriculum Services Canada.

Curry, M., Gearhart, M., Kafka, J. and Little, J. W. (2003). Looking at student work for teacher learning, teacher community and school reform. *Phi Delta Kappan, 85*(3), 185–92.

Frederiksen, J. R. and White, B. Y. (2004). Designing assessments for instruction and accountability: An application of validity theory to assessing scientific inquiry. In M. Wilson (Ed.) *Towards coherence between classroom assessment and accountability. The 103rd Yearbook of the National Society for the Study of Education Part 2* (pp. 74–104). Chicago: National Society for the Study of Education.

Fullan, M. (2005). *Leadership and sustainability: System thinkers in action.* Thousand Oaks: Corwin Press.

Gipps, C. (1994). *Beyond testing: Towards a theory of educational assessment,* London: Falmer Press.

Gipps, C. and Murphy, P. (1994). *A fair test? Assessment, achievement and equity.* Buckingham: Open University Press.

Harlen, W. (1994). *Concepts of quality in student assessment.* Paper presented at the American Educational Research Association conference, New Orleans.

Harlen, W. (2005). Trusting teachers' judgement: Research evidence of the reliability and validity of teachers' assessment used for summative purposes. *Research Papers in Education, 20*(3), 245–70.

Klenowski, V. (2007). Evaluation of the effectiveness of the consensus-based standards validation process. Retrieved from http://education.qld.gov.au/corporate/newbasics/html/lce_eval.html

Klenowski, V. and Adie, L. (2009). Moderation as judgement practice: Reconciling level accountability and local level practice. *Curriculum Perspectives, 29*(1), 10–28.

Klenowski, V. and Wyatt-Smith, C. M. (2008). *Standards driven reform Years 1–10: Moderation an optional extra?* Paper presented at the Australian Association for Research in Education Conference, Brisbane.

MacBeath, J. (1999). *Schools must speak for themselves.* London: Routledge.

Maxwell, G. S. (2002a). *Are core learning outcomes standards?* Brisbane, Queensland: Queensland Studies Authority. Retrieved from www.qsa.qld.edu.au/downloads/publications/ research_qscc_assess_report_1.pdf

Maxwell, G. S. (2002b). *Moderation of teacher judgments in student assessment* (Discussion paper). Brisbane: Queensland School Curriculum Council.

Maxwell, G. S. (2008). *Setting standards: Fitting form to function.* Paper presented at the 34th IAEA Annual Conference, Cambridge, UK.

National Curriculum Board (2008). The shape of the national curriculum: A proposal for discussion. Retrieved from www.ncb.org.au/our_work/preparing_for_2009.html

Newmann, F. (1991). Linking restructuring to authentic student achievement. *Phi Delta Kappan, 72*(6), 458–63.

O'Neill, O. (2002). *A question of trust: The BBC Reith Lectures.* Cambridge: Cambridge University Press.

Ralston, F. and Newman, H. (1999). *Towards consistency of teacher judgement: Moderation in all things.* Paper presented at Australian Curriculum Studies Association Conference, 29 September – 2 October, Perth.

Sadler, D. R. (1987). Specifying and promulgating achievement standards. *Oxford Review of Education, 13*(2), 191–209.

Sahlberg, P. (2006). Raising the bar: How Finland responds to the twin challenge of secondary education? *Professorado, 10*(1), 1–26.

Sahlberg, P. (2007). Education policies for raising student learning: The Finnish approach. *Journal of Education Policy, 22*(2), 147–71.

Stobart, G. (2005). Fairness in multicultural assessment systems. *Assessment in Education, 12*(3), 275–87.

Torrance, H. (1997). Assessment, accountability and standards: Using assessment to control the reform of schooling. In A. H. Halsey, H. Lauder, P. Brown and A. S. Wells (Eds) *Education culture, economy and society* (pp. 320–31). Oxford: Oxford University Press.

Wiggins, G. (1989). A true test: Toward more authentic and equitable assessment. *Phi Delta Kappan, 70*(9), 703–13.

Wiggins, G. (1991). Standards, not standardization: Evoking quality student work. *Educational Leadership, 48*(5), 18–25.

Wilson, M. (2004). Assessment, accountability and the classroom: A community of judgment. In M. Wilson (Ed.) *Towards coherence between classroom assessment and accountability. The 103rd Yearbook of the National Society for the Study of Education Part 2* (pp. 1–19). Chicago: National Society for the Study of Education.

7

SOCIAL JUSTICE VISIONS AND CURRICULUM REALITIES IN THE EARLY YEARS OF EDUCATION

Susan Grieshaber

Equity is an important part of curriculum and syllabus design but has only recently found its way into curriculum documents used in the years before compulsory schooling. The inclusion of equity in curriculum and syllabus design is much more likely if equity is integral to the vision of a nation and supported by policies and funding arrangements that are aimed at producing social, cultural, economic, and educationally equitable outcomes. This chapter explores the relationship between a national vision for a socially just society, policies, and financial commitment; and the importance of including social justice and equity in syllabus and curriculum documents in before school settings. It begins with a discussion of the terms "curriculum," "syllabus," and "equity," and how they relate to early childhood education in the Australian context. An exploration of societal vision, policies, and financial commitment in the Nordic countries (Denmark, Finland, Iceland, Norway, Sweden) follows and includes discussion about the implications for children, families, immigrants, and early childhood education. The inequities that can be involved in play are highlighted by drawing on a number of qualitative studies to show how young children can use skin color, size, proficiency with English, and so on to marginalize others. These acts of marginalization are contrasted with responses to the draft Australian national curriculum (Commonwealth of Australia, 2009) for children aged 0–5 that claimed it is too politically correct. The chapter concludes that syllabus and curriculum documents should be framed using principles of equity aimed at a socially just society, and that this works best when accompanied by a national vision, appropriate policies, and proper financial support.

Curriculum in Early Childhood Education

"Curriculum," "syllabus design," and "equity" are words that have not traditionally been associated with early childhood education, especially in Australia with respect to the years prior to formal schooling. Until recently, the word "curriculum" was rarely used in discussions about settings that cater for children aged from birth to five years. It is still uncommon for "syllabus" to be used in before-school settings. Ten years ago, equity was not part of the everyday language of those working with young children and their families. "Curriculum" and "syllabus design" are much more familiar to those working in the first few years of formal schooling because of the centrality of these documents to teaching and learning in the compulsory years. Curriculum is the totality of what occurs in classroom and school settings, and a syllabus provides a plan or outline that does not prescribe details of curriculum, pedagogy, and assessment (see Luke, Weir & Woods, 2008). However, these terms are used variously by different authorities and authors. In several states of Australia in the past five or so years, documents with the word "curriculum" in the title have been created for teachers in the years prior to compulsory schooling. In the state of Queensland, the *Early Years Curriculum Guidelines* (Queensland Studies Authority, 2006) were written for teachers of children aged 4.5–5.5 years attending preparatory classes and have been made mandatory for use in these settings.

Prescribing any curriculum document for the pre-compulsory years has been the exception rather than the rule in Australia and is ironic given that the preparatory year in Queensland is not a compulsory year of education. Perhaps it is an effect of the great acclaim attached to the significance and benefits of early childhood education in recent times. Alternatively, it could be part of neoliberalism and the "schoolification" (OECD, 2006) of the pre-compulsory years, which were once the preserve of free play, where children were able to develop "naturally." Whatever the reason, "curriculum" should now be a more familiar term for those in the pre-compulsory years as the documents from most systems include this nomenclature in their titles. Equity should also be a familiar term, as it too is integrated in more documents, including examples from Australia such as the *South Australian Curriculum, Standards and Accountability Framework Early Years Band: Birth to Year 2* (Department of Education, Training and Employment, 2001) and the Queensland *Early Years Curriculum Guidelines* (Queensland Studies Authority, 2006).

All curriculum, syllabus documents, and resource materials should be founded on principles of equity. Not to be confused with equality, equity is about fairness and justice, and makes visible the imperative to overcome factors that potentially impede the creation of equity and equitable circumstances. Equity involves power relations because it seeks a more equitable distribution of social and economic resources. However in Australia, and other similar nation states, the divide between the rich and the poor continues to increase despite a "lingering attachment to egalitarian ideals" (Stilwell & Jordan, 2007, p. 1). A lingering attachment to egalitarian ideals will never be enough to create a more equitable distribution of social and economic resources. The neoliberal preoccupation with efficiency and growth has come at the expense of social justice (Stilwell & Jordan, 2007) and the potential of egalitarian policies to contribute to efficiency and growth has been ignored by the "proponents of incentivation" (p. 200). Stilwell and Jordan claim that the damage from economic inequality seeps into all aspects of society, as it "undermines social cohesion, corrupts democratic political processes and impairs the possibilities of dealing with the looming environmental crisis" (p. 199). To Stretton (2005), a redirection in public policy aimed at more equitable social outcomes can be achieved through policies related to education, housing, health, childcare, pensions, work, natural resources, and social security. The number of policy areas implicated is an indication of the magnitude and complexity of the problem, as well as the time and effort required to address it. A more equitable distribution of social and economic resources starts with a vision of a socially-just society and is followed by appropriate policies and financial commitment. Infusing principles of equity in early childhood curriculum and syllabus documents would then be a matter of process.

A National Vision, Policies, and Financial Support: The Nordic Countries

The social welfare systems of the Nordic countries (Denmark, Finland, Iceland, Norway, Sweden) have had some success in creating more equitable social and economic circumstances than those countries subscribing to neoliberal approaches (e.g., the USA, Australia). The "Nordic welfare model" is similar in general principles and implementation across the five countries, but the effects are different in each country due to "country-specific economic realities and varying social and political traditions" (Kristjansson, 2006, p. 14). What characterizes the Nordic social welfare system is a vision of an egalitarian society with a high standard of living and personal and social well-being for all, including children. More importantly, this vision is supported by educational policies, specifically early childhood education policies; as well as family policies that center on "enhancing gender equality within the family, and, in families with children, between the parents" (Kristjansson, 2006, p. 14). These policies have produced a number of benefits for individuals as well as society as a whole, and include the fact that Scandinavian societies have been recognized for some time as the most equal in the world economically, as well as between genders (United Nations [UN], 2004). The child and family policies are based on Nordic traditions of "democracy, equality, freedom and emancipation, solidarity through cooperation and compromise, and a general concept of the 'good childhood,' or what life should be like for all children" (Wagner & Einarsdottir, 2006, p. 4). The "good childhood" is a revered and fiercely protected aspect of Nordic social welfare systems.

The Nordic vision manifests itself in the provision of statutory parental leave during the first year of life, paid at greater than 50% of earnings (to a maximum ceiling) and in the process maintains equal opportunities for women (OECD, 2006). Social welfare policies have also resulted in low child poverty rates of 2.8% in Finland, 3.4% in Norway, and 4.2% in Sweden (after government taxes and transfers), which are the lowest of the OECD countries (UNICEF, 2005). The child poverty rate in Denmark is the lowest in the world at 2.4% (after taxes etc.) (UNICEF, 2005) and

Norway is the only OECD country where the rate is "very low and continuing to fall" (UNICEF, 2007, p. 7). An assessment of child well-being in rich OECD countries, using six child well-being dimensions, produced an average rank that placed the Netherlands first, Sweden, Denmark, and Finland second, third, and fourth respectively, and Norway seventh (UNICEF, 2007). These figures sit in sharp contrast to the USA, which was ranked 20 of 21 countries on the same assessment (UNICEF, 2007), and which has a child poverty rate of 21.9% (UNICEF, 2005). Public expenditure on early childhood education and care services in Denmark, Sweden, Norway, and Finland are the highest of the OECD countries, with Denmark spending 2.1% of GDP on services for children aged 0–6 years and Sweden 1.7% (OECD, 2006). More support is provided for children aged 6–7 years attending pre-school in Denmark, Sweden, and Finland. In comparison, the UK spends 0.5%, the USA just under 0.5%, and Australia 0.45% of GDP on early childhood education and care services for children aged 0–6 years (OECD, 2006). The recommendation in 1996 by the European Commission Network on Childcare was that at least 1% of GDP should be spent on early childhood education and care services for children (OECD, 2006). The UNICEF (2007) report *Child Poverty in Perspective* showed that higher government spending on "family and social benefits is associated with lower child poverty rates" (p. 7). From these figures, it is apparent that government vision and expenditure, backed by policies, make a difference to quality of life in the Nordic countries.

Nordic educational policies have also produced results better than most at the secondary school level. The OECD Programme for International Student Assessment (PISA) for students aged 15 years assesses the acquisition of knowledge and skills required for full participation in society. According to the 2000 PISA reading results, schools in Finland, Sweden, Iceland, and Norway produce high quality outcomes and are highly equitable because student social background exerts little influence on literacy performance (A Report by the Council for the Australian Federation [ARCAF], 2007; OECD/UNESCO, 2003). The 2003 PISA results for mathematics showed that Finnish schools were of high quality and highly equitable in terms of the relationship between student background and mathematical performance. Another analysis of the 2003 mathematics data has shown that schools in Iceland, Finland, and Norway are highly equitable because there is very little variation in performance between schools (ARCAF, 2007). This means that the school students attended in these countries made little difference to their performance on the PISA tests and that choice of school had little effect on the test results. In both within school and between school measures of equity, these Nordic countries produced excellent results. In Australia, the 2000 PISA reading data showed high quality but low equity because of the extent of the association between social advantage and higher educational performance (ARCAF, 2007). Analysis of the 2003 PISA mathematics data revealed very little between school variation in Iceland, Finland, and Norway (about 4%), while variation in Australia was approximately 20%. Thus schooling is not as equitable in Australia (ARCAF, 2007) and there is a greater chance that the school attended makes a difference to outcomes.

While the PISA results for students aged 15 are impressive for the Nordic countries, the early years are a fundamental part of the Nordic vision. Nordic conceptions of childhood and early childhood education policies are unique. This is due to:

- the way they have handled childcare and the links between preschool and compulsory schooling;
- the approach to children's rights and relationship-building between adults and children;
- the way in which the role of play is conceptualized;
- the inclusion of postmodern theories and ideas; and
- the way in which "local distinctiveness" has been preserved "amid rapid globalization" (Wagner & Einarsdottir, 2006, p. 5).

In Finland, policy aims at the creation of a socially just society which encompasses concern for the rights and responsibilities of all (OECD, 2006). The Ministry of Social Affairs and Health is responsible for national policy for children (0–6 years) and families, and for the provision of allowances to parents and service providers, including maternity grants, health care, child and family counseling, child welfare, and home help services (OECD, 2006). The *National Curriculum Guidelines on Early Childhood Education and Care* (OECD, 2006), provide a core curriculum that is used as the basis for locally articulated design. The guidelines focus on the importance of "care, upbringing and education as an integrated whole for young children … no requirement about specific pedagogies is imposed" (OECD, 2006, p. 322). The curriculum guidelines are conceptualized as an important part of the educational continuum of lifelong learning, and in conjunction with this, smooth transition from one educational setting to another (such as from preschool to school) has received close attention.

With the exception of Iceland, immigration has featured in recent changes to the Nordic countries and has brought questions about Nordic conceptions of childhood and early childhood education that relate to equity. In Denmark for instance, migrants constitute 4.1% of the population and in Finland there are over 100 different migrant groups, with most coming from Russia and Somalia (OECD, 2006). Norway has an indigenous population of 1.7% and 3% of the population are migrants, while in Sweden 14% of children in early childhood education and care services have a first language other than Swedish (OECD, 2006). However in Denmark, there has been significant public debate about migrants and the way in which Nordic life and traditions might change as a result of immigration. In some ways this debate contradicts the Nordic ideals of democracy, equality, freedom, emancipation, solidarity, and the "good childhood." As a result of this debate, a study of peer relationships in 21 elementary classrooms in 10 schools in two Danish cities investigated "whether anti-immigrant sentiments and stereotypes track into Danish public school settings" (Wagner, 2006, p. 304). Results showed that this was not the case as there was no more than a random chance of majority and minority children disliking each other.

What might be called "subtle prejudice and marginalization" (p. 304) emerged primarily as an effect of majority children tending to favor other majority children, rather than "outright discrimination against minority children" (p. 304). While minority children were more likely to "cross ethnic boundaries in selecting liked classmates," it was unclear whether "this represented a healthy accommodation to social realities for minority children or a threat to their ethnic identity development" (p. 304).

Of concern to researchers in the Wagner (2006) study was the revelation that in more than 75% of the classrooms there were no minority boys in the high-status popular category (no comments were made about girls). Researchers questioned the implications for children when members of their minority group were rarely seen as having high social status within their own classroom peer group. The researchers concluded that two aspects of Nordic tradition may be working against each other: "egalitarianism may prohibit open hostility toward minority children, while ... solidarity may promote strong in-group favouritism among majority children" (Wagner, 2006, p. 205). Recommendations included that early childhood educators consider anti-bias and multicultural curricula that focus on inclusion and fairness because they are at the core of democratic and egalitarian principles of the good childhood and central to beliefs about solidarity. As a way of preventing prejudice, marginalization, and discrimination from developing, further research with young children was suggested to identify ways of promoting positive relationships at individual and group levels between majority and minority children. A similar concern about solidarity was raised a few years ago when Norwegian society was becoming multi-ethnic (OECD, 1999). The OECD Country Note suggested that in the circumstances, Norwegian preschools, which were based so distinctly on Norwegian values and behavior, needed to recognize Norwegian families from other ethnic backgrounds by developing values and educational frameworks to which all could relate. The Nordic countries are not alone in facing the educational implications of globalization and changed patterns of immigration, and the attention to equitable provision that this entails.

Play

Promoting positive relationships between minority and majority children in early childhood education is at the heart of equitable approaches. Yet even some of the Nordic countries with their history of democracy and egalitarianism are finding that these very values might be marginalizing those from non-Nordic backgrounds. One of the key tenets of Nordic ideology, policy, and practice is the value placed on the "good childhood" and the concept of free play. Free play in the Nordic sense is taken to mean play that is "free from excessive adult control, oversupervision, and interference" (Wagner, 2006, p. 293). Being free from excessive adult control is one way in which the principle of emancipation is enacted and experienced. Spontaneity and free exploration of indoor and outdoor environments typify childhood experiences in the Nordic countries. This extends to risk taking, which is acknowledged as an important part of free play in Norway (Sandseter, 2009; see Wyver et al., 2010).

In contrast to the Nordic countries, Wagner (2006) described free play in the USA as something where

> adults have specified a brief time, say 15 to 30 minutes, in the pre-established daily schedule when children *are allowed* to do what they want to do, often *if* they have finished the tasks the adults have given them. In many settings, especially in the kindergarten and primary grades, children earn the right to play on Friday afternoons if they have behaved nicely and complete their work on Monday through Thursday.
>
> *(p. 293)*

In the Nordic countries, children are expected to engage in democracy as an ongoing part of their experiences at home, school, and in their communities. Early childhood education policy documents and curriculum guidelines make statements to this effect and children take an active role in democratic processes in early childhood settings. For instance, the Swedish curriculum for children aged 1–5 years, *Curriculum for the Pre-school Lpfö 98* (Swedish Ministry of Education and Science 2006), makes strong statements about the democratic principles on which Swedish preschools are established and explains that the preschools are charged with assisting children to acquire the democratic principles on which Swedish society is based. By USA standards, children in early childhood settings in the Nordic countries have a large say in decisions that affect them throughout the day, making the experience not only democratic but also egalitarian (Wagner, 2006).

While what happens in the Nordic countries may seem idyllic and idealistic, how democracy and egalitarianism are enacted as part of everyday life is what sets them apart from experiences in the USA, the UK, and Australia. These disparities come from Nordic visions for society that are based on long traditions of democracy and equality, which are backed up by policy and financial support, and which become visible in everyday occurrences such as how children's play is conceptualized and enacted in early childhood settings.

Play is one of the time-honored principles of early childhood education and is considered to be one of the best ways for young children to learn and develop (see Moyles, 2005). It is enshrined in Article 31 of the United Nations Convention on the Rights of the Child (UNICEF, 2009) and nearly every book about children and early childhood education. It is accepted unquestionably as an undeniable right of every child. However, a small but growing number of qualitative studies have provided insight into how play situations involving young children can be inequitable (Danby & Baker, 1998; Brooker, 2002; Campbell, 2005). Thus the relationship between teacher intentions for play and what actually transpires in play contexts deserves further scrutiny. Creating contexts for equitable play is important not only for those who write policy, but also for those who use syllabus and curriculum documents. Like the situation in Norway and Denmark where awareness has been raised about the possible marginalization of children from non-Nordic backgrounds, play needs to be investigated because it is not always innocent, fun, and natural. It can be political and involve morals and ethics: "Play can be fun, but play is also the very serious business of childhood where power relations are played out in terms of 'race', class, gender, ethnicity, age, size, skin color, sexuality, heteronormativity, proficiency with English, and more" (Grieshaber, 2008, p. 30). At times play can be downright unfair and involve rejection, discomfort, and alienation. Teachers can also unknowingly be complicit in perpetuating its unfairness.

Researchers around the globe have documented the ways in which children's play can be unfair and how some children use sophisticated techniques to marginalize others. One of the earliest and most infamous examples is Walkerdine's (1981) feminist poststructuralist analysis of interactions among boys and girls in the block area of a nursery school in the UK. The sexist and highly derogatory comments from one of the boys, who called one of the girls "a stupid cunt" and degraded the teacher with a parody (p. 15) are dismissed by the teacher as "silly" and developmentally innocent "play." More recently, researchers have turned their attention to "race" and skin color, as well as the intersection of these factors with gender, size, proficiency with English, and so on. In Australia, Mundine and Guigni (2006) depicted how children in one child care center were included/excluded from playing because of their clothing, knowledge of popular culture, and "black skin" (p. 13). They concluded that "issues of racism" were being used by children to "make the rules about who could play and who could not" (p. 14). Skattebol (2005) too, has commented on how certain understandings of "whiteness" associated with entitlement are a feature of children's social worlds and operate as a type of power associated with particular social practices. An example from Grieshaber and McArdle (2010) explains how the act of two children colluding and using physical force to take toys from a child (twice in a matter of several minutes) was aided by his small physical stature, non-membership of the dominant Anglo-Australian group, and the fact that no educators appeared to see what happened. Similar events have been reported in the USA by Derman-Sparks and Ramsey (2006), who noted:

> You see a group of children laughing at a new class member who speaks with an accent. Three little girls (all white) play in the costume corner, and one says, "I get to be the princess 'cuz I've got blonde hair," and the other girls agree without comment. You hear a child refuse to play with a dark-skinned doll, because it's "dirty."
>
> *(p. 11)*

Some of the more recent analyses incorporate strategies that practitioners are using to assist children to learn about the unfairness of play. However, the challenge for educators is to learn to identify unfair play and deal with it equitably; to teach children about how and why it is inequitable, and in the process, teach about playing fair.

In some cases, educators have unknowingly contributed to the marginalization of children through their words and actions. The study by Campbell (2005) showed how 5-year-old Mick, a boy from the Pacific Islands and an English language learner in a child care setting in Melbourne, Australia, was doubly compromised in his attempts to play. First, two middle class Anglo Australian boys stopped him from playing with construction materials because he did not know how to play "properly." Second, when the teacher intervened, she suggested to Mick that the way he could learn to play was from the very boys who were refusing to let him play; thus sealing his fate in the short term and quite probably ensuring his lack of inclusion in the future. In this example, skin color, ethnicity, social class, and proficiency in English were used by the Anglo boys to marginalize Mick, and the teacher's actions located the problem with Mick. The bigger and older boys in Danby and Baker's (1998) account of *How to be masculine in the block area* provided gender lessons for the younger boys (the apprentices) that drew on strength, size, and power and involved threats of violence such as "bashing you." The play was frightening for the newcomers as they were not familiar with the ritual. When the teacher attended to a crying child in the block area, the silent but menacing threats of the older boys ensured that the younger boy wasn't able to voice his concern about the conflict that was occurring. The teacher's words and actions inadvertently supported the position of the older boys who were the instigators of the threats and conflict, which had the effect of legitimizing the "play" and would have done little to reduce the distress of the crying younger boy. While not all play is inequitable, the growing number of published articles suggests that the incidents mentioned here are by no means isolated and that inequities seem to occur during times of free play (Grieshaber & McArdle, 2010). Nevertheless, incorporating notions of equitable play in the development of recent Australian policy documents has not been without tension. In the section that follows I use the development of an Australian early years curriculum document as an example to explicate this point further.

The Australian Early Years Learning Framework

Recent developments in Australia indicate that there is some reluctance to consider equity as part of early childhood curriculum and no sign of the lingering egalitarianism about which Stilwell and Jordan (2007) spoke, at least in regard to particular journalists and developing *Belonging, being & becoming: The early years learning framework for Australia* (for children aged birth to 5 years) (Commonwealth of Australia, 2009). Contestation and negotiation characterize the process of creating curriculum frameworks and what occurred with this document was no exception (see Sumsion et al., 2009). Attempts to make social justice and equity a fundamental part of this document were ridiculed by a journalist and the editor from the national newspaper, *The Australian,* in response to a draft:

> POLITICAL correctness in the playground is the theme of the nation's first curriculum for childcare centres ... CHILDHOOD is an age of innocence, imagination and curiosity. Trust the bureaucracy to spoil it by writing a

childcare curriculum infested with politically correct jargon and philosophical gobbledygook … Thankfully it is only a draft, so it is not too late for the bureaucrats and academics writing it to inject a dose of common sense.

(Bita, 2008, p. 3; emphasis in original)

This journalist (Bita) and several of those who made online responses to Bita's article positioned childhood as a period of innocence and did not countenance equity as relevant for a national learning framework for children aged birth to 5 years. The editor also commented, declaring that children would be able to finger-paint "on the back of its ludicrous, politically correct pages" and that the writers should "go back to the playpen" (The Editor, 2008, p. 11). On the same day, the Shadow Minister for Early Childhood Education, Childcare, Women, and Youth, Mrs Sophie Mirabella (2008), issued a press release titled *Let children be children – stop the PC* [politically correct] *brainwashing*. It stated: "This is a document aimed at blatant social engineering, not early childhood education." Despite the growing amount of research, these responses highlight the impossibility (for some) of conceiving that discrimination and prejudice are part of the everyday lives of young children. Social engineering is not new to early childhood education, having been a fundamental part of Montessori's program for children of the slums in Rome. Further, it is still evident today in the compensatory Head Start programs in the USA that aim to counteract the effects of poverty; and in the vision of the Council of Australian Governments (Commonwealth of Australia, 2009) that aspires to provide all children with the best start in life through early childhood education to "create a better future for themselves and the nation" (p. 5).

Arguments about early childhood educational settings being natural and normal places for young children are tempered by the fact that all early childhood settings are artificial creations and as such engage in social engineering of one sort or another. Many early childhood institutions in Australia began life with the aim of getting the children of the poor and working class off the streets – what Brennan (1994) called a mission of "child-saving" (p. 7). Any semblance of the "naturalness" of early childhood education disappears when history comes into play as arguments about political correctness being social engineering join the long list of attempts to regulate the poor, working class, working mothers, unhealthy children, children with special needs, and family life in general. That this "politically correct" draft curriculum caused media concern can be linked to the dominance of ideas about young children being innocent, vulnerable, and in need of protection. These enduring and very powerful ideas make it difficult for children to be seen as competent in their own right and, correspondingly, as able to take action that discriminate against and marginalize selected others; and indeed to learn to do otherwise. In their analysis of the "work" of community in *Belonging, being & becoming: The early years learning framework for Australia* (Commonwealth of Australia, 2009), Millei and Sumsion (2011) use Rose's (1999) notion of "radical ethico-politics" (p. 196) to argue that in the final version of the document there is space for working toward a more socially just society. Opportunities are created because of the way in which "a normative position about politics develops dissensus and maintains a focus on the way in which 'groups' or 'communities' can hold a view and espouse values that are not part of a majority view" (p. 81). Creating and preserving such a space generates possibilities and reduces some of the tension that comes with pressure to remove anything too "politically correct." Thus the potential for children to be able to experience socially-just and equitable play situations has been secured in the Framework. Aspirations for educators to learn about equitable play, and to teach children about playing equitably, are more likely to be realized if they are supported by curriculum materials and become essential parts of ongoing professional learning, both formal and informal.

Conclusion

Framing syllabus and curriculum documents using principles of social justice and equity is not new in education. Different global circumstances and alternative theoretical principles are new, which necessitate changes in social priorities and the way principles of social justice and equity operate in the 21st century. More is now known about children and their social worlds and the political way in which they can operate, which mean that children's social worlds are often a microcosm of the surrounding culture. Having a national vision that embodies the principles of a just society and that is supported fiscally and by relevant policies improves the likelihood that social, economic, and educational conditions will be more equitable. Basing a vision on deficit notions of "fixing" the children of the working class has not been nearly as successful as the social activism of the Nordic welfare models. Dewey's (1938) ideas of education being the impetus for reforming democratic community life in the USA and of curriculum holding the potential for society to remake itself still have currency today. However, the effectiveness of and commitment to these ideas is questioned in a country (USA) that spends comparatively little of the GDP on early childhood education, has over 21% of its children living in poverty, and relies on standardized testing of children to determine educational accountability. Friere's (1972) aim of achieving social justice in capitalist societies through teaching the oppressed and Pinar's (1978) reconceptualist curriculum theory that is value laden and politically emancipatory in its intent are examples that have been used to create more equitable curricula. All syllabus documents and curriculum materials reflect underlying beliefs (that may be explicit or implicit) about the nature of knowledge, how knowledge is used, the nature of humans, the process of learning, and the relationship between society and education (Weber, 1984). The key is to build equity into syllabus and curriculum documents in explicit ways from the start, but this must occur in conjunction with national visions, policy, and fiscal support of and for children and families. Combining national visions of social justice and equity, supportive family and education policies, and sufficient government funding with principles of egalitarianism, quality of life, social and economic equity, will improve chances of enacting equitable curriculum and ensuring that learning in the early years is not only oriented to, but can affect, socially-just outcomes. Such outcomes might include reducing within and between school variation in countries like Australia so that the school attended makes little difference to educational performance, improving economic equality across all groups in society, children learning how to play equitably, and enhancing gender equity in families.

References

A Report by the Council for the Australian Federation (ARCAF). (2007). *Federalist Paper 2: The future of schooling in Australia* (Rev. Ed.). Department of the Premier and Cabinet: Melbourne.

Bita, N. (2008). Plan to teach tots calls for PC play. *The Australian*. 18 December (p. 3).

Brennan, D. (1994). *The politics of Australian child care: From philanthropy to feminism*. Cambridge: Cambridge University Press.

Brooker, L. (2002). *Starting school: Young children learning cultures*. Buckingham: Open University Press.

Campbell, S. (2005). Secret children's business: Resisting and redefining access to learning in the early childhood classroom. In N. Yelland (Ed.) *Critical issues in early childhood education* (pp. 146–62). Berkshire, England: Open University Press.

Commonwealth of Australia. (2009). *Belonging, being & becoming: The early years learning framework for Australia*. Canberra, ACT: Department of Education, Employment and Workplace Relations (DWEER) for the Council of Australian Governments.

Danby, S. and Baker, C. (1998). How to be masculine in the block area. *Childhood, 5*(12), 151–75.

Department of Education, Training and Employment. (2001). *South Australian curriculum, standards and accountability framework early years band: Birth to Year 2*. Government of South Australia.

Derman-Sparks, L., & Ramsey, P. G., with Edwards, J. O. (2006). *What if all the kids are white? Anti-bias and multicultural education with young children and families*. New York: Teachers College Press.

Dewey, J. (1938). *Experience and education*. New York: Macmillan.

Friere, P. (1972). *Pedagogy of the oppressed*. Harmondsworth: Penguin.

Grieshaber, S. (2008). Fun, play-based education. *Every Child, 14*(3), 30–31.

Grieshaber, S. and McArdle F. (2010). *The trouble with play*. Maidenhead: Open University Press.

Kristjansson, B. (2006). The making of Nordic childhoods. In J. Einarsdottir and J. T. Wagner (Eds) *Nordic childhoods and early education: Philosophy, research, policy and practice in Denmark, Finland, Iceland, Norway, and Sweden* (pp. 13–42). Greenwich, CT: Information Age Publishing.

Luke, A., Weir, K. and Woods, A. (2008). *Development of a set of principles to guide a P-12 syllabus framework: A Report to the Queensland Studies Authority*. Brisbane, Qld: Queensland Studies Authority.

Millei, Z. & Sumsion, J. (2011). The "work" of community in Belonging, Being and Becoming: The Early Years Learning Framework for Australia. *Contemporary Issues in Early Childhood, 12*(1), 71–85.

Mirabella, S. (2008). *Let children be children – Stop the PC brainwashing*. Shadow Minister for Early Childhood Education, Childcare, Women and Youth; Press release 18 December. Liberal Party of Australia. Retrieved from www.liberal.org.au/news.php?Id=2341

Moyles, J. (Ed.) (2005). *The excellence of play* (2nd edition). Maidenhead: Open University Press.

Mundine, K. and Guigni, M. (2006). *Diversity and difference: Lighting the spirit of identity.* Watson, ACT: Early Childhood Australia.

OECD (2006). *Starting strong II: Early childhood education and care.* OECD: Paris, France.

OECD (1999). *Early childhood education and care policy in Norway.* OECD Country Note. June 1999.

OECD/UNESCO (2003). *Literacy skills for the world of tomorrow: Further results from PISA 2000.* Institute for Statistics. Paris/Montreal: OECD/UNECSO-UIS.

Pinar, W. F. (1978). The reconceptualization of curriculum studies. *Journal of Curriculum Studies, 10*(3), 205–14.

Queensland Studies Authority (2006). *Early years curriculum guidelines.* Brisbane: The State of Queensland.

Rose, N. (1999). *Powers of freedom: Reframing political thought.* Cambridge: Cambridge University Press.

Sandseter, E. B. H. (2009). Children's expressions of exhilaration and fear in risky play. *Contemporary Issues in Early Childhood, 10*(2), 92–106.

Skattebol, J. (2005). Insider/outsider belongings: Traversing the borders of whiteness in early childhood. *Contemporary Issues in Early Childhood, 6*(2), 189–203.

Stilwell, F. and Jordan, K. (2007). *Who gets what? Analysing economic inequality in Australia.* Port Melbourne, Victoria, Australia: Cambridge University Press.

Stretton, H. (2005). *Australia fair.* Sydney: University of New South Wales Press.

Sumsion, J., Barnes, S., Cheeseman, S., Harrison, L., Kennedy, A. M. and Stonehouse, A. (2009). Insider perspectives on developing Belonging, Being & Becoming: The Early Years Learning Framework for Australia. *Australasian Journal of Early Childhood, 34*(4), 4–13.

Swedish Ministry of Education and Science (1998). *Curriculum for the pre-school Lpfö 98.* Stockholm: Swedish Ministry of Education and Science.

The Editor (2008). Let the children play. *The Australian.* 18 December.

United Nations (2004). *Human development report 2004: Cultural liberty in today's diverse world.* New York: United Nations Development Program.

UNICEF (2005). *Poverty in rich countries, 2005. Innocenti report card no. 6.* The United Nations Children's Fund 2005. Florence: UNICEF Innocenti Research Centre.

UNICEF (2007). *Innocenti report card 7. Child poverty in perspective: An overview of child well-being in rich countries.* Florence: UNICEF Innocenti Research Centre.

UNICEF (2009). Fact sheet: A summary of the rights under the Convention on the Rights of the Child. Retrieved from www.unicef.org/crc/files/Rights_overview.pdf

Wagner, J. T. (2006). An outsider's perspective: Childhoods and early childhood education in the Nordic countries. In J. Einarsdottir and J. T. Wagner (Eds) *Nordic childhoods and early education: Philosophy, research, policy and practice in Denmark, Finland, Iceland, Norway, and Sweden* (pp. 289–306). Greenwich, CT: Information Age Publishing.

Wagner, J. T. and Einarsdottir, J. (2006). Nordic ideals as reflected in Nordic childhoods and early education. In J. Einarsdottir and J. T. Wagner (Eds) *Nordic childhoods and early education: Philosophy, research, policy and practice in Denmark, Finland, Iceland, Norway, and Sweden* (pp. 1–12). Greenwich, CT: Information Age Publishing.

Walkerdine, V. (1981). Sex power and pedagogy. *Screen Education, 38,* 14–21.

Weber, E. (1984). *Ideas influencing early childhood education: A theoretical analysis.* New York: Teachers College Press.

Wyver, S., Tranter, P., Naughton, G., Little, H., Sandseter, E. B. H. and Bundy, A. (2010). Ten ways to restrict children's freedom to play: The problem of surplus safety. *Contemporary Issues in Early Childhood, 11*(3), 263–77.

8

CURRICULAR CONVERSATIONS

Literacy Teaching and Learning in the Middle Years

Donna E. Alvermann and James Marshall

Introduction

A curriculum that seeks "equity of engagement in common and diverse cultural conversations" has set for itself an educationally critical but politically challenging agenda. Embedded within these few words are powerful conceptual binaries that have animated some of the most significant educational discussions of the last quarter century. While frequently deconstructed in the theoretical literature, these binaries have remained stubbornly resistant to resolution in the worlds of curricular and teaching practice. In what follows, we will describe three of these binaries, placing them briefly in their historical and political contexts, explaining the challenges they represent, and arguing for their importance within a comprehensive literacy curriculum for the middle-years.

Common and Diverse Cultural Conversations

The "and" that both joins and separates "common" and "diverse" in this phrase represents a politically charged pivot point that has shaped decisions across schooling contexts, from state and district-wide funding formulas to textbook design, to assessment practices. Fueled by the culture wars (Bennett, 1993; Bloom, 1987; Hirsch, 1987; Ravitch & Ravitch, 2007) and the political configurations that abetted and extended those wars (Cross, 2004), the 1980s and 1990s saw a series of extended, often networked, efforts to establish common cultural materials as the central core of the literacy curriculum. These efforts essentially defined themselves as a specific opposition to educational movements that were often labeled as "softening," "weakening," or "diluting" the more traditional cultural curriculum. The latter represented an effort to extend the boundaries of the literacy curriculum to include multicultural texts and multimodal forms of media – an inclusion that invited a range of new pedagogies and literacy practices (Cope & Kalantzis, 2000; Freedman, Simons, Kalnin & Casareno, 1999).

In curricular practice, this tension was often resolved in district curricula and syllabus documents, and in textbooks by attempting inclusion while providing a stable range of traditional literature and genres. In such efforts, a canonical poem might be thematically paired with an Aboriginal song, say, or a lyric from South Africa, Afghanistan, or Tibet. These pairings would in turn invite comparisons and contrasts between the texts, resulting in arguments that usually took the form of "In spite of these differences, we can see important similarities in these texts."

While the effort to include a wider range of texts is both necessary and overdue, it seems important to recognize that curricula that combine texts across cultures without highlighting and problematizing the boundaries between those cultures, may end by erasing critical differences between the cultures. (Willinsky, 1998). In other words, the very reason for curricula to become more inclusive – that is, to help students to recognize and learn to respect difference – is undermined by the curricular frame in which the materials are introduced. To resolve such a dilemma, a coherent curricular effort to offer both common ground and diverse voices must emphasize differences as well as similarities, contrast as well as comparison. Developing curriculum, then, would be less an occasion for rendering invisible the boundaries that separate groups than of mapping and critically examining the boundaries as they are.

One approach to mapping existing boundaries with an eye to critically examining the extent to which a curriculum provides room for common ground and diverse voices involves the use of principled practices. The concept of principled practices (Duffy & Hoffman, 1999, 2001; Smagorinsky, 2002) directs attention from the "one size fits all" or "best" practice model of, say, literacy comprehension instruction, to the study of classroom cultures that embed such instruction. Specifically, its aim is to move the conversation beyond debates about the value of instructional methods tested in lab-like experiments (Alvermann & Moore, 1991; National Reading Panel, 2000) to a dialogue about the cultural dimensions of a curriculum and the choices it offers.

Principled practices applied to curricular designs with equity of engagement as a goal might look something like this:

- Students from diverse cultural and linguistic backgrounds experience opportunities to learn in a respectful environment – one characterized by high expectations, trust, and caring teachers (Li, 2006; Nieto, 1999).
- Students' cultural identities and personal background knowledge are viewed as strengths, not deficits (Sturtevant et al., 2006).
- Teachers exercise their moral authority to search for connections between themselves and students as well as among students themselves (Valenzuela, 1999).

- Existing home/school differences become resources for curricular discussions, not barriers (Gonzalez, Moll & Amanti, 2005; Lee, 2004).
- Students' affective filters, especially those associated with their motivation to learn, are keen, and often influence directly how they perceive themselves as learners and as members of a larger, diverse academic community (Abi-Nader, 1993; Morrell & Duncan-Andrade, 2006).

Curricular Content and Literacy Skills

A second important tension resonates with the first, but has a somewhat longer history and somewhat broader curricular dimensions. This is the tension between those who argue for the primacy of curricular content, specified by grade level and subject area (e.g., Bennett, 1993; Carnegie Council on Advancing Adolescent Literacy, 2010; Ravitch & Finn, 1987) and those who argue instead for the primacy of students' learning processes, which are less amenable to scope-and-sequence divisions (e.g., Bruner, 1997). This argument extends back almost to the beginnings of English as a school subject: one of the major arguments for the founding of the National Council of Teachers of English, in fact, was the need felt for secondary teachers to resist the universities' power to specify the literary content of the high school curriculum. In his history of the teaching of English, Applebee (1974, p. 245) concludes that "teachers of English have never successfully resisted the pressure to formulate their subject as a body of knowledge to be imparted." And three major reform efforts in literacy teaching over the last quarter-century – the Whole Language movement, the Writing Process movement, and reader response approaches to teaching literature – all positioned themselves as opposed to those who would unilaterally specify literacy content without reference to readers and their context.

As with the first tension, curriculum and textbook developers have often attempted to resolve these differences by combining elements from both frameworks in their products. Thus secondary students might be assigned a highly specific genre in which to write (persuasion, say) with a highly specific prompt, but at the same time be asked to employ drafting strategies borrowed from writing process pedagogies such as pre-writing or peer-reviewing (e.g., Common Core Georgia Performance Standards, 2008). They might be asked to closely read a highly canonical text and later be asked how they felt about the characters or if the text reminded them of anything in their own lives (Pirie, 1997; Willinsky, 1990).

This second tension overlaps with the first because an argument *for* content always moves swiftly toward an argument *about* content, but it also extends beyond the boundaries of pedagogy and beyond the borders of literacy education. Debates within mathematics, for example (National Council of Teachers of Mathematics Standards, 2007), and social studies education (National Council of Social Studies Standards, 2007), have frequently centered on arguments about whether curricular content should be selected because it provides an occasion for learning critical skills in the discipline or whether it should be selected because of its intrinsic, disciplinary importance. Thus a small episode in US History such as the early 1970s mining strike in West Virginia (Moffett, 1988) might be given short shrift in a traditional overview of 20th-century history. But it might be expanded upon in an alternative kind of history where students are given opportunities to explore issues such as geographical region, working class labor, and committed religious beliefs in more finely grained detail. Curricula in any subject always represent a highly selective choice from a vast array of potentially valuable materials, and the political agendas and political agents shaping those agendas must be acknowledged in any curriculum that aims for comprehensiveness.

The tension generated when considering how much emphasis to place on content in relation to literacy skills in curriculum development has fueled an endless debate about the degree to which content or skills instruction will influence literacy outcomes. In an extensive review of how curricular decisions affect students' literacy engagement and academic performance, Guthrie and Wigfield (2000) concluded that various approaches, including skills, strategy, and content instruction, while important, do not have a direct impact on most student outcome measures (e.g., time spent reading independently, achievement on standardized tests, performance assessments, and beliefs about the value of reading and writing).

Instead, the *level* of student engagement (including its sustainability over time) is the mediating factor, or avenue, through which instruction influences student outcomes. Guthrie and Wigfield's (2000) conception of the engagement model of reading calls for instruction that fosters: student motivation (including self-efficacy and goal setting); strategy use (using prior knowledge, self-monitoring for breaks in comprehension, analyzing new vocabulary); growth in conceptual knowledge (reading trade books to supplement textbook information, viewing videos, experimenting with hands-on devices); and social interaction (discussing an internet search with the teacher, text messaging a friend about a missed assignment).

Although Guthrie and Wigfield's (2000) engagement model is theoretically sound and backed by research, it does not sufficiently address the curricular demands specific to reading in the subject matter areas. Over three decades ago, Hirst (1974) advanced the notion that discrete forms of knowledge and language distinguish one discipline from another and systematically affect a person's understanding of subject matter derived from different domains. Much later, a research agenda having curricular implications that came out of the RAND Reading Study Group's (2002) deliberations emphasized that "a reader's domain knowledge interacts with the content of the text" (p. 14) and has a critical bearing – along with a text's vocabulary load, linguistic structure, and genre – on what a reader comprehends. The importance of domain knowledge is particularly evident as school districts in the United States transition from standards-based instruction associated with the No Child Left Behind era to the new Common Core State Standards recently adopted by 43 states and the District of Columbia (Long, 2011).

Increased attention to domain knowledge and how it interacts with content to affect a reader's comprehension led subsequently to a commissioned work by the

Carnegie Corporation of New York entitled *Literacy Instruction in the content areas: Getting to the core of middle and high school improvement* (Heller & Greenleaf, 2007). This report has both clarified and expanded the agenda for adolescent literacy reform in the United States by calling on district, state, and federal policymakers to ensure, among other things, that "members of every academic discipline define the literacy skills that are essential to their content area and which they *should* be responsible for teaching" (Heller & Greenleaf, 2007, p. 1, emphasis in the original). This responsibility does not include providing basic reading instruction to struggling readers (a task assigned to reading specialists in the secondary schools), but it does assume the availability of initial and ongoing professional development in teaching the literacy skills that are essential to the various academic disciplines. Access to this kind of professional development is also at the core of recommendations made by a 12-member European team of adolescent literacy educators in the ADORE Project *Teaching Struggling Adolescent Readers*, which is funded within the Socrates Programme, an educational initiative of the European Commission (Garbe, Holle & Weinhold, 2010).

In a review of the research on text comprehension from a developmental learning perspective, Alexander and Jetton (2000) also pointed to the importance of domain or disciplinary knowledge in determining what a reader will understand. Although different disciplinary texts have some things in common, they also have distinguishing features that set them apart and bear implications for classroom instruction in the content areas. For instance, comprehending a history textbook requires expertise in systematically locating problem/solution frames, explanations, and agents of change within a chronological lens (or a critique of that lens). Science texts, on the other hand, are typically organized around systems and subsystems. Knowledge domains are also distinguished by their lexicons, or technical vocabulary, and by their modes of inscription – the ways in which concepts and processes within a particular domain are represented in symbolic form (Jetton & Dole, 2004). Moreover, ways of reading and writing about science, engaging in science experiments, or being recognized as a scientist are vastly different from the ways of reading a history text, writing a historical essay, or being recognized as a historian. These discourses and their corresponding differences make it imperative that a reader approach any given text by asking critical questions about whose message is being conveyed, by what means, and for what purposes.

Easing the tension inherent in curricular models that emphasize content over literacy skills (process) or skills over content is possible. The following tenets, developed by Herber in 1970 and refined eight years later, require viewing curriculum as context, content as vehicle, and literacy skills as the processes by which one learns the content. With this in mind, consider how:

- Content determines process. That is, implicit within the content of subject matter texts are the reading processes (or skills) students need to comprehend the material.

- There need not be a dichotomy between the content of a subject and the skills for learning the content. As noted earlier, skills are the means by which students comprehend the content of the curriculum, although not singularly nor in isolation from a reader's background knowledge and any number of other factors.
- Curricular decisions that lead to pull-out programs (e.g., teaching literacy skills separate from the context and content in which they are needed) confound efforts to develop students' independence in reading and responding to texts (Herber, 1978, pp. 4–5).

While viewing curriculum as context, content as vehicle, and literacy skills as the processes by which one learns can theoretically ease the tension between those who argue for the primacy of curricular content (specified by grade level and subject area) and those who argue for the primacy of students' learning processes, practically speaking this tension remains. It is reflected most notably in the confusion that surrounds implementation of content area reading and writing instruction at the secondary level. As Heller and Greenleaf (2007) pointed out in their review of the research literature on disciplinary literacy instruction,

> Generations of researchers and educators have drawn a sharp distinction between the teaching of basic skills and the teaching of academic content, with reading and writing assigned to the former. Indeed, it is sometimes argued that students should master the basics of literacy by the fourth grade *so that* (emphasis in the original) they can go on to study advanced subject matter, such as mathematical theorems, historical events, scientific methods, great works of literature, and so on.
>
> *(p. 16)*

The oft-repeated maxim that students must learn to read before they read to learn is not only lacking in research evidence but also potentially damaging from an instructional point of view. Separating the act of reading from one of its functions – reading to learn *something* – makes little sense. Though it can be argued that developmentally, beginning readers are different from skilled readers, the difference between these two age groups lies more with the content or subject matter materials they are expected to read than with any overall purpose for reading.

However, if the practical tension between teaching curricular content versus literacy skills remains, it isn't simply due to the separation of reading from one of its functions (to learn content). Perhaps more importantly, subject matter teachers feel pressured to cover the content specified in state and professional organizations' standards or system syllabus and curriculum documents in a timely manner, or at least in time for the high-stakes assessments. These pressures, coupled with unclear messages to content area teachers as to whether or not they are individually accountable for students' gains in academic literacy, led Heller and Greenleaf (2007) to speculate the following: until teaching is treated as a learning profession and teachers are provided opportunities for practising the integration of reading, writing, and reasoning in their academic disciplines, it is unlikely that the tension between curricular content and literacy skills will ease, at least on a practical level.

An opportunity to practise the integration of content and literacy skills, while necessary, is insufficient. Both teachers and students in the middle grades can benefit from an improved understanding of how disciplines differ from one another and why that difference requires different decoding processes for different symbolic representations (e.g., mathematical, linguistic, sound, visual), as well as strategies for producing, inquiring into, comprehending, and critiquing textual authority (Bain, 2000; Moje, 2008).

Learning Processes and Assessment Technologies

A conventional but still useful way of conceptualizing curricula in its various iterations is to think of curricula as (1) planned or written, (2) taught or enacted, and (3) assessed, either formally or informally. Framed in this way, we can see how curricular intentions are transformed as they move across the contexts in which they are worked upon and by the agents (politicians and policy makers, teachers and students, assessment agencies and psychometric consultants) who do the working.

In an increasingly familiar and highly political process, curricula are generated in a three-stage manner that reflects the three-part conceptual frame just described. First, curricular standards for grade levels and subject areas are developed by agencies at the state or national level (e.g., Hargreaves, 2003; Hillocks, 2002). These usually state, as bulleted items of varying length, the goals to be achieved by students within the subject area at a particular grade level and usually include both the skills to be mastered and the content to be covered (e.g., the Common Core Georgia Performance Standards, 2010).

In a second, sometimes overlapping phase, teaching materials, textbooks, and pedagogical protocols are developed that purport to reflect the standards and that promise to help teachers "teach" the standards if followed as intended. Because some of the central goals of a literacy curriculum at any grade level ("mastery" of standard English, competence in persuasive writing, comprehension of canonical texts) are not only lofty but ill-defined, the match between those goals and the specific teaching strategies embedded in pedagogical materials and textbooks is often hard to track. Once a set of standards is produced, however, there is usually enormous political pressure – and enormous commercial pressure – to produce swiftly a set of materials that will "teach" to those standards. But textbook companies, freighted by immense investments in earlier products, are seldom able to produce entirely new approaches to teaching on short notice (Apple, 2001). Thus the "new" teaching approaches on offer are more cosmetic than substantive, employing the vocabulary of the state mandated standards as a frame for teaching the same content and skills. And, of course, even if the teaching materials and textbooks successfully offered thoughtful and practical implementation strategies to teachers, the teachers themselves need to interpret and apply those strategies based on their own students' strengths and their own teaching expertise.

Perhaps the most critical phase in the lives of curricula, though – certainly the phase where the stakes are the highest – is the point where curricular standards as devised and taught become the basis for the assessment of student performance. Here, too, attention must be paid to the match between the standards that have been generated and to the practical instruments that will measure students' competency on those standards. But attention must also be paid to the match between those practical assessment instruments and the teaching strategies teachers chose or were able to employ with the students in their care.

To claim that mandated assessments are measuring student progress on mandated standards begs three related questions:

- What is the evidence that teachers have had the resources, the skills, and the opportunities to teach the standards across a wide range of socioeconomic and cultural contexts to a wide range of students?
- What is the evidence that the assessments employed reliably measure what is most important in the standards in ways that reflect the complexity of the learning goals specified in the standards?
- What is the evidence that the very process of mandating high-stakes assessment changes the nature of teaching and learning in ways that have not been anticipated and in ways that do not square with some of our deepest commitments to public schooling (e.g., Nichols & Berliner, 2007)?

That high-stakes tests have already reshaped the nature of teaching, especially the teaching of literacy, seems increasingly beyond dispute. As Nichols and Berliner (2007) have argued, such tests in the United States have narrowed the curriculum by reducing the range of school subjects taught to those that are regularly tested and by reducing the complexity of the remaining school subjects so that they can be assessed in standardized, "objective" formats. High-stakes tests have also restricted the resources upon which teachers can draw (Marshall, 2009). Thus the curriculum in literacy becomes a heavily scripted set of routine performances where grammar and usage exercises replace student writing and the definitions of literary terms replace students' engagement with literary texts. Nichols and Berliner argue further that high-stakes tests erode the integrity of test scores themselves, but more important to the discussion here is that the tests may erode the integrity of the curriculum being offered to students.

What happens to teachers when the nature of teaching changes in these ways? How are the changes affecting teachers' understanding of their work? And to what extent are they contributing to the number of teachers who leave teaching after only a few years? Graham, Marshall and Power (2007), in a study of seasoned teachers asked to prepare underachieving students for high-stakes tests, found the teachers angry and in their own words, "schizophrenic" about their work. It was not simply that the literacy curriculum had been impoverished in the ways already described. It was that their professional identities and sense of professional agency had been taken from them in the name of standardized reform. Because they could no longer make curricular decisions tailored to the needs and interests of their students, they felt they were becoming *less* effective as classroom teachers – an ironic outcome given the reform agenda. Their commitments to their students, who needed to pass the exams, complicated their frustrations with the exams themselves.

The intensification and de-skilling of teaching brought about by high-stakes testing may not only push experienced teachers to new levels of professional doubt, it may also invite a different kind of young person into the profession – a person more comfortable with standardized, teacher-proof curricula and less committed to a nuanced classroom practice that is informed by a knowledge of students and their community. If new teachers of literacy are different enough from their senior colleagues in their sense of curricular normalcy and professional agency, then the project of achieving "equity of engagement in common and diverse cultural conversations" may represent an even more serious and long-term challenge than anticipated. On the one hand, it would mean that high-stakes tests may have changed the environments of schooling in much the same way that ecological disruptions have changed the global environment. On the other hand, it would mean that the process of preparing candidates to teach would become one of preparing them for that new environment. At such a point, the ideological structures impeding curricular equity and cultural conversations may have become both systemic and self-perpetuating. More than ever, then, it seems essential to examine and reinforce our commitments to curricular reform.

One of those commitments is to increase the chances that large-scale reform efforts will contribute in a positive manner to how young people perceive themselves as readers and writers – even to how they use literacy to mediate their identities in a school curriculum, a neighborhood, or a larger community in which they live. The importance of attending to students' perceptions of themselves as readers and writers in an era of externally-mandated reforms and high-stakes tests is paramount and not to be taken lightly. For as Holland, Lachicotte, Skinner and Cain (1998) remind us, "People tell others who they are, but even more important, they tell themselves and then try to act as though they are who they say they are" (p. 3).

We find this conception of identity a useful one, especially when one's goal is to conceptualize a curriculum that seeks equity of engagement in common ground and diverse cultural conversations. We also find it conducive to exploring the following set of literacy related questions – the answers to which may suggest a need for monitoring and adjusting whatever curricular tensions exist between students' learning processes and an all too-pervasive assessment environment.

- Are young people's perceptions of themselves as readers and writers inextricably tied to their teachers' perceptions of how they have fared in today's high-stakes testing arena?

- Do students value reading against the grain – sometimes described as reading the subtexts or "hidden" messages of texts that authors may have consciously or unconsciously concealed?
- More to the point, have they been taught to read in this manner, and if so, do they recognize that texts of all kinds (print, visual, aural, digital) position them in ways that produce certain meanings and literate identities from the cultural and material resources available within specific social situations (Ladson–Billings, 2006; Morgan, 1997)?

Young people's interests in the internet and other interactive communication technologies suggest the need for a curriculum that emphasizes reading with a critical eye toward how writers, illustrators, and the like represent people and their ideas – in short, how individuals who create texts make those texts work. All texts, including academic textbooks, routinely promote or silence particular views and in doing so influence to no small degree how students in the middle grades take up (or not) the identities that are produced and made available to them. Yet concerns about young people and their literate identities seldom rank high in the midst of curricular reform efforts.

Historically it has been shown that the shifts in distribution of cultural and material resources that accompany curricular change are only a few of the tensions that coexist in the form of uneasy balances and alliances (Luke, 1989). This is especially the case when such reform occurs in a high-stakes assessment climate. As the push to increase young people's literacy achievement continues to mount, it is important to not lose sight of middle-grade students who struggle to keep up with, or even fail to meet, the increased expectations of a new curriculum. These are typically the same students who for different reasons experience difficulty in reading, discussing, and writing about a wide range of curricular materials.

Attempting to define the term *struggling reader* is like trying to nail Jell-O to a wall, as evidenced in a collection of articles aimed at addressing the need to equip adolescents (some of whom *can* read but choose not to) with the skills and dispositions necessary for comprehending subject matter texts (Moore, Alvermann & Hinchman, 2000). The term itself takes on different characteristics depending on the person who is defining it and for what purpose. Indeed, a cursory analysis of almost any mainstream literacy journal will reveal that the term *struggling* can refer to youth with clinically diagnosed reading disabilities as well as to those who are unmotivated, disenchanted, or generally unsuccessful in school literacy tasks. A smorgasbord of descriptors, these labels tell little or nothing about the cultural construction of even a single struggling reader. They do, however, provide ways of thinking about culture and struggling that are seldom addressed in the literature on teaching students in the middle grades who, for whatever reason, are thought to be achieving below their "full potential" as readers.

Some Parting Thoughts

The conceptual binaries we have used here to frame our argument cannot be usefully seen as independent, separate problems to be somehow "solved" in efforts to develop curricula. Rather, when taken together, those binaries map the discursive space within which competing curricular models can be located. When a particular curricular model takes a position about one term in a binary (arguing for subject matter content, say, over the teaching of critical skills), it necessarily invites dissenting response from the opposing term. The binaries cannot be resolved, the conversation cannot be concluded, because conversations about the binaries themselves constitute the dialectic, ongoing, and always politically framed discourse about public education. Any specific curriculum, then, especially one with literacy in the middle years as a pivotal point, must acknowledge these binaries while at the same time recognizing itself as a viable means of critically examining the nature of the political and economic tensions they represent. Just as the discontinuities expressed in the three binaries that frame this paper call for discussion when developing a curriculum that seeks equity of engagement, so too is there a need for rethinking the teaching of youth whose motivations to read and write hinge on a range of factors that include but are not limited to social, cultural, and political influences. To participate fully in curricular discussions of these influences, we perceive a need for judiciously discarding some of the rhetoric surrounding literacy teaching and learning in the middle years – rhetoric that would claim (or wish) to be above interrogation, yet is firmly ensconced in the binaries we propose to keep, if for no other reason than to engage with the challenges they present.

References

Abi-Nader, J. (1993). Meeting the needs of multicultural classrooms: Family values and the motivation of minority students. In M. J. O'Hair and S. J. Odell (Eds) *Diversity in teaching: Teacher education yearbook I* (pp. 212–36). Fort Worth, TX: Harcourt Brace Jovanovich.

Alexander, P. and Jetton, T. L. (2000). Learning from text: A multidimensional and developmental perspective. In M. L. Kamil, P. B. Mosenthal, P. D. Pearson and R. Barr (Eds) *Handbook of reading research* (Vol. 3, pp. 285–310). Mahwah, NJ: Erlbaum.

Alvermann, D. E. and Moore, D. W. (1991). Secondary school reading. In R. Barr, M. L. Kamil, P. Mosenthal and P. D. Pearson (Eds) *Handbook of reading research* (Vol. 2, pp. 951–83). New York: Longman.

Apple, M. (2001). *Educating the "right" way: Markets, standards, God, and inequality.* London, UK: Routledge/Falmer.

Applebee, A. N. (1974). *Tradition and reform in the teaching of English.* Urbana, IL: National Council of Teachers of English.

Bain, R. (2000). Into the breach: Using research and theory to shape history instruction. In P. Stearns, P. Seixas and S. Wineburg (Eds) *Knowing teaching, and learning history: National and international perspectives* (pp. 331–53). New York: New York University Press.

Bennett, W. (1993). *The book of virtues.* New York: Simon and Schuster.

Bloom, A. (1987). *The closing of the American mind.* New York: Simon and Schuster.

Bruner, J. S. (1997). *The culture of education.* Cambridge, MA: Harvard University Press.

Carnegie Council on Advancing Adolescent Literacy (2010). *Time to act: An agenda for advancing adolescent literacy for college and career success.* New York: Carnegie Corporation of New York.

Common Core Georgia Performance Standards (2010). Retrieved from www.gadoe.org/CCGPS.aspx

Cope, B. and Kalantzis, M. (Eds) (2000). *Multiliteracies: literacy learning and the design of social futures.* London: Routledge.

Cross, C. (2004). *Political education.* New York: Teachers College Press.

Duffy, G. G. and Hoffman, J. V. (1999). In pursuit of an illusion: The flawed search for a perfect method. *The Reading Teacher, 53*(1), 10–16.

Freedman, S., Simons, E., Kalnin, J. and Casareno, A. (1999). *Inside city schools: Investigating literacy in multicultural classrooms.* New York: Teachers College Press.

Garbe, C., Holle, K. and Weinhold, S. (Eds) (2010). *ADORE – Teaching struggling adolescent readers in European countries.* Germany: Frankfurt am Main.

Georgia Department of Education (2008). *Georgia performance standards.* Atlanta, GA: Author.

Gonzalez, N., Moll, L. C., & Amanti, C. (2005). *Funds of knowledge: Theorizing practices in households and classrooms.* Mahwah, NJ: Erlbaum.

Graham, P., Marshall, J. and Power, C. (2007). The way we teach now: Teachers of English in the new world of high-stakes assessment. *English Leadership Quarterly, 30*(2), 2–5.

Guthrie, J. and Wigfield, A. (2000). Engagement and motivation in reading. In M. L. Kamil, P. B. Mosenthal, P. D. Pearson and R. Barr (Eds) *Handbook of reading research* (Vol. 3, pp. 403–22). Mahwah, NJ: Erlbaum.

Hargreaves, A. (2003). *Teaching in the knowledge society: Education in the age of insecurity.* New York: Teachers College Press.

Heller, R. and Greenleaf, C. L. (2007). *Literacy instruction in the content areas: Getting to the core of middle and high school improvement.* Washington, DC: Alliance for Excellent Education.

Herber, H. L. (1970). *Teaching reading in content areas.* Englewood Cliffs, NJ: Prentice-Hall.

Herber, H. L. (1978). *Teaching reading in content areas* (2nd edition). Englewood Cliffs, NJ: Prentice-Hall.

Hillocks, G. (2002). *The testing trap.* New York: Teachers College Press.

Hirsch, E. D. (1987). *Cultural literacy.* Boston: Houghton Mifflin.

Hirst, P. H. (1974). *Knowledge and the curriculum.* London: Routledge & Kegan Paul.

Hoffman, J. V. and Duffy, G. G. (2001). Beginning reading instruction: Moving beyond the debate over methods into the study of principled teaching practices. In J. Brophy (Ed.) *Subject-specific instructional methods and activities: Advances in research in teaching* (Vol. 8, pp. 25–49). New York: Elsevier Science.

Holland, D., Lachicotte, W., Jr., Skinner, D. and Cain, C. (1998). *Identity and agency in cultural worlds.* Cambridge, MA: Harvard University Press.

Jetton, T. L. and Dole, J. A. (2004). *Adolescent literacy research and practice.* New York: Guilford.

Ladson-Billings, G. (2006). From the achievement gap to the education debt: Understanding achievement in U.S. schools. *Educational Researcher, 35*(7), 3–12.

Lee, C. D. (2004). Double voiced discourse: African American Vernacular English as resource in cultural modeling classrooms. In A. Ball & S. W. Freedman (Eds) *New literacies for new times: Bakhtinian perspectives on language, literacy, and learning for the 21st century.* New York: Cambridge University Press.

Li, G. (2006). *Culturally contested pedagogy: Battles of literacy and schooling between mainstream teachers and Asian immigrant parents.* Albany: SUNY Press.

Long, R. (2011). Common Core State Standards: Approaching the assessment issue. *Reading Today, 29*(1), 23–25.

Luke, A. (1989). Literacy as curriculum: Historical and sociological perspectives. *Language, Learning and Literacy, 1*(2), 1–16.

Marshall, J. (2009). *Divided against ourselves: Standards, assessments, and adolescent literacy.* In L. Christenbury, R. Bomer and P. Smagorinsky (Eds) *Handbook of adolescent literacy research* (pp. 113–25). New York: The Guilford Press.

Moffett, J. (1988). *Storm in the mountains.* Carbondale, IL: Southern Illinois University Press.

Moje, E. B. (2008). [Commentary] Foregrounding the disciplines in secondary literacy teaching and learning: A call for change. *Journal of Adolescent & Adult Literacy, 52,* 96–107.

Moore, D. W., Alvermann, D. E. and Hinchman, K. A. (Eds) (2000). *Struggling adolescent readers: A collection of teaching strategies.* Newark, DE: International Reading Association.

Morgan, W. (1997). *Critical literacy in the classroom.* London: Routledge.

Morrell, E. and Duncan-Andrade, J. (2006). Popular culture and critical media pedagogy in secondary literacy classrooms. *International Journal of Learning, 12*(9), 273–80.

National Council of Social Studies Standards (2007). Retrieved www.ncss.org/standards

National Council of Teachers of Mathematics Standards (2007). Retrieved from www.nctm.org/standards

National Reading Panel (2000). *Teaching children to read: An evidence-based assessment of the scientific research literature on reading and its implications for reading instruction* (NIH Publication Number 00–4769). Washington, DC: National Institute of Child Health and Human Development.

Nichols, S. and Berliner, D. (2007). *Collateral damage: How high-stakes testing corrupts America's schools.* Cambridge, MA: Harvard University Press.

Nieto, S. (1999). *The light in their eyes: Creating multicultural learning communities.* New York: Teachers College Press.

Pirie, B. (1997). *Reshaping high school English.* Urbana, IL: National Council of Teachers of English.

RAND Reading Study Group (2002). *Reading for understanding: Toward an R&d program in reading comprehension.* Santa Monica, CA: Science & Technology Policy Institute, RAND Education.

Ravitch, D. and Finn, C. (1987). *What do our seventeen year olds know?* New York: Harper & Row.

Ravitch, D. and Ravitch, M. (2007). *The English reader: What every literate person needs to know.* New York: Oxford University Press.

Smagorinsky, P. (2002). *Teaching English through principled practice.* Upper Saddle River, NJ: Merrill/Prentice Hall.

Sturtevant, E. G., Boyd, F. B., Brozo, W. G., Hinchman, K. A., Moore, D. W. and Alvermann, D. E. (2006). *Principled practices for adolescent literacy: A framework for instruction and policy.* Mahwah, NJ: Erlbaum.

Valenzuela, A. (1999). *Subtractive schooling: U.S.-Mexican youth and the politics of caring.* Albany, NY: SUNY Press.

Willinsky, J. (1990). *The new literacy.* London: Routledge.

Willinsky, J. (1998). *Learning to divide the world.* Minneapolis: University of Minnesota Press.

9

IMPROVING SECONDARY SCHOOLS[1]

Ben Levin

The Challenge of Secondary School Improvement

Completion of secondary education is now seen as a necessity for all young people if they are to have a reasonable opportunity to contribute to and benefit from modern societies. According to the Organisation for Economic Co-operation and Development (OECD), the international average rate of completion of secondary education among its member countries is 80%, but this rate ranges from about 75% to nearly 100% (OECD, 2006). Yet even Singapore, with a high school completion rate of more than 95% (Sclafani, 2008), is seeking further improvement. The evidence we have suggests that it should be possible for virtually all students to complete a challenging secondary education.

At the same time, there is a view among education change experts that, hard as it is to create lasting change in elementary schools, it is much more difficult to do so in secondary schools (Fullan, 2006; Hargreaves & Goodson, 2006). And of course, the higher the current completion rate, the more difficult it will be to make further gains.

In secondary education, as in elementary education, the literature is full of examples of individual schools, or sometimes small numbers of schools, that have been able to show dramatic improvements in student outcomes, retention rates and areas of school reform, and sometimes under very difficult circumstances (e.g. Muijs, Harris, Chapman, Stoll & Russ, 2004). At the same time, there are very few examples of system-wide improvement (Reynolds, Stringfield & Schaffer, 2006), although system-wide improvement is what we need. Improving large numbers of schools is much harder to do than single site (or small cluster) reform because it cannot be a matter of relying on a small number of outstanding leaders or teachers, which so often seems to be the situation in the cases of exemplary schools. Instead, we need strategies that will work across many schools with people with average levels of skill and commitment.

There are many reasons why system-wide improvement in secondary schools is difficult. One has to do with size. Secondary schools are typically much larger, which means that there is more anonymity and less ability to know each student well. Compounding larger size is the rotation of students among classes taught by specialists, so that teachers encounter many more students in a day or week than they do in elementary schools and students have less contact with any individual teacher. A further issue is the division of secondary schools and their teachers into sections or departments by discipline or area of study, which tends to reduce the sense of professional community across the school and makes whole-school approaches to change harder to deliver. Public confidence in secondary schools, the *sine qua non* for the system's progress, also tends to be lower than for elementary schools.

However, these structures are not the only barriers to better student outcomes. A major dilemma lies in the basic purpose of secondary schooling. In a 2005 report, the World Bank (2005) outlined the central dilemmas that face secondary education all around the world. Secondary schools, the Bank said, are trying at one and the same time to be

> terminal and preparatory, compulsory and post compulsory, uniform and diverse, meritocratic and compensatory, ... serving both individual needs ... and societal and labor market needs, ... offsetting disadvantages but also, within the same institution, selecting and screening students ... , [and] ... offering a common curriculum for all students and a specialized curriculum for some.
>
> *(p. 14)*

The report includes an apt and powerful quote from Aristotle's *Politics* showing that this diversity in roles and expectations is longstanding, but as completion of secondary education has become the minimum expectation for virtually all students, the contradictions have become more prominent and more difficult to manage.

The World Bank report also stressed the extraordinary homogeneity in secondary schooling around the world, and the equally extraordinary commonality and stability in basic areas such as curriculum and school organization. Secondary schools everywhere tend to be organized in similar ways and to teach similar subjects and courses. Yet countries around the world are making efforts to increase quality and also increase equity of outcomes in their secondary education systems. This chapter puts forward a direction for achieving those dual purposes, particularly in industrialized countries that already have close to universal secondary participation. The situation in many developing countries is quite different and would require a different strategy.

The approach proposed here is derived from several sources. The extensive literature on educational change generally and in secondary schools in particular provides a considerable amount of guidance. Other important elements are derived from my experiences over more than 30 years, in government and academia, to create and understand change in secondary schools. Much of the thinking in this paper comes from the efforts in Ontario, Canada, since 2004 to increase high school graduation rates significantly (Ungerleider, 2007) and the ensuing reflections of the author, who held the role of the chief civil servant responsible for this effort for several years, as to the implications of these efforts for our overall understanding of secondary school improvement (Levin, 2008a,b). Not everything proposed in this chapter has been done in Ontario, but the Ontario reforms are based on and consistent with the general thinking outlined here.

Sustainable Improvement

Before moving to the body of this chapter it is worth discussing briefly an interesting recent debate that has developed around the notion of sustainable school improvement (e.g. Hargreaves & Fink, 2003; Datnow, 2005; Hargreaves & Goodson, 2006; Lai, McNaughton, Amituanai-Toloa, Turner & Hsiao, 2009). Real improvement in schools must be sustainable – that is, must be embedded in the work of the institution in a way that allows it to continue even when the initial impetus changes. To be sustainable in this sense, improvement strategies must not only yield better outcomes, but must do so in a way that has professional and public support. One might define sustainable school improvement as that which improves important student outcomes while also reducing inequities in those outcomes, does this in a way that builds skill, engagement and morale among educators, and is well received and supported by students, parents and the broader community. All three elements of the definition – improvement, support by educators and public acceptance – are equally important, since the lack of any one of these is likely to make improvement unsustainable (Levin, 2008a).

The Requirements for Secondary School Improvement

This chapter focuses on those factors that can be affected by policy and practice in secondary schools, while recognizing that schools cannot do everything, and that even how much they can do is in dispute (Thrupp, 1999; Mortimore & Whitty, 2000; Levin, 2006). Student background continues to be the strongest single predictor of student outcomes (Levin, 2004). There is no doubt that changes outside the school in areas such as early childhood development, employment, housing, income supports and community services are important to improving students' welfare and school achievement, no matter what schools do (Levin, 2009). Educators should continue to lobby for and support these broader social policy changes.

At the same time, there is every reason to think that schools could also do better. Every study of relative school achievement, whether within or across countries, shows large variations in school outcomes even among schools with very similar student and community demographics. All of this suggests that we do not yet know what the limits of improvement are. So without in any way putting the entire responsibility for better outcomes onto schools, the research does identify the following school factors affecting secondary school success.

Most secondary school reform programs in industrialized countries have focused on one or more of three areas: (1) changing curriculum requirements or achievement standards; (2) increased testing and assessment, often of the "high stakes" variety or (3) some degree or combination of choice and specialization within and among schools, often referred to as "pathways," including various ideas about the appropriate role for vocational or technical programs.

These strategies are inadequate if not largely incorrect in their impetus, because they are inconsistent with what we know about the factors supporting and inhibiting improved student outcomes. These include:

- The most important single factor under the control of schools is whether students see secondary schools as places where they belong, are cared for, supported and engaged as the "owners" of their own education;
- Central to creating this sense among students is to have stimulating daily teaching and learning practices as well as respectful and caring relationships among students and adults;
- Good teaching and learning are themselves supported (but not created) by course requirements and curricula that recognize the diversity among students without creating a hierarchy of quality (i.e., avoid streaming or tracking); and
- Student engagement in secondary education requires strong links between the school and the broader community, including important connections to students' education, work and life futures.

However, identifying the right changes, while essential, is not sufficient. A program of change for secondary schools that is intended to deliver real and sustained improvement as just defined must: a) attend to five important areas of effort simultaneously; b) pay careful attention to implementation, not just policy and design and c) take into account and manage effectively the main barriers to progress.

Five interactive and mutually supportive areas of attention for improving secondary school outcomes are required.

1. A focus in every school (and in the districts or other regional structures that support or control schools) on student success. This focus requires a safe school environment in which every student has a sense of belonging and of adult care, and where diverse student identities are affirmed.
2. A focus on improvements in daily teaching and learning practices across all classrooms and teachers, including improvements in student assessment policy and active engagement of students in their own learning.
3. Appropriate programs and pathways, including less specialization in curricula, and varied pathways only insofar as all of them provide real opportunities for meaningful employment and further education.

4. Connection of the school to the worlds of citizenship and work, including effective bridges and transitions to post-secondary education, employment, volunteer work and the development of essential life skills, such as political engagement, that are beyond the standard high school curriculum.
5. Community engagement that brings parents into the educational process and draws the broader community into supporting students' learning and welfare.

While these change variables are key to sustainable school reform, simply describing these changes, or even putting them into policy, will not be enough. One of the largest problems in school improvement has been the absence of implementation efforts commensurate to the scale of the change being sought. Real implementation requires the creation of focus in every school and district through effective leadership, strong teamwork, capacity-building for staff and effective use of data. Reform initiatives also need to be aligned (across levels), coherent, respectful of all parties and evidence-informed.

The main barriers to secondary school change can be understood as:

- The dominance of post-secondary admission requirements in shaping secondary school programs and structures;
- The organization of secondary schools (curriculum, staffing, timetabling, credits) around subjects and disciplines; and
- The never-ending demand to include more specific content elements, which in turn leads to fragmentation of student experience and neglect of overarching educational goals and skills such as problem-solving, research, application, citizenship and knowledge integration.

These practices are deeply embedded in the thinking of educators and also of students, parents and policy makers, to the extent that they are seen as impossible to alter. This means that improvement must also be seen as a political exercise that engages the thinking of all parties and tries to shift beliefs to be more consistent with evidence. Reforms have little chance of success if they ignore what teachers, students or parents believe to be true, and changes in those beliefs cannot be mandated, but must be created through dialogue (Robinson, 1995).

Given the limitations of a single chapter, each of the five areas of attention for improving secondary school outcomes can be discussed here only very briefly, but a fuller discussion, especially of the political factors, is available in Levin, 2008a. In the section that follows, each component is unpacked.

1 A Focus in Every School on Student Success

A large amount of research shows that students' sense of connection to the school is a prime factor in their persistence (Ferguson, Tilleczek, Boydell, Rummens, Cote & Roth-Edney, 2005; Furlong & Christensen, 2008). Students who have dropped out of school report feeling that nobody cared or made any attempt to keep them in school; indeed, often they felt encouraged to leave. Similarly, the literature on resilience (e.g., Ungar, 2005) shows how powerfully students can be affected by even a single adult who they see as believing in and supporting them. No amount of change in curriculum or policy will compensate for school environments that students, especially those with the greatest challenges, find alienating and unsupportive. As noted later in the discussion of standards, caring for students does not mean the acceptance of poor quality work or inappropriate behavior; tolerating those would in fact indicate an absence of real concern.

There are several elements to creating a caring environment in secondary schools. Although policy measures such as small schools, house systems or teacher-advisor systems may help support a successful approach, the primary required change is cultural and attitudinal, and this will not be created by mandating particular structures. Instead, there must be a deliberate focus in the entire school, involving professional and support staff as well as students and parents, that practices and communicates a genuine interest in, understanding of and respect for the situation and needs of every student. The central task is to make each secondary school a place that believes that its mission is success for students rather than seeing high failure or dropout rates as an indicator of "standards" and quality. Clear goals and a school leadership team committed to their achievement are essential.

This task is rendered more difficult because the student population in most countries is becoming more diverse demographically, while students are also living in a world of popular culture and technology that is more removed from typical school life than at any time in at least the last 40 years. Successful schools find ways of recognizing and respecting student identity without compromising their demand that students apply themselves to learning.

 A range of specific practices can help create a caring and supportive environment, including greater cultural awareness of the real lives of students among staff, outreach to minority student groups, advising and mentoring systems and various approaches to early intervention and support for students experiencing difficulty. One example would be the creation in Ontario of the new role of the "student success teacher" with specific responsibility for knowing, supporting, advocating for and otherwise assisting students who are having problems. Another would be the Ontario practice of reviewing the status of every student part way through each term so that interventions can be made early enough to prevent failure (Ungerleider, 2007). This practice in itself has helped reduce course failure rates significantly in Ontario high schools. The details of the practices matter less than the overall atmosphere created. However, rhetoric about caring is no substitute for specific practices that turn caring into actions. Without these, the talk is empty and breeds cynicism. It is essential to have in every school clear goals for improvement (for example to reduce course failure rates), effective leadership and a team orientation that creates, supports, monitors and reinforces the necessary practices until they become taken for granted ways of working.

2 A Focus on Improvements in Daily Teaching and Learning Practices

While many secondary teachers are exemplary professionals doing outstanding work, surveys of students in secondary schools still report significant levels of disengagement and boredom (Cullingford, 1991; Yazzie-Mintz, 2006). In PISA 2003, an average of 32% of students across countries considered "that school has done little to prepare them for life" (OECD, 2004, p. 125). The traditional response to this analysis is to say that school is not about fun or enjoyment, so whether students are interested is largely irrelevant. However, student engagement is clearly linked to better outcomes (Furlong & Christiansen, 2008) and is also highly contextual; even highly disengaged students will identify particular classes or teachers where they experience a much greater degree of interest and success. Nor are students asking for "fun"; they seek school activities that challenge them in ways that matter to them.

Elementary schools and teachers have had quite a bit of professional development on pedagogical approaches such as differentiated instruction and co-operative learning. Much less appears to have been done in secondary schools around how to create engaging, stimulating and intellectually challenging classes across a wide range of subject areas, especially for students with weaker backgrounds in the discipline or less ability. There is evidence (e.g., Ladwig, Smith, Gore, Amosa, & Griffiths, 2007; Grubb, 2008) that students in less challenging tracks or streams tend to get less interesting or varied instruction, a situation entirely consistent with the finding in PISA that countries with more tracking and streaming have poorer performance (OECD, 2004).

Improving instruction is more difficult in secondary schools because teachers are all specialists and each subject will require, at least to some extent, its own approach to effective instruction. The disciplinary associations, such as organizations of mathematics or science or language teachers, provide an important vehicle for this change; they should be deeply engaged in efforts to improve instruction in secondary schools since teachers are much more likely to be accepting of changes put forward by their disciplinary colleagues.

At the same time, there are some common areas across subjects for attention, two of which – student engagement and student assessment – are particularly important. At least some of the practices of effective student engagement, such as choice in work and assignments, clear understandings of purposes and desired outcomes for learning, or connecting work to students' out-of-school experiences and interests are relevant across subject boundaries.

Assessment is a critical area of instructional policy and practice. As noted later, high school change must always be about developing real skills at the highest possible level. A growing literature on effective assessment practices shows that steps such as ensuring that assessments are fair measures of key goals, ensuring that students understand the criteria for quality work and regularly giving substantive feedback without grades can also improve student engagement and performance (Reeves,

2008). Effective assessment is clearly linked to real performance (rather than narrow measures of recall), meaningful curricula and skills that go beyond any single subject area.

Schools can also learn much from careful analysis of their current data on student performance. The growing literature (e.g., Bernhardt, 2003; Earl & Katz, 2006) and experience on using data to guide improvement offers many useful ways to create discussion in schools about how student performance might be improved – for example, by comparing student performance across subject areas. However, learning to use data effectively is not at all a simple matter and requires its own infrastructure and support (Campbell & Levin, 2009).

Large-scale assessments, such as state or national exit examinations, can be an appropriate part of a high standards secondary school system, particularly because they are highly popular with the public and so can contribute to public confidence. However, there are dangers associated with large-scale assessment as well, especially where it is the main determinant for entry to post-secondary education. These problems include high levels of anxiety among students, narrowing of curriculum and teaching and an increased rather than reduced focus on university admission as the only outcome of secondary school that really counts. Countries with high stakes examination systems, such as Japan, Korea, France, England or New Zealand, have all been struggling with ways to soften these negative impacts.

Much remains to be learned about how we might best work to improve instructional practice and student engagement in secondary classrooms, but this remains a vital area for any real effort to improve student outcomes.

3 Appropriate Programs and Pathways

An important starting point for any discussion of curriculum and pathways is that students aged 16 and 17 do not know where their lives will take them. Adult confidence that we can predict individual student outcomes is not supported by the evidence, which shows that such predictions are often wrong (Gleason & Dynarski, 2002). Given the diversity in students' life paths, it is not possible to have a secondary education that is appropriate to all the different choices students might make. Increased specialization in secondary school curriculum is counterproductive.

The default position in many school systems has been to see preparation for university as the best and most flexible option, even though there is abundant evidence that the "academic" option does not work for many students while they are in school, and that university is not the immediate destination for a majority of students. Other pathways, such as vocational education, have suffered from low public and student regard (a situation that seems unlikely to change any time soon) and often do not show positive outcomes in terms of employment or earnings (World Bank, 2005) – perhaps because often students are placed in these programs to suit the school rather than because of students' own interests. The desire of other sectors, such as technical training institutions or apprenticeships, to be able to attract competent students has led to their increasing their own entrance requirements even where (as is also the case for universities) the requirements cannot be demonstrated to be strongly related to later performance.

Different pathways in secondary school are only justifiable if each path leads to real opportunities for meaningful and decently-paid employment, to broadly-accepted labor market qualifications, tertiary study or – even better – to more than one of these. Given an assumption of many changes of plan for most young people, this principle would suggest that:

- Movement across pathways should be supported, whether in secondary schools or after, as young people make the inevitable adjustments to changes in their life circumstances and plans; and
- A strong focus in curriculum and outcomes on generic skills that apply across pathways (and are relevant to students with diverse backgrounds and interests) is desirable, as it reinforces similarities rather than stressing differences in content.

A further concern is excessive curriculum specialization in secondary schools, most of which results from the focus on university preparation as well as the specialized training and subject organization of teachers and courses. Only a small minority of students benefit from highly specialized secondary school curricula. A good example of the problem is mathematics, where most countries want to have more students take increasingly advanced maths in secondary schools despite the fact that only a very small percentage of these students, let alone of the larger labor force, ever uses these skills. Yet maths skills with much broader applicability and utility both to employment and everyday life are not taught to most students. There is relentless pressure in secondary schools to increase the number of courses and hence degree of specialization, a pressure that produces undesirable results in just about all possible respects and should therefore be strongly resisted.

One further way to address pathway and curricular issues as well as increasing student engagement is by providing more opportunities for students to undertake self-directed learning. Given the importance of independent learning in the current and future labor market, it would seem desirable to require all secondary students to complete a meaningful piece of self-directed learning, a move that would also create greater flexibility in curriculum and more possible pathway options.

Further implications for pathways are also outlined in the next section, which discusses connections of the school to the worlds of citizenship and work.

4 Connection of the School to the Worlds of Citizenship and Work

The disconnection between secondary education and students' worlds beyond the school has been recognized for a very long time (e.g., Coleman, 1961). For example, although preparation for work remains an important stated goal of schools, they have tended to see students' out of school employment as a problem that interferes with academic performance instead of being an opportunity to support learning about work and the labor market.

Similarly, active citizenship and political engagement is a stated goal of secondary schools, but in practice most secondary schools are institutions in which students have fewer rights and freedoms than they have when they leave the school building.

Both these areas are also connected to academic achievement, since students will perform better where they see the institution as taking more account of their interests and realities. Connections to citizenship and work can reinforce engagement, which in turn can reinforce academic achievement.

A real secondary school reform program, then, must give attention to building meaningful connections with employment, including students' part time and summer employment, and to creating opportunities for meaningful civil and political participation in the school as well as in the broader community. To do so would require substantial change in many aspects of school culture and organization. However, there are some feasible steps that could lead in the right direction.

One example would be the use of portfolios that would both allow and require students to demonstrate a broad range of skills, such as teamwork or problem solving, across their high school experience independently of any particular course. Such portfolios would be useful to students in seeking employment and possibly in entry to post-secondary education, but would also push schools to think about how they recognized and provided these broader learning opportunities. Portfolios are also a way to recognize the enormous energy and commitment that many students show for extra-curricular activities in areas such as the arts, sport or volunteerism.

A second example would be around civic engagement. Unless schools set out to promote engagement actively, in classrooms and in the school as well as in the broader community, ideas of participation will remain entirely abstract to students, if not the subject of cynicism. Active measures are required to give students more voice in what happens in their classrooms and schools. A significant literature (e.g., Thiessen & Cook-Sather, 2007; Mitra, 2008) gives many specific examples of how this can be done.

A third example is related to pathways to work and involves building bridges that allow students to work at more than one level simultaneously. For example, models that encourage students to undertake advanced technical training while still in high school, or that connect study to simultaneous meaningful employment could be expanded and encouraged. Models such as career academies, dual credit systems, early college systems (e.g., Hoffman, Vargas, Venezia & Miller, 2007) or Ontario's new high skills majors all provide students with opportunities to explore their interests in more depth and to make more rapid progress when they have a defined area of interest.

Schools can effectively combine several purposes here by engaging students in the process of researching the outcomes of their predecessors. Many examples exist (e.g. Fielding & Bragg, 2003; Rudduck & Flutter, 2004; Jones & Yonezawa, 2008) of high school students taking on this research as part of their program of studies while also increasing their knowledge of post-school options and providing schools with important, but often neglected, information about the destinations of former students.

5 Engagement of Parents and the Community in Supporting Students' Learning and Welfare

As already noted, student outcomes in every school system continue to be linked more strongly to socio-economic status than to any other single factor. Schools cannot be successful unless they are strongly linked to the families and communities in which students live. Yet parent and community liaison is usually an afterthought, done when someone has leftover time, energy or money.

There are two main respects in which these connections are important. First, parents and families remain the third side of the triangle of student success (Coleman & Collinge, 1998; Desforges, 2003; Corter & Pelletier, 2005). Schools and parents need to work together to support students' engagement and success. This requires active measures by schools to reach out to parents, especially parents who are considered "hard to reach" due to such barriers as language, poor experiences with their own schooling or problems and challenges in their own lives such as poverty or physical or mental health problems. Creating these linkages requires dedicated resources in schools, with personnel for whom this is a primary responsibility. It cannot just be an additional load placed onto teachers, although teachers must play an important role as well. Moreover, engagement is a two-way proposition and is not the sole responsibility of parents; parents have to be heard with attention as well as spoken to about their responsibilities.

Second, especially for many students with the greatest risks, the community provides avenues for outreach and engagement through vehicles such as youth agencies, ethnic organizations, religious institutions or sports or arts groups. Engagement with these local resources can help schools deepen their understanding of students' worlds as well as sometimes finding new ways to reach students. Local communities can also offer resources such as mentors and employment opportunities that can help reinforce for students the value of secondary education in terms of achieving their life goals.

A Note on Standards

One of the main criticisms of many proposals to reform secondary education is that these proposals will "lower standards" and reward students for poor work. A further danger is that increased student success will be taken as a prima facie indicator of falling standards – that is, if more students are graduating, that must mean school is easier and standards lower. The standards argument has high public resonance so must be taken very seriously. It cannot be defused by arguing that there are multiple standards for different kinds of work and interests, since there is wide recognition that not all of these multiple standards lead to good outcomes for students. Rather, all secondary school reform must expressly commit to the achievement of high standards for all students in a range of activities, all of which can be shown to lead to positive outcomes. This does not mean that all students must do the same work or have the same curriculum. There will be some areas in which all students must have a basic competence, primarily in regard to written and oral communication as well as the broader skills of teamwork and problem-solving, but these should be kept to the minimum. High standards are achieved when education stretches and challenges students to perform at high levels. This can and should be done in areas and in ways that students perceive as relevant to their lives and goals.

A Note on Equity

Much of the focus of this paper is on strategies that can be used in all schools, though always with local flexibility. These strategies, evidence suggests, will improve overall outcomes including those for students with greater challenges. An across-the-board approach, however, will not be sufficient to make significant reductions in the inequities in outcomes among various ethnic and socio-economic groups. Accordingly, generic improvement strategies must be combined with targeted efforts to reduce disparities in these groups. This issue is covered in other sections of this collection and is itself a subject for a substantial paper, but what can be said here is that reducing gaps in achievement requires not so much entirely different approaches, but intensification and customization of the approaches already described. For example, parent and community outreach is both more important and more difficult in high poverty communities or with recent immigrants or indigenous peoples. Additionally, as noted earlier, students with poor skills may get less interesting and challenging instruction, so the task of addressing instructional quality in high need programs or schools, and particularly the need to attract and retain highly skilled teachers and principals in those schools, requires explicit attention. The key point is to retain a clear focus on reducing inequities in outcomes for all groups, which necessarily also means having data to know if progress is being made.

Implementation

Governments often make the mistake of thinking that promulgating some new policies, providing some project funding, and providing a few days of training to teachers and principals is sufficient to create lasting change. Much experience and research shows that this is not the case. If the goal is to create sustained improvement in hundreds of schools and thousands of classrooms, then the implementation effort has to be carefully designed and of a significant order of magnitude at several levels. Schools need to have some resources to support improvement, of course, and so do intermediate bodies such as districts. But money is not generally the primary concern. Human capacity to understand and promote innovation is in shorter supply than cash. Very few ministries of education have the capacity to support real change in school practices, being typically focused on rules, funding and issue management. Very few schools or school systems are organized around improvement. Jurisdictions that have experienced success have set up special-purpose infrastructures to support key initiatives while also connecting these carefully both to other parts of government and to the broader education sector.

Several other important elements of implementation can be briefly mentioned. One is coherence. A main challenge to many reforms is that schools feel beleaguered by a large number of initiatives that do not seem to connect with or reinforce each other, so it is important to avoid too many separate strands of reform. Relentless attention to a small number of key, simple goals over a period of years is essential. There are no short cuts. Having the appropriate data to judge current status and improvement, and making it available to people in usable ways, is another important implementation requirement. So is the presence of sufficient effective leadership with commitments to clear, public goals at all levels of the system.

Thoughtful communication is required to maintain stakeholder and public support for reforms. Educators often assume that the virtues of improvement are self-evident, but in reality they require constant, intensive and open dialogue with all the parties to ensure that they are not derailed by other issues or interests. Those responsible for improvement programs have to invest significant time and energy in an open dialogue with all parties. Communication is a core feature of improvement, not a distraction from it. In particular, classroom teachers need to feel involved in shaping the agenda, not just as the recipients of orders from on high. Systems must be willing to adjust plans in light of feedback from teachers, just as teachers must be willing to adjust their teaching in light of feedback from students. If we have learned anything in the last 20 years it is that reform cannot be done to teachers, any more than learning can be imposed on students. Teachers must be full partners in the improvement enterprise, just as students must be full partners in the classroom.

The importance of maintaining public confidence in standards of secondary education has already been mentioned. Schools will have to find new ways of reporting on their progress and challenges to the community as this is the only way to generate the support and goodwill needed to sustain improvement. People are too smart to believe propaganda from schools, but they will respond to honest communication. Both the political level and civil service have to be involved in the communications so that they work in a coordinated way toward success.

Successful implementation of sustainable improvement requires attention, resources and skilled management. It is not an afterthought or a distraction; without it any reform program, no matter how well designed or thoughtful, will flounder.

Conclusion

It is possible to improve student outcomes in secondary schools. We know a lot about what is required in order to have more students reach higher levels of skills and knowledge, leading to better career and life outcomes. This paper outlines a strategy that is well grounded in evidence, and is achievable given enough care, determination and persistence.

Note

1 Many of the ideas in this paper are developed more extensively in Levin, 2008a and 2012. I wish to acknowledge the influence on my thinking of many colleagues in academia, students at OISE and colleagues in the Ontario Ministry of Education.

References

Bernhardt, V. (2003). *Data analysis for continuous school improvement*. Larchmont, NY: Eye of Education.

Campbell, C. and Levin, B. (2009). Using data to support educational achievement. *Educational assessment, evaluation and accountability, 21*(1), 47–65.

Coleman, J. (1961). *The adolescent society: The social life of the teenager and its impact on education*. New York: Free Press of Glencoe.

Coleman P. and Collinge, J. (1998). *Parent, student and teacher collaboration*. Thousand Oaks, CA: Corwin.

Corter, C. and Pelletier, J. (2005). Parent and community involvement in schools: Policy panacea or pandemic? In N. Bascia, A. Cumming, A. Datnow, K. Leithwood and D. Livingstone (Eds) *International handbook of educational policy* (pp. 295–327). Dordrecht, NL: Springer.

Cullingford, C. (1991). *The inner world of the school: Children's ideas about schools*. London: Cassell.

Datnow, A. (2005). The sustainability of comprehensive school reform models in changing district and state contexts. *Educational Administration Quarterly, 41*(1), 121–53.

Desforges, C. (2003). *The impact of parental involvement, parental support and family education on pupil achievement and adjustment: A review of the literature*. London. Department for Education and Skills. Research Report RR433. Retrieved from www.dcsf.gov.uk/research/data/uploadfiles/RR433.pdf

Earl, L. and Katz, S. (2006). *Leading in a data rich world: Harnessing data for school improvement*. Thousand Oaks, CA: Corwin.

Ferguson, B., Tilleczek, K., Boydell, K., Rummens, J. A., Cote, D. and Roth-Edney, D. (2005). *Early school leavers: Understanding the lived reality of student disengagement from secondary school*. Final Report submitted to the Ontario Ministry of Education, May 31, 2005.

Fielding, M. and Bragg, S. (2003). *Students as researchers: Making a difference*. Cambridge: Pearson.

Fullan, M. (2006). *Turnaround leadership*. San Francisco: Jossey-Bass.

Furlong, M. J. and Christensen, S. L. (Eds) (2008). School engagement [Symposium]. *Psychology in the schools, 45*(5), 365–69.

Gleason, P. and Dynarski, M. (2002). Do we know whom to serve? Issues in using risk factors to identify dropouts. *Journal of Education For Students Placed At Risk, 7*(1), 25–41.

Grubb, W. N. (2008). Multiple resources, multiple outcomes: Testing the "improved" school finance with NELS88. *American Educational Research Journal, 45*(1), 104–44.

Hargreaves, A. and Fink, D. (2003). Sustaining leadership. *Phi Delta Kappan, 84*(9), 693–700.

Hargreaves, A., & Goodson, I. (2006). Educational change over time: The sustainability and non-sustainability of three decades of secondary school change and continuity. *Education Administration Quarterly, 42*(1), 3–41.

Hoffman, N., Vargas, J., Venezia, A. and Miller, M. (2007). *Minding the gap*. Cambridge, MA: Harvard Education Press.

Jones, M. and Yonezawa, S. (2008). Student-driven research. *Educational Leadership*, *66*(4), 65–69.

Ladwig, J., Smith, M., Gore, J., Amosa, W. and Griffiths, T. (2007). *Quality of pedagogy and student achievement: Multi-level replication of authentic pedagogy.* Paper presented to the Australian Association for Research in Education, Fremantle, November.

Lai, M. K., McNaughton, S., Amituanai-Toloa, M., Turner, R. and Hsiao, S. (2009). Can sustained acceleration of achievement in reading comprehension be achieved through schooling improvement? *Reading Research Quarterly*, *44*(1), 30–56.

Levin, B. (2004). Students at-risk: A review of research. *Educators Notebook, 15* (3), March issue. Retrieved from www.mcle.ca/notebookvol15no3.pdf

Levin, B. (2006). Schools in challenging circumstances: A reflection on what we know and what we need to know. *School Effectiveness and School Improvement, 17*(4), 399–407.

Levin, B. (2008a). *How to change 5000 schools.* Cambridge, MA: Harvard Education Press.

Levin, B. (2008b). Sustainable, large-scale education renewal. *Journal of Educational Change, 8*(4), 323–36.

Levin, B. (2009). Enduring issues in urban education. *Journal of Comparative Policy Analysis, 11*(2), 181–95.

Levin, B. (2012). *More high school graduates.* Thousand Oaks, CA: Corwin Press.

Mitra, D. L. (2008). Balancing power in communities of practice: An examination of increasing student voice through school-based youth–adult partnerships. *Journal of Educational Change, 9*(3), 221–42.

Mortimore, P. and Whitty, G. (2000). Can school improvement overcome the effects of disadvantage? In T. Cox (Ed.) *Combating educational disadvantage* (pp. 156–76). London: Falmer.

Muijs, D., Harris, A., Chapman, C., Stoll, L. and Russ, J. (2004). Improving schools in socially disadvantaged areas – a review of research evidence. *School Effectiveness and School Improvement, 15*(2), 149–76.

Organisation for Economic Co-operation and Development (2004). *Learning for tomorrow's world: First results from PISA 2003.* Paris: OECD Publishing.

Organisation for Economic Co-operation and Development (2006). *Education at a glance: OECD Indicators 2006.* Paris: OECD Publishing.

Reeves, D. (Ed.) (2008). *Ahead of the curve: The power of assessment to transform teaching and learning.* Bloomington, IN: Solution Tree.

Reynolds, D., Stringfield, S. and Schaffer, E. (2006). The High Reliability Schools Project: Some preliminary results and analyses. In J. Chrispeels and A. Harris (Eds) *School improvement: International perspectives* (pp. 56–76). London: Routledge.

Robinson, V. (1995). Organisational learning as organization problem solving. *Leading and Managing, 1*(1), 63–78.

Rudduck, J. and Flutter, J. (2004). *How to improve your school: Giving pupils a voice.* London: Continuum.

Sclafani, S. K. (2008). Two roads to high performance. *Educational Leadership, 66*(2), 26–30.

Thiessen, D. and Cook-Sather, A. (Eds) (2007). *International handbook of student experience.* Dordrecht, NL: Springer.

Thrupp, M. (1999). *Schools making a difference: Let's be realistic!* Buckingham: Open University.

Ungar, M. (Ed.) (2005). *Handbook for working with children and youth: Pathways to resilience across cultures and contexts.* Thousand Oaks, CA: Sage.

Ungerleider, C. (2007). *Evaluation of the Ontario Ministry of Education's student success strategy.* Ottawa: Canadian Council on Learning.

World Bank (2005). *Expanding opportunities and building competencies: A new agenda for secondary education.* Washington, D.C.: World Bank.

Yazzie-Mintz, E. (2006). *High school survey of student engagement.* Bloomington, IN: School of Education, Indiana University. Retrieved from http://ceep.indiana.edu/hsse

10

GENERALIZING ACROSS BORDERS

Policy and the Limits of Educational Science[1]

Allan Luke

Introduction

Two related questions are the focus of this chapter. The first is a question about policy, and in a period where bodies, capital and information cross borders with unprecedented scale and speed – it queries how well policy crosses these same borders. The second relates to queries about what the substantive consequences of attempts to move educational innovation and educational science from one cultural context to another, from one nation to another, from one jurisdiction and system to another, might be. This is all in an era characterized by moves towards a transnational management model of education where the focus is on the drive to standards, and where equity is couched in a new technical vocabulary of risk management, market choice and quality assurance.

I write the chapter with an acute understanding of the shifting standpoints put forward throughout the chapter, and a clear understanding that these shifting standpoints are as a result of my own journeys across borders. So I write as outsider and insider; born and educated as Chinese American, I have worked in Canada, Australia, Singapore and in numerous East Asian and Pacific Island education systems as a teacher, teacher educator, researcher and policy consultant. I have written critical theory and I also have been involved in large-scale empirical studies. My current research is on Aboriginal and Torres Strait Islander school reform in Australia. Ten years ago, I crossed the unmarked boundary between the university and government bureaucracy. I left an academic and leadership role at a large university and moved into the position of Deputy Director General and Ministerial Advisor, directing large state system reform in the state of Queensland: 1,200 schools, 40,000 teachers and a million students. From there I shifted across another set of borders and ten years ago, I helped establish Singapore's first national research center in education. This involved building that country's first large-scale evidence base for government policy.

The relationships between research and the making of policy, between policy and classroom practice, between evidence and reform are not abstract. They are everyday problems facing politicians and bureaucrats, school boards, parents and principals, teacher educators and teachers. Additionally, matters of culture, ideology and political economy are not incidental burrs in the making and implementation of policy. They are essential considerations. Effective policy makers consider not just bureaucratic capacity and implementation, they also anticipate local uptakes and the likely collateral effects of policy. Courageous policy makers lead by building public understandings, engaging with complexity across real and imagined boundaries, moving towards durable educational settlements around shared values and social contracts. Such policy making requires a close eye on the local articulation and recontextualization of policy: a kind of narrative scenario planning based on rich interpretive historical, cultural and political understandings. A narrow managerial science cannot suffice such a task.

Researchers, all of those who work in state systems and government and those who sit on school boards or in university boardrooms, must raise troubling questions in current policy settings where we are all pushed to take on the new common sense of accountability through narrow metrics, and deal with standards that do not always do justice to what is educationally and culturally meaningful. Institutions in these neoliberal accountability contexts are involved in a process of silencing. There is a sometimes stated and sometimes unstated notion that critique is not productive, and even anti-scientific, that somehow foundational issues are irrelevant to the real politick of systems reform and policy business. These are important assumptions to resist, and this call to resistance is not a matter of romanticism or political correctness. Rather it is testimony to the fact that the normative, the cultural, and matters of value have quietly slipped from policy discussions (Ladwig, 2010), overridden by a focus on the measurable, the countable and processes of cost efficiency and quality assurance. After a decade of implementation of such centralized policy in the US and UK, there is ample evidence that the actuary's approach can make for reductive approaches to educational science, short-term policy orientations and a plethora of collateral effects at the school and classroom level.

In this chapter I will examine the scientific and policy rationales for transnational and national standardization, focusing on two examples of policy export: early childhood standards in one of North America's oldest indigenous communities and the development of international standards for university teaching. I then shift focus to the current calls for American educational systems to look elsewhere for reform and innovation – to Finland, Canada and Singapore – and document the cultural and political contexts of these places and systems. My aim is to address two affiliated issues: (1) the possibilities of a principled policy borrowing that begins from an understanding of cultural and historical context and (2) the possibilities for a meditative, multidisciplinary educational science that might better guide such an approach.

My tools are story, metaphor, history and philosophy, leavened with empirical claims. There are truths, and indeed policies that can be obtained through travel across place and time, through argument, history and philosophy as readily as through field experiments and meta-analyses. So here I make a deliberate attempt to take readers elsewhere, to new and different places: to Australia, to Ontario, to Asia, but as well as to indigenous communities just down the road or across the waters – and in so doing perhaps make the educationally familiar seem more strange.

Policy debates and educational science alike can and should begin from a recognition of the centrality of history, place and culture – and, following Dewey, a recognition of the primacy of issues of equity, morality and value. The case I make is that effective policy requires a richer, broader cultural science of education. In his 1973 article "Speech and language: On the origins and foundations of inequality among speakers," Dell Hymes explained this as a "mediative" rather than "extractive" science – a science with the requisite theoretical humility to represent and engage with rather than override and overwrite communities' and cultures' everyday practices and rights.

Following the Leader

Writing in the *New York Times*, columnist Nicolas Kristoff (2011) recently argued that America should look to China for examples of education reform. He praised the discipline and focus of Chinese teachers and students. Also in the *New York Times*, globalization writer Thomas Friedman (2011) proclaimed the value of Singapore mathematics education, though he cautioned against also borrowing their approach to individual freedom. In Linda Darling-Hammond's important book, *The Flat World and Education* (2008), she discusses Singapore and Finland as models for reform. A month ago, Secretary Arne Duncan convened a summit of OECD countries featuring discussions by systems and union representatives – with Ben Levin (2008), former Deputy Minister of Ontario, outlining Canadian reforms. Reporting on the gathering, the *New York Times* (Dillon, 2011) quoted Andreas Schleicher, the scientific director of the OECD, on the status of teachers and teaching in "high quality/high equity" performing countries.

Could it be that American education is at this time on the cusp of "outside in" reform – that the historical flows of expertise, innovation, educational science and policy from the US have reversed? If this is the case then it is vital that some discussion be had about what a principled policy "borrowing" should look like and on what grounds it could proceed.

When my own academic generation began graduate studies in the 1970s, we inhabited a very different educational world than we all do today. The term "globalization" was yet to be invented. In that world the public good was the national good, the domestic good was the world good. In the United States, we were taught then what we now call American exceptionalism: that the American public good – whether defined in terms of economic growth, politics or the newfound postwar discourses of civil rights and equity – was good for everybody, everywhere, and that this was the case on a world scale.

This concept extended to the history of the education field, where American educational innovation – from Dewey and Thorndike onwards – was taken as generalizable to other parts of the world, as providing universal educational truths about universal human learners. In my doctoral research in the early 1980s, I traced the 25 year movement of US-based testing and behaviorist approaches to reading from Teachers College and Chicago, across the border to Toronto, and across the continent to Ministry offices on Vancouver Island (Luke, 1988). I recall one of my late Chinese aunties telling me about meeting John and Edith Dewey in Shanghai in the interwar period. Dewey's lectures in Japan and China after WWI, which I discuss later in this essay, have a continuing influence in these countries. When I taught in Thailand in the 1990s, I was struck by how closely the graduate training programs of major universities resembled those of the American Midwest – where our Thai colleagues had gone to study under Vietnam-era aid programs. For the last century, American educational research, innovation and reform have travelled across borders, just as European colonial education did in centuries before.

There has been a transnational generalizing across borders. Often this generalization process has proceeded with little critique, as part of aid and development programs, and often with little close analysis of its cultural and social effects. In a field that is concerned about the dangers of generalizing across states, school systems and student cohorts without the gold standard of evidence, there has been little hesitation in transporting curriculum, pedagogy, models of leadership, school governance and reform, assessment and evaluation, models of learning – and, as I'll argue here, marketization and privitization – to other education contexts. The transportation process is conducted through aid programs, research fellowships, through UNESCO, the World Bank and the Asia Development Bank, through international journal publication, citation and ranking systems and through the training of international graduate students. It may also be conducted through the shipping of in-service programs or exportation of textbooks, tests or performance indicators. The upshot is that there has been much educational expertise and commodities parachuted in to "other" contexts without substantive engagement with local histories, cultures and difference.

This is despite the fact that the work of American educational research is culturally produced. It is the product of a distinctive configuration of educational histories, problems, issues, systemic and ideological constraints. So a question that must be asked is how generalizable is American educational research beyond its national borders?

Even after the 1972 Arab oil crisis, after A Nation at Risk in the 1980s, there was little domestic discourse on globalization within the US. Additionally, with the exception of the work of Paulo Freire and the well-documented Anglo-American reinterpretation and appropriation of Vygotsky, examples of any outside-in importation of ideas and paradigms have been extremely rare. Educational systems in Asia, Africa and the Americas were defined principally in terms of a development paradigm. Hence, the work of American educational research in a Cold-war and Post-war era replicated an inside-out model of innovation and policy that was predicated on the rest of the world playing developmental "catch-up" with American schooling. It is important not to caricature the effects of this development paradigm. Work in poverty amelioration, the education of girls and women, language-in-education planning and the expansion of universal free education and university infrastructure were important moments in postwar modernization and development of many postcolonial states. Yet the point for this paper is that even critical work had an Anglo/American focus on class and gender, and distinctively American work on cultural and linguistic minorities has always been, and continues to be, generalized to other populations and cultural millieux without critical and empirical recalibrations. In the context of the current dilemmas of school reform – to continue to define American education as the apotheosis of the development of the school and the center of educational science is, at the least, ironic and, at best, in need of critical scrutiny and discussion.

Those of us working in Australia and New Zealand, Canada and Europe are not exempt from the pitfalls of the post-war aid model. As an example, in the mid-1990s, I evaluated an AusAid program on Tarawa Atoll in the island state of Kirbati. We were examining the Australian construction of middle schools on North Tarawa Atoll. We took a long ride in an open boat across the seven mile lagoon to arrive at small villages without electricity and running water. Students and teachers used palm walled/coral floored constructions, which provided cool, all weather learning environments, where they blended English-medium instruction with vernacular language use. At the same site, we found concrete block, Australian-style classrooms, school fittings and textbooks which were disused and disintegrating in the sun and salt air.

There are two key considerations from the literature on globalization for our world with its non-synchronous and uneven development. These are that (1) other nations/countries are not on a linear evolutionary development aspiring towards the status of American schooling and (2) global equality and inequality are linked; that is, that the transnational division of labor and modes of information mean that domestic policy and multinational corporate action here has ramifications for jobs, workers and the ownership of means of production elsewhere. We live in a complex world of push/pull effects, where social and economic policies and practices with specific domestic effects have collateral effects elsewhere. But there are lessons that increasingly fall outside of the discourses and practices of school reform as we have known it. These are related to understanding that other pathways, pedagogic/curricular traditions, forms of knowledge, forms of childhood and childrearing and other forms of school leadership and organization are possible and necessary. They may offer sustainable ways forward in the pursuit of equitable access to a useful education for all. However, it is important to investigate how transferrable or transportable these understandings are.

Policy Crossing Borders

In this section I will outline two cases of policy crossing borders: early childhood standards for the Pueblo indigenous communities in New Mexico and quality teaching metrics as part of the competitive ranking and funding of universities.

Mary Eunice Romero-Little is a Cochiti Pueblo researcher at Arizona State University. Over the last decade, her work has documented Pueblo childrearing and childhood, and the experience of Cochiti Pueblo children as they move from family, home and community to early childhood education. The Pueblo communities are among the original peoples of North America – and, further, despite a history of mission and federal boarding schools and displacement and removal of their children in the last century, the Pueblo communities have had documented success in intergenerational maintenance of languages and traditional practices.

In *Standardized Childhood* (2007), Bruce Fuller describes the national and transnational push for "standards" in early childhood. The general rationale for state, federal and national policy makers is that children from poor and cultural minority backgrounds are most at risk of not succeeding in school learning, and that early intervention can lead to improved educational achievement, cognitive, linguistic, social and emotional capabilities. Longitudinal studies of the effects of early institutional intervention by economists are cited as evidence of these propositions. The stated goal of standards for infancy to age four are equity of access to infant care, childcare and quality educational and health services such as Headstart. In policy documents the aim is to develop state regulatory "blueprints" and "learning guidelines" (Shumacher, Hamm, Goldstein & Lombard, 2006). These will set the foundations for expanded professionalization of early childhood workforces, licensing and accreditation of programs and facilities and performance in the allocation of funding. Comparable approaches have been developed across many OECD countries (Tobin, 2005).

Romero-Little (2010) describes the context of Cochiti Pueblo childrearing:

> traditional ways to care for and teach young children were carried out through an intricate and dynamic socialization process shaped by indigenous languages and guided by indigenous epistemologies for thousands of years. In Cochiti Pueblo, ... newborns are considered highly intelligent beings who come into the world with universal knowledge of both the spiritual and physical realms.
>
> *(p. 12)*

She describes a distinctive epistemic connection between the physical and spiritual world: "a sacred trust" and responsibility that is not "spoken" in conventional terms (Romero, 2003, pp. 147–48). It is carried out through daily interactions in the home and performed in seasonal activities and events held in the community such as in kivas (ceremonial chambers). New Mexico's 2005 state standards are viewed by elders, leaders and families in the Pueblo community as a threat to language retention, to cultural ways of childhood and childrearing and indeed to their people's sacred knowledges and languages:

> we spoke to him only in Keres at home and he was speaking it well. But then he went to headstart. The first day he came back and said to us in imperfect English: "Don't speaky to that way (Keres), speaky me Ingles."
> *(Romero-Little, 2010, p.12)*

Yet Romero-Little does not reject out of hand Western approaches to early childhood. Instead, she develops community-based criteria for the selection of programs. These include a focus on essential cognitive, linguistic skills for community and mainstream learning – but also, requisite conditions for indigenous language use and retention and the development of "congruent" cultural knowledges, ways of interaction and learning. Through detailed ethnographic fieldwork and participant observation, Romero-Little is able to establish new parameters for policy that might work without deleterious cultural and language effects.

This example of Hymes' "mediative" science is not the current early childhood science that is used to generate monocultural/universalist standards and targets. Further, Romero-Little's work sets the grounds for the adaptation of particular Western/European based approaches that, to borrow from Carol Lee (2001), "culturally model" community interaction, learning and vernacular language practices.

My second case is the development of standards for transnational comparison and ranking of university teaching. In 2009, I represented my university at the 3rd International Conference on World Class Universities at Shanghai Jiao Tong University (Centre for World Class Universities, 2009), where the top 100 university rankings are announced annually. The conference was sponsored by Thomson-Reuters. There were over 200 delegates from universities from around the world: a curious mixture of university presidents, marketing reps, heads of international student recruitment, government bureaucrats, freelance consultants and some higher education scholars. The discussions were unique: a senior administrator of a leading Mexican university discussed the recruitment of international students; a Ministry official discussed the intention to establish Arab rankings systems of world class education; several Eastern European academics viewed citation indices as extending English language hegemony and, in the background, representatives of a leading American business magazine were recruiting consultants to generate their own patented ranking system. This cast of characters is not accidental. In the boardrooms of university management, the issues of government regulation and funding, university personnel management, marketing and branding, faculty human resources, regional partnerships and co-branding, international student recruitment, intellectual property, metrics and comparative ranking sit in an uneasy mix.

Several presentations at the conference discussed the impacts of the global financial crisis on funding of land grant institutions and endowments, other papers focused on the use of journal ranking metrics, indicators of comparative research performance.

Metrics around research productivity have been on the table for some time now since the invention of the SSCI and Web of Science in the 1960s at the University of Pennsylvania. The new development was the announcement by researchers working for the OECD and EU on standards for quality university teaching and research supervision. Some of the discussion focused on current indicators (e.g., seminar versus lecture), ratios of tenured versus casualized staff, staff qualifications, class size, outcome indicators (e.g., employment levels of students) and student satisfaction surveys. The notion of a universal metric for quality university teaching is intriguing, given the distinctive curricular and linguistic traditions of universities and qualitative research on particular cultural and interactional styles of university pedagogy, where gender, class and cultural/linguistic backgrounds make a difference (Unterhalter & Carpentier, 2010). At the conference I asked whether assessment tied to rankings will have the effect of driving university teaching towards the production of, for example, increased student exit survey ratings. A panel of technical experts working on OECD/EU measures explained that the metrics would be sophisticated enough to accommodate this.

My principal objection to these general shifts to standardization, is that the general corporatization of universities is already showing signs of ironing out difference, local academic and intellectual eccentricity, eliminating courses and programs that do not generate revenue and gradually re-normalizing national, regional and cultural traditions of university teaching. The ongoing debates in Oxford, along with French and German universities – characterized in *The Economist* (2005) as the protection of tenured academics' elitism, privilege and ungovernability – are manifestations of the general move towards corporate managerialism. In Australia, universities and their faculties are given overall numerical rankings and funding based on measured teaching quality, despite the unreliability and sampling problems of surveys used. In 2010, all universities were supplied with lists of tiered journals field by field, performance against which has been used to rank individual schools, faculties and universities on government quality rankings. By current estimates, the combined cost to government and universities including additional staff time, infrastruture, consultants and software development has been $100 million AUD (Rowbotham, 2011). In universities, then, as well as in schooling, the total bureaucratic rationalization of every operational component is well apace, accelerated by declines of government funding, endowment returns and philanthropic funding.

Thomson Reuters provides principal funding for the Shanghai Jiao Tong Ranking, it also funds the Times Higher Education Supplement Universities Ranking system, the IELTS English Language proficiency test and the Web of Science citation ranking system, and is one of the largest producers of university textbooks in the world. Its principal corporate rival is Elsevier, owner of the Scopus rankings system. Thomson Reuters' Prometrics testing and online assessment arm was sold to the Educational Testing Service in 2007 for $435 million, and now constitutes that organization's "for profit" subsidiary. In effect, the systems for monitoring and generating standards for the international comparison of university teaching and research, proficiency and entry tests and a corpus of textbooks are the provenance of several multinational corporations (Graham & Luke, 2011). The international movement is driven by a new political economy of higher education, where governments, transnational organizations such as the OECD and corporations together drive an ideology of equity through market and standards. The result has been that most of our universities have now developed core administrative infrastucture for performance metrics, compliance and strategic engagement with ranking systems. This infrastructure is costly and yet few institutions are now outside of the reach of this higher education global marketplace (Naidoo, 2003).

These two brief cases, one about early childhood education and the other university teaching, illustrate the policy push across borders to transnational standards. Moves toward standardization and corporate management have not overridden the role of the national regulation in Asia or Europe – there are and will continue to be significant local adaptations, critiques and resistances (Rizvi, 2007; Mok, 2010; Shahjahan, 2011). Yet in board rooms and staff rooms there is a new commonsense evident. This relates firstly to a notion that standards will enable equity, that equity is about self-evident basics, that teachers and professors will perform better if there are stronger, merit incentives and performance benchmarks. Similarly, this new commonsense involves logic that to catch up with other countries, those painted as leaders in the field of the competitive production of human capital, requires a relentless approach to outcomes. It is predicted on the assumption that parents or communities or international students must be able to access transparent information to enable market choices of educational goods and services. But in each case, standardization of educational practices has the potential to flatten out cultural and linguistic, intellectual and educational diversity, with potentially deleterious effects on residual and emergent educational traditions.

Borrowing and Recontexualizing Educational Policy

I return now to where I began and consider the prospects of the "importation" of reform from other systems to the US. The question is how and on what grounds principled borrowings of policy can occur. My point so far has been that educational reforms are complex and embedded contextual cultural and historical stories. The extrapolation and recontextualization of innovation, reform and method needs to be undertaken with caution.

But before commenting on the question above, I will provide a negative exemplar of policy borrowing, from Australia. In 2009, the Australian Labor federal government took office proclaiming its own "Education Revolution." It featured calls for a knowledge economy to be achieved through a national curriculum that focused on the basics, a one-laptop-per-child policy for secondary students and an expanded testing/accountability system. Several colleagues and I made our contributions to the reform debate in separate reports to the state governments of South Australia (Luke, Graham, Sanderson, Voncina & Weir, 2006) and Queensland (Luke, Weir & Woods, 2008).

Our argument was as follows: Citing reanalyses of PISA literacy tests for 14 year olds, we focused on what Schleicher (2008) refers to as "high quality, high equity systems." In regression analyses, Canada and Finland have been more successful than most systems in ameliorating the impacts of socioeconomic background of students on literacy performance. Australia and New Zealand follow slightly behind, with US and UK results leading to markedly steeper equity slopes on the regression analysis. Broadly speaking, the countries with more equitable results on conventionally measured achievement have longstanding commitments to public education and comprehensive social welfare, health care and pension systems. On the other hand, countries that have highly stratified income disparity, measured by the Gini Coefficient of income variability, have much greater difficulty creating a level playing field for achievement. In the most simple terms, poverty matters, and school achievement does not work independently of combinatory suites of social and economic conditions and intervention policies.

Moving from these metrics to contextual and historical policy analysis, we attributed the success of high quality/high equity systems to the policy balances of "informed prescription" and "informed professionalism," that is, a modicum of centralized prescription via assessment/curriculum dictates and strong levels of investment in teacher education, in-service and professional development (see Chapter 2 of this volume for further explication of these concepts). Finland and Ontario have several common features:

- highly qualified teacher education candidates and graduates;
- extensive investment in in-service and ongoing teacher development;
- what we have termed low-definition or less prescriptive curriculum: with a strong emphasis on local board, municipal and school level curriculum interpretation and planning; and
- low to moderate emphasis on standardized testing.

Note that these policy suites from high quality, high equity systems do not follow the standardization/marketization models. But as importantly, we pointed out in these government reports that Ontario and Finland, like Australia, had strong social democratic commitments to public education, to educational principles of social justice – and that these sat within compatible commitments to universal access to childcare, health care and social welfare infrastructure. We argued that it was logical for Australia in any quest for policy borrowings to consider closely systems with comparable social contracts.

Our intervention failed. Then Education Minister and now Prime Minister, Julia Gillard sought policy advice directly from Joel Klein. In forums sponsored by Newscorp in Sydney and New York, in accounts published in Newscorp's national newspaper *The Australian*, in talks at the Brookings Institute, Gillard publicly lauded the New York model of school reform.[2] With few historical, curricular, governance, industrial and sociodemographic similarities between Australian schooling and the New York system, the Australian government has imported and adapted many reforms from this system and the United States more generally. These have included: expanded census testing in literacy and numeracy, published comparative school test score performance, a push to a national curriculum as part of a high-profile back to basics movement, support for a Teach for Australia program (modelled on Teach for America), greater principal budgetary and staffing decision-making, continued funding for the independent/private school sector and, most recently, the announcement of budgeting for comparative teacher rankings and one-off merit payments. We are now three years down the road of reform: staffroom morale is low, teaching to the test has begun in earnest, and the first cases of test score fraud are in play. The statutory body established to manage these systems has admitted that the metrics used on its website to compare the socioeconomic background of schools were flawed, and school test score comparisons have unresolved technical issues of sampling and measurement error (Luke, 2010).

These policy moves were made without a published or publicly presented analysis by the government of current system performance, which is consistently in the top tier of OECD countries. Those who have criticized elements of this policy agenda have been attacked in editorials and op ed pieces in *The Australian* (see Snyder, 2008 as one example).

In effect, the Australian federal government chose to borrow reforms that a decade of US research tells us have had at best mixed and conditional, and at worst negative effects. It ignored and, in instances, mocked cautions raised by a broad spectrum of educational researchers and teacher educators, unions and professional organizations as self-interested, politically correct and not in the public interests. This speaks to the transnational push to use highly selective versions of educational research to buttress ideologies around markets, around standards, parental choice and around teachers and unions, teaching and professionalism.

To examine the alternatives, I want to focus on the broader contextual variables that sit alongside some of the successful systems' reforms on offer. I want to briefly revisit Ontario and Singapore in light of my earlier claims about science and policy travelling across borders. My emphasis here is on the constituent role of cultural historical context, and political economic factors in the formation of policy and practice. A decade ago, Ontario began a major push toward educational reform. One of its key architects was Ben Levin (2008), then Deputy Minister of Education under the McGuinty Liberal government, now Professor at OISE. The Ontario reforms followed the general parameters of the informed prescription, informed professionalism model. Ontario teacher education programs are oversubscribed, with excellent students competing for positions – and universities such as York and Toronto run urban teacher education programs with strong focus on cultural diversity and equity. Levin and colleagues worked with the unions to develop a strong performance-based equity orientation, with simple messages about professionalism, about equity and learning and about public accountability to community. In contrast with the aforementioned breakdown in relationships between the educational research community and policy-makers, it is also worth noting that many key Canadian researchers have participated in policy development and implementation processes at the provincial and school board level.[3]

A modicum of curriculum specification was undertaken, schools were asked to set and track targets for test score improvement, but high levels of support for teacher and school development were provided. This included large scale inservice and the establishment of a literacy and numeracy secretariat with over 100 staff to assist principals and teachers to develop and model effective programs. Currently, many boards have moved towards developing and implementing assessment for learning and teacher moderated assessment systems. There has been no scripted instruction or scientific curriculum mandate – just consistent support of teacher professionalism to respond to mandates for school-level planning and analysis that required high levels of principal and teacher expertise. This was about the expansion of adaptive professional expertise, rather than the rote reproduction of routinized teaching (cf. Darling-Hammond & Bransford, 2005). The results over the past five years have been solid initial test score gains, now with some plateau effects, improvement in the achievement of second language learners and, according to PISA data, comparative success at ameliorating the impacts of socioeconomic background. Importantly, this foundational success has set the grounds for continued professional development and curriculum work in areas such as critical literacy, indigenous studies, middle school literacy and numeracy, assessment for learning and so forth.

In 2009, the Ontario government supported a province-wide call for "A Renewed Vision for Public Education" (People for Education, 2009). At the heart of these reforms are not teaching method, correct instructional model or finding the right package – they represent a distinctive Canadian commitment to equity, multiculturalism and to a social contract between government, communities and professional educators around education and the public good. This is about education and equity as core Canadian values, not a search for scientifically derived technique.

To consider a very different educational context I now detail the Singapore schooling reform moves. Singapore schooling was a key component of former Prime Minister Lee Kwan Yew's agenda for nation building. His People's Action Party (PAP) has won every election since nationhood in 1963. Over that 48 year history, Singapore has emerged as one of the world's leading economic powers. It has the tenth largest foreign reserves in the world, fourth largest banking exchange sector, the busiest port and logistics center of any country and produces 10% of the world's microchips. When I arrived in Singapore in 2002, the Minister of Education explained that in a country of 5 million people, on an island of about 250 square miles and with no natural resources to speak of, Singapore's education system was its core business. Singapore's educational success as a top ranked TIMMS country on mathematics, science and literacy is a national source of pride – its secondary school completion rate is over 95%. Its higher education sector is well funded and supported: in 2005, the per capita government funding support for each undergraduate education student was approximately six times what an Australian teacher education faculty was funded per student.

The Singapore education system is tasked with the production of human capital, but also with maintaining an official multilingual state and racial harmony amongst its Chinese, Malay and Indian populations. This is an education obsessed country: where fast-food outlets in shopping malls reportedly put up "no studying allowed" signs to keep students from hogging the tables.

When I arrived in Singapore, the push from the system was to import specific education innovations from the West. These included moderated assessment, constructivism, higher order and critical thinking, genre-based instruction, multi-literacies and digital learning into a system that they believed focused too much on rote, traditional, didactic knowledge. Locals refer to this as "East Asian chalk-and-talk." My academic colleagues and I at the National Institute of Education advised that it was far better to begin from a rigorous empirical description of classrooms and schools, and then make policy choices about reform with a fuller estimation of cultural and social consequences (Luke, Freebody, Shun & Gopinathan, 2005). The results of this research is featured in important work by Singaporean researchers and colleagues, but the general picture includes high levels of time-on-task, teacher-centered pedagogy that is focused on curriculum content, and a very strong emphasis on basic skills (e.g., Liu, 2007; Teo & Chia, 2007; Koh & Luke, 2009; Luke, 2008; Kwek, 2011). At the same time, classroom observation and assessment documented clear thresholds and limits in autonomous, critical and higher order work.

Singapore's success at mathematics and science education, and the strengths and weaknesses of traditional pedagogy are not in and of themselves the product of a specific technical approach. The system works through a structural isomorphism where state, family and corporation are linked together to create a face-to-face culture where education, Confucian respect for teachers and elders' authority are at the heart of the social order. Further, this particular multiracial social contract and its educational achievement patterns are not without empirical complexity, internal contestation and debate (Hogan, Liau, Tan, Aye, Ladwig & Lacson, 2005).

So these systems are successful, but what would the result be of a suggestion to "import" East Asian chalk-and-talk to Tennessee, or Ontario multiculturalism to Arizona? Caveat emptor – let the borrower beware or, at the least, borrow carefully. The relative success of each of these models is contingent upon context. In Ontario, Singapore and Finland public education is part of a total cultural and social settlement, and is geared to the production of a particular educational habitus (e.g., Simola, 2005). Simply, all of their particular reforms – Finnish research-based teacher training, Ontario's literacy programs, multiculturalism, gender-equity and anti-homophobia programs, Singapore's mathematics education – are produced and work in situ. They are the products of history and cultures, and in each country they work as part of a larger governmental and community commitment to specific visions of education as a public good.

Policies – successful and unsuccessful – are ultimately epic narratives with problems to be solved, heroic agents, participants, false starts and dead ends, and with endings, at times happy and at times tragic. A principled policy borrowing depends upon an interpretive analysis of a whole educational system in operation: an understanding of cultural practices, communities and demographics, ideologies and relations of power and of the human beings who make that system what it is. The stories of Singapore and Ontario are not about the triumph of scientific methods, and they are not about the triumph of markets or successful standardization. They are about cultural and governmental settlements, about durable historical social and cultural commitments to particular forms of education and, indeed, forms of life.

A Cultural Science of Education

Given my initial claims about the problems of science, borders and colonization, it would be ironic and hypocritical for me to write as an external expert with normative solutions for the very complex problems facing American educational research, schooling and society. Certainly, after my description of Australian reform, you would not want to emulate us emulating you.

There are two salutary historical lessons here. First, policies do not always travel well. In fact, too often selective versions of educational science, selective minings of educational research are undertaken in the service of particular economic and ideological interests. To paraphrase Michael Apple (1979), "the selective traditions" of educational research – like selective traditions of curriculum – are fraught with exclusions, with omissions and silences. Further, as Apple's (2000) later work went on to argue, these decisions are often driven by a collusion of multinational corporate and partisan political interests, often intricately linked with the work of those transnational institutions that play an increasing role in the setting of standards for educational evidence and performance.

At times, these organizations make principled efforts at evidence-based policy. In other cases, governments are part of cynical efforts to create policy-based evidence – to reconstruct after the fact, scientific rationale and data for overtly political and ideological decisions. Educational researchers know how interpretative and contingent our science is – our work places us within schools and other complex settings where multilevel solutions to complex performance and demographic data are played out. But many systems and educators now face a push for standardization that exceeds the imperatives for interoperability, where rationalizations of fairness are used to justify sameness. This is not the science of social transformation that Dewey envisioned. Instead it is an ideology of marketization and standardization, aided and abetted by multinational educational enterprises.

I have argued in this paper that considering policy borrowing possibilities requires an understanding that many of the effective educational policy suites currently available are not methods or approaches that can be removed from their contexts. They are themselves the products of longstanding settlements of the order described in Herbert Kliebard's (2004) epic work on American curriculum. What is needed in any process of reform is a broad and encompassing social and cultural debate, rich, multidisciplinary evidence and a settlement not just on a vision for democratic education, but as well, for a just and equitable society. Policy borrowing can only begin from a consideration of local cultural context, of historical genealogy and of contending ideologies. There are no scientific, quasi-scientific or pseudo-scientific fixes that can escape this.

To return to my other initial question about the possibility of a generalizable science of education. It was Thorndike's belief that the generalizable science of education would be based upon behaviorist educational psychology: that is, a psychology of individual measurable difference. It was Dewey's belief, drawing from a larger canvas of pragmatism and symbolic interactionism, that educational science necessarily would start with the social and end with the social, working through the complex dialectics of individual and society, culture and economy, empirical and hermeneutic. In this way, in a problem-based and problem-solving science, matters of ethics and values would never be taken as subordinate or adjunct issues. Since the very issues of science and art were ethically and value laden, so the conduct of that science would also necessarily need to be.

In *Democracy and Education* (1916), Dewey proposed a philosophy of education that focused on "social efficiency"; that is, the production of human capital, of laboring subjects. This ideal he shared with Thorndike (1940/1974), but he also argued for foci on citizenship and, indeed, on cultural transmission. What I have described within this chapter is a move towards a global curriculum settlement around educational basics and "new economy" competences, with a focus almost exclusively on the measureable production of human capital, that pushes for interoperability and equity of exchange. However in so doing, the current approach simply excludes other goals of democratic education – debates and learnings about civics, civility, language and culture, about diverse and common cultural touchstones and about learning to live together – and it altogether ignores indigenous lessons about the stewardship of cultures, the land and the planet.

So what of educational science? In work on ecosystemic approaches to science, Jay Lemke (1995), Michael Cole (1996) and others describe an educational science that does not attempt to eradicate diversity and colonize difference. Diversity is necessary for the survival of biosocial systems. Those systems that flatten out or destroy diversity risk becoming homeostatic, closed and ultimately unable to meet new ecosystemic and biosocial challenges (Wilden, 1987). In digital terms, the very notion of "bandwidth" refers to a system's capacity to handle requisite diversity of information (Lemke, personal communication, 2011). If we began from definitions of cultures as being tool and artefact based (Cole, 2010), we would have to question the effects of educational systems whose central aim is to standardize and constrain tools and their use, and to limit and delimit displays of what might indeed count as an artefact.

Instead I propose a cultural science of education that asks these questions: At what point does standardization go beyond any purported need for interoperability – and instead become a repressive limitation of the available, imaginable cultural tools and artefacts and, thereby, a sociogenetic limitation and constraint on what can be thought, felt, done and created? At what point does this standardization become a liability, a risk rather than an enabling condition for cultural and species survival?

Acknowledgements

Thanks to Kris Gutierrez and Joanne Larson for support, Queensland University of Technology colleagues and students for their criticisms and revisions, Eunice Romero-Little for access to her work and Jay Lemke, Michael Cole, Courtney Cazden, James Ladwig, Tara Goldstein, Ben Levin, Alfredo Artiles and James LaSpina for their ideas and comments.

Notes

1 This paper was first presented as the AERA Distinguished Lecture in April 2011 [Luke, Allan. *Generalizing Across Borders: Policy and the Limits of Educational Science*. AERA Distinguished Lecture. 8 April, 2011]. It is published in another form in the *Educational Researcher*, vol 40, no 8, 367–77.
2 See, for example, an account of these comments in: www.brookings.edu/events/2009/0619_australian_education.aspx
3 Michael Fullan, Andy Hargreaves, Kenneth Leithwood and others have provided key input at the provincial, board and regional school levels. Many of us in the literacy education community have worked with the Ontario Ministry of Education Literacy and Numeracy Secretariat and with local school boards.

References

Apple, M. W. (1979). *Ideology and curriculum*. London, UK: Routledge and Kegan Paul.
Apple, M. W. (2000). *Official knowledge*. New York, NY: Routledge.
Centre for World Class Universities (Ed.) (2009). *Proceedings: 3rd international conference on world-class universities*. Shanghai: Shanghai Jiao Tong University.
Cole, M. (1996). *Cultural psychology*. Cambridge: Cambridge University Press.
Cole, M. (2010). What's culture got to do with it? Educational research as a necessarily interdisciplinary exercise. *Educational Researcher*, *39*(6), 461–70.
Darling-Hammond, L. (2008). *The flat world and education*. New York, NY: Teachers College Press.
Darling-Hammond, L. and Bransford, J. (Eds) (2005). *Preparing teachers for a changing world*. San Francisco, USA: Josey-Bass.
Dewey, J. (1916). *Democracy and education*. New York, NY: Collier Macmillan.
Dillon, S. (2011). US urged to raise teachers' status. *New York Times 16/3/11*. Retrieved from www.nytimes.com/2011/03/16/education/16teachers.html?hp
The Economist (2005). Free Oxford University. Retrieved from www.economist.com/node/3986918?story_id=E1_PJRGJTR
Friedman, T. L. (2011). Serious in Singapore. *New York Times*. Retrieved from www.nytimes.com/2011/01/30/opinion/30friedman.html
Fuller, B. (2007). *Standardized childhood*. Stanford, CA: Stanford University Press.
Graham, P. and Luke, A. (2011). Critical discourse analysis and political economy of communication: Understanding the new corporate order. *Cultural Politics: An International Journal*, *7*, 103–31.

Hogan, D., Liau, A. K., Tan, T. K., Aye, K. M., Ladwig, J. and Lacson, W. (2005). *Meritocracy in Singapore education.* Unpublished manuscript. National Institute of Education, Nanyang Technological University, Singapore: Centre for Research on Pedagogy and Practice.

Hymes, D. (1973). Speech and language: On the origins and foundations of inequality among speakers *Daedalus, 102*(3), 59–85.

Kliebard, H. M. (2004). *The struggle for the American curriculum, 1893–1958* (3rd edition). New York, NY: Routledge.

Kristoff, N. (2011). China's winning schools. *New York Times.* Retrieved from www.nytimes. com/2011/01/16/opinion/16kristof.html?_r=1&scp=1&sq=%22chinese%20schools%22 &st=cse

Koh, K. and Luke, A. (2009). Authentic and conventional assessment in Singapore schools: An empirical study of teacher assignments and student work. *Assessment in Education, 16*(3), 291–318.

Kramer-Dahl, A., Teo, P., & Chia, A. (2007). Supporting knowledge construction and literate talk in secondary social studies. *Linguistics and Education, 18*(2), 167–99.

Kwek, D. (2011). Weaving as frontload and backend pedagogies. In C. Day (Ed.) *The Routledge international handbook of teaching and school development.* London, UK: Routledge.

Ladwig, J. G. (2010). Beyond academic outcomes. *Review of Research in Education, 34*(1), 113–41.

Lee, C. (2001). Is October Brown Chinese? A cultural modeling system for underachieving students. *American Educational Research Journal, 38*(1), 97–142.

Lemke, J. L. (1995). *Textual politics.* London, UK: Taylor & Francis.

Lemke, J. L. (2011). Personal communication.

Levin, B. (2008). *How to change 5000 schools.* Cambridge, MA: Harvard Education Press.

Liu, Y. (2007). Teacher-student talk in Singapore Chinese language classrooms: A case study of the initiation/response/follow-up. *Asia Pacific Journal of Education, 28*, 87–102.

Luke, A. (1988). *Literacy, textbooks and ideology.* London, UK: Falmer Press.

Luke, A. (2008). Pedagogy as gift. In J. Albright and A. Luke (Eds) *Pierre Bourdieu and literacy education* (pp. 68–91). New York, NY: Routledge.

Luke, A. (2010). Will the Australian national curriculum up the ante in primary schools? *Curriculum Perspectives, 30*(3), 59–64.

Luke, A., Freebody, P., Shun, L. and Gopinathan, S. (2005). Towards research-based innovation and reform: Singapore schooling in transition. *Asia Pacific Journal of Education, 25*, 5–28.

Luke, A., Graham, L., Sanderson, D. Voncina, V. and Weir, K., (2006). *Curriculum and equity: An international review of research and theory.* Adelaide, SA: Department of Education and Children's Services.

Luke, A., Weir, K. and Woods, A. (2008). *Development of a set of principles to guide a P-12 syllabus framework.* Brisbane, Qld: Queensland Studies Authority.

Mok, K. H. (Ed.) (2010). *The search for new governance of higher education in Asia.* New York, NY: Palgrave Macmillan.

Naidoo, R. (2003). Repositioning higher education as a global commodity: Opportunities and challenges for future sociology of education work. *British Journal of Sociology of Education, 24*(2): 249–59.

People for Education (2009). *The annual report on Ontario's public schools.* Toronto, CA: People for Education.

Rizvi, F. (2007). Internationalization of higher education: An introduction. *Perspectives in Education: South Africa Journal of Education, 24*(4), 1–11.

Romero-Little, M. E. (2010). How should young Indigenous children be prepared for learning? A vision of early childhood education for Indigenous children. *Journal of American Indian Education, 49*(4), 7–28.

Romero, M. E. (2003). *Perpetuating the Conchiti way of life: Language socialization and language shift in a Pueblo community.* Unpublished doctoral dissertation, University of California-Berkeley.

Rowbotham, J. (2011). Research results raise concerns. *The Australian*, *24/8/11*, 24.

Schumacher, R., Hamm, K., Goldstein, A. and Lombard, J. (2006). *Starting off right: Promoting child development in state early care and education initiatives.* Washington, DC: Center for Law and Social Policy.

Schleicher, A. (2008). Schooling through the prism of PISA. In A. Luke, K. Weir and A. Woods *Development of a set of principles to guide a P-12 syllabus framework* (pp. 72–85). *Brisbane, Qld: Queensland Studies Authority.*

Shahjahan, R. A. (2011). Engaging the faces of "resistance" and social change from decolonizing perspectives: Toward transforming neoliberal higher education. *Journal of Curriculum Theorizing*, *27*(3), 273–86.

Simola, H. (2005). The Finnish miracle of PISA: Historical and sociological remarks on teaching and teacher education. *Comparative Education*, *41*(4), 455–70.

Snyder, I. (2008). *The literacy wars.* Sydney, NSW: Allen & Unwin.

Thorndike, E. L. (Clifford, J. Ed.) (1940/1974). *Human nature and the social order.* Cambridge, MA: MIT Press.

Tobin, J. (2005). Quality in early childhood education: An anthropologist's perspective. *Early Education and Development*, *16*(4), 422–34.

Unterhalter, E. and Carpentier, V. (Eds) (2010). *Global inequalities and higher education. Whose interests are we serving?* Houndmills, USA: Palgrave MacMillan.

Wilden, A. (1987). *The rules are no game: The strategy of communication.* London: Routledge and Kegan Paul.

CONTRIBUTORS

Donna E. Alvermann is University of Georgia Appointed Distinguished Research Professor of Language and Literacy Education. She studies young people's digital media practices and their implications for academic literacy across disciplines. Her books include *Reconceptualizing the Literacies in Adolescents' Lives* (3rd ed.), *Content Area Reading & Literacy: Succeeding in Diverse Classrooms* (7th ed.) and *Adolescents' Online Literacies*.

F. Michael Connelly is Professor Emeritus at the Ontario Institute for Studies in Education of University of Toronto (OISE/UT), long time Editor of Curriculum Inquiry, former Chair of the Department of Curriculum and founding Director of the OISE/UT Center for Teacher Development. He has published widely with close to 200 publications across the fields of science education, curriculum studies, teacher education, multiculturalism and narrative inquiry. He has worked with schools, school boards and teacher organizations, and has written policy papers for Ministries and Professional Associations in Ontario and a variety of other systems. He received AERA's Division B Lifetime Achievement Award, the Canadian Society for the Study of Education's Outstanding Canadian Curriculum Scholar Award, the Canadian Education Association Whitworth Award, the Ontario Confederation of University Faculty Association's award for excellence in teaching and the 2010 Best Publication Award (with Shijing Xu) for the Narrative Inquiry SIG, AERA. He is involved with a China–Canada sister school network studying the narrative histories of immigrant family knowledge structures and ways of knowing.

Gerry Connelly is an Adjunct Professor in Leadership Development and Co Director of the Sustainable Education Academy at York University. She is also Director of Policy and Research for the Learning Partnership (TLP), a national charitable organization dedicated to championing a strong public education system in Canada. She is the former Director of Education of the Toronto District School Board (TDSB), the largest board in Canada. Gerry has served as Director of the Curriculum and Assessment Policy Branch, in the Ontario Ministry of Education. She was responsible for developing the K-12 Ontario Curriculum and standard report card. Gerry is the recipient of the *Distinguished Educator Award* from OISE/University of Toronto, the *Government of Ontario Teacher Dedication Award* by the Royal Conservatory of Music and Learning Through the Arts, and the Ontario Supervisory Officers' provincial award for *Leadership in Public Education*. Several other awards have acknowledged her commitment to equity, and to community engagement. These include the *City of Toronto Bob Marley Award*, *the Fraser Mustard Award* and the *University of Toronto Arbor Award*.

Zongyi Deng is an Associate Professor in Curriculum, Teaching and Learning Academic Group, National Institute of Education (NIE), Nanyang Technological University, Singapore. A former Associate Professor at the University of Hong Kong (HKU), he is currently a Research Associate with Wah Ching Centre of Research on Education in China, HKU. He is an Executive Editor of *Journal of Curriculum Studies (JCS)*. Representative publications appear in *The Sage Handbook of Curriculum and Instruction*, *Curriculum Inquiry* and *JCS*.

Susan Grieshaber is a Professor of Early Years Education at the School of Early Childhood, Queensland University of Technology, Brisbane, Australia. Her research interests include early childhood curriculum, policy, gender and families, with a focus on equity and diversity. She has published widely in a range of areas that reflect her research interests and co-edits the international, refereed online journal *Contemporary Issues in Early Childhood*. Sue has interests in a variety of theoretical and methodological perspectives including critical, feminist and postmodern approaches, and uses these in her research and teaching.

Val Klenowski is a Professor of Education at the Queensland University of Technology in Brisbane, Australia. She has research interests in the use of social moderation in the context of standards-driven reform, culture responsive assessment and pedagogy and the use of digital portfolios. Val has published in the fields of curriculum, evaluation, assessment and learning.

Ben Levin is Professor and Canada Research Chair in Education Leadership and Policy at the Ontario Institute for Studies in Education, University of Toronto, Canada. In addition to a distinguished academic career he has also served as Deputy Minister (chief civil servant) for Education in both Ontario and Manitoba. His most recent books are *Breaking Barriers: Excellence and Equity* (with Avis Glaze and Ruth Mattingley, Pearson Canada, 2011) and *More High School Graduates* (Corwin

Press, 2012). His interests are in large-scale change, poverty and equity and linking research more effectively to policy and practice.

Allan Luke is a Research Professor in the Faculty of Education at the Queensland University of Technology, Brisbane, Australia. He is known for his work in multi-literacies, literacy, education policy, classroom pedagogical coding and school reform. He is currently engaged in projects related to digital literacies, school reform for improved outcomes for indigenous students, syllabus and curriculum.

James Marshall is a Professor of Language and Literacy Education and Associate Dean for Academic Programs in the College of Education at The University of Georgia. His research and teaching focus on educational policy, teacher education and the teaching of literature.

Patrick Shannon is a Professor of Education at Penn State University and Director of the Integrated Undergraduate/Graduate Programs in Special Education and Curriculum and Instruction. He runs the program's Summer Reading Camp, which matches IUG students and elementary and middle school students positioned as struggling to learn to read at school in the construction of museum exhibits for Discovery Space in State College, PA. His most recent book is *Reading Wide Awake* (Teachers College Press).

Katie Weir is a Senior Lecturer at Griffith University's Gold Coast campus in Queensland, Australia. Her focus in research and teaching is on understanding curriculum and educational assessment. She also works as a consultant with schools and education providers across Australia and internationally to improve student learning outcomes by building the capacity of teachers to design and implement quality assessment for learning purposes.

Annette Woods is a Senior Lecturer in the Faculty of Education at Queensland University of Technology in Brisbane, Australia. She researches and teaches in literacy, curriculum, pedagogy and assessment, social justice and school reform. Her current research includes an investigation into teachers' use of syllabus documents, a school reform study that investigates the links between digital learning and print literacy outcomes and an evaluation of a large-scale reform project to improve outcomes of indigenous students in Australia.

INDEX

Note: 'N' after a page number indicates a note; 'f' indicates a figure; 't' indicates a table.